THIRD EDITION

The Grocers
The rise and rise of the supermarket chains

Andrew Seth and
Geoffrey Randall

KoganPage

LONDON PHILADELPHIA NEW DELHI

First published in 1999
Reprinted 1999
Second edition 2001
Third edition 2011

120 Pentonville Road	1518 Walnut Street, Suite 1100	4737/23 Ansari Road
London N1 9JN	Philadelphia PA 19102	Daryaganj
United Kingdom	USA	New Delhi 110002
www.koganpage.com		India

© Andrew Seth and Geoffrey Randall, 1999, 2001, 2011

The right of Andrew Seth and Geoffrey Randall to be identified as the authors of this work has been asserted by them in accordance with the Copyright, Designs and Patents Act 1988.

ISBN   978 0 7494 6104 1
E-ISBN   978 0 7494 6105 8

British Library Cataloguing-in-Publication Data

A CIP record for this book is available from the British Library.

Library of Congress Cataloging-in-Publication Data

Seth, Andrew.
  The grocers : the rise and rise of supermarket chains / Andrew Seth, Geoffrey Randall.
      p. cm.
  Includes bibliographical references and index.
  ISBN 978-0-7494-6104-1 – ISBN 978-0-7494-6105-8 (ebk) 1. Supermarkets–Great Britain–History. 2. Grocery trade–Great Britain–History. 3. Chain stores–Great Britain–History. 4. Supermarkets–United States–History. 5. Grocery trade–United States–History. 6. Chain stores–United States–History. 7. Supermarkets–Europe–History. 8. Grocery trade–Europe–History. 9. Chain stores–Europe–History. I. Randall, Geoffrey, 1938- II. Title.
  HF5469.23.G72S46 2011
  381'.4564130941–dc22
                            2010036873

Typeset by Saxon Graphics Ltd, Derby
Production managed by Jellyfish
Printed in the UK by CPI Antony Rowe

CONTENTS

FOREWORD

T he food retailing and supermarket industries are some of the biggest and most competitive in the world. The development of this industry, particularly in the markets on both sides of the Atlantic, has been an exciting journey for the participants – as I know from my own experience. Both in the UK at Asda, later when we sold our company, happily, to Walmart stores, and now at Loblaws in Canada I have been lucky enough to engage in this journey close up. It's been a learning experience and one where I have seen successes as well as failures, luckily more of the former than the latter! But a business like food retailing produces winners as well as losers and the challenges to provide our customers with great innovations never stop coming.

Andrew Seth and Geoffrey Randall have been studying this business for many years and in their different ways they know it well. Andrew was an international manager at Unilever for thirty years, and sold Lever's brands, such as Dove and Persil, to retailers like me. In fact we first met more than twenty years ago when I was Asda's CEO at Leeds and he was Lever UK's CEO. Nobody has been closer than Andrew to the inner workings of our industry and nobody understands the relationships that exist between supplier and retailer better than he does. I can tell you, as he can himself, that we didn't always agree. I can also tell you that companies as strong as Lever and Asda are well able to sort out approaches and events that create a good consumer response.

The relationships between the brand owners and retailers are one of the topics that this book covers and it's an area that both authors know well from their different viewpoints. Geoffrey Randall is a seasoned business academic who led the business studies department at Greenwich University and who then consulted to a range of leading consumer and retail companies. He has authored several books on consumer and trade marketing in his own right, and in previous collaborations with Andrew their work has become recognized as the definitive study of British and international supermarkets. The fact that they have complementary backgrounds obviously adds substance to their work, and gives authority to their conclusions about today's industry, as well as their forecast of what is likely to happen ahead.

I unhesitatingly recommend their latest book *The Grocers* to British as well as world readers. British food retailing is a terrific story and it is told here with authority as well as genuine excitement. This is a fine book not just for the professional but for the general reader, for consumers who want to understand the big changes that are taking place in their shopping lives in the UK, USA and Europe. It shows how a small handful of companies have come to dominate the food retailing scene, and analyses brilliantly the strategies and tactics that have enabled them to grow their companies.

Allan Leighton
President and Deputy Chairman, Loblaws

ACKNOWLEDGEMENTS

Without the full and unstinting cooperation of many people, we could not have written this book. They are all busy, many of them carrying serious executive responsibilities, yet they all made themselves available and gave us the benefit of their knowledge and experience. We acknowledge their help with gratitude:

Tesco: Sir Terry Leahy, Lucy Neville-Rolfe, Laura Wade-Gery, Steve Webb. Asda: Andy Bond, Nick Agarwal. Morrisons: Richard Pennycook, Angus McIver. Waitrose: Mark Price. Marks and Spencer: John Dixon. The Cooperative Society: Peter Marks. Ocado: Andrew Bracey. Lidl: anonymous. Fresh and Easy: Ricardo Munoz. Enotria: Rufus Weston. McBride: Chris Bull.

Ivor Bramley, farmer; Robert Clark, Retail Intelligence Network; Edward Garner and Richard Herbert, Kantar Worldpanel, GfK; Andrew Kasoulis, Credit Suisse; David McCarthy, Evolution Securities; Elizabeth Rigby, *Financial Times*; Matthew Taylor, UBS; Matthew Truman, Nomura.

All opinions, and any errors of fact, are the authors' own responsibility.

Introduction

A visit to the supermarket in 2010

Vicky pulls into the supermarket car park. It is crowded, as usual, and she finds a place on the outer ring. She has already been to the farm shop to buy local meat, and vegetables that are grown in the adjoining field. Entering the supermarket, she is confronted by the fresh produce section (her husband has told her that it is designed to give an aura of freshness and authenticity to the whole store, but to her it's just the fruit and veg). Facing her is a display of special offers: buy one get one free; three for the price of two. She doesn't buy any of these, and indeed is a bit irritated by them: she and her husband are on their own now, and they can't possibly eat that much before it goes off. Choosing what she wants, she moves on to buy fish; they like to eat it at least once a week, and the supermarket is the only place to buy it now.

She picks up supplies of detergent, floor cleaner and toilet paper. Her husband has asked for some specific oats for the muesli he makes for himself, and she chooses some biscuits and adds supplies of essentials such as tea bags. She then remembers that they are a bit short of wine, so she goes back to select from the wide range on display. She finds the labelling and price guides helpful, and anyway knows some of the ones they like. Getting to the checkout, she is relieved to find a short queue, and she knows the checkout assistant (it's not just girls on the checkouts any more, but boys too, and one woman who looks old enough to be *her* mother).

Leaving, Vicky fills up with diesel at the supermarket's filling station; they usually buy their fuel there, simply because it's cheaper. She is going on to Lidl, where her husband has asked her to buy some olive oil and parmesan cheese. He does most of the cooking now that he has time, and in fact often does the shopping too. She hates cooking, and is not much fonder of shopping, at least not this sort. Last week, they visited a new Waitrose about 20 minutes' drive away, and she wonders if they might try online ordering from there: some of the products were new to them both. Although they prefer to shop in Sainsbury's, they sometimes use Asda for convenience; neither of them likes the nearby Tesco Extra – just too huge and too crowded. The new owners of the post office in their village have transformed their stock of groceries, so they can use that for any extras they need.

This story happens to be true, but we can draw from it some generalizations about the grocery market today:

- Most shoppers have a choice of grocery outlets, and will use several of them at different times for different purposes.
- Many people are increasingly looking for local food, the more authentic the better.
- There is a large and growing segment consisting of older couples and single people, and the big supermarkets are not very good at catering to their needs.

That is what is happening today. What might the future be like?

Well, it could happen

Deborah Smith looked out of her suburban London window and smiled happily. It was a big day in her life, 21 May 2030, her son Jamie's 14th birthday, and she saw the sun was shining, just as she had hoped. She began to plan the events of the day, which would not really start until her eldest son came home that afternoon. He was getting a bit old for birthday parties, she appreciated, but had fixed himself and a group of close friends with a day out at the weekend at Stamford Bridge, home of his favourite football team. Today, however, would be a family event with Jamie's younger brother Oliver and her husband Patrick, who had arranged to be home early from his City job for the occasion. Debbie had even managed to commandeer two sets of grandparents to be there. Jamie would certainly feel it was a special occasion.

Of course, he had already organized many of his requirements in advance. The family all had their individual shopping accounts at BQF (Best Quality Foods), the best of the three or four gourmet food shops on their local high street. BQF, a dynamic Indian-owned enterprise, had food interests in a dozen developed countries, as well as the UK, but it had to compete with the one truly strong local company, Tesco, in its red, white and blue regalia, as well as the Chinese-owned multiple, Cho-Han Gourmet, and of course Wal-Mart Neighbourhood, which Debbie's parents still liked to call Asda, its former British name. Debbie could remember the days when the British high street was just as dull as ditchwater, full of estate agents and building society branches, and flashing shop fascias in an amazing range of garish colours. But those days were long gone, and now she and her family had more choice than they needed where food shopping was concerned, and in a style they all found a lot more congenial. There were four very go-ahead shops all within walking distance, which meant none of them needed to use their own or the community bikes that were parked on racks at both ends of their own street. Now and again they had considered buying a car to take the family to the seaside or visit friends, but in the end Patrick always vetoed this as 'not a cost-effective solution'. No cars were needed for shopping any more, that's for sure. The cab companies were ready at five minutes' notice to provide a charged-up electric Hung-Lee saloon or even a convertible, and the boys liked ringing the changes in the type they chose to hire. Of course, if you lived in the wilds of the country, where Debbie's own parents lived, this was a bit difficult, and her own parents kept an ancient hybrid vehicle just to go to their local quaintly named superstore, which was several miles away. These were a dying breed. There were only a few hundred of them still surviving, and they were pathetic relics of what had once been an advanced shopping model, where everybody had gone in their owned car and loaded up with food for a week. What an amazing habit, Debbie reflected to herself. And with petrol at €6 per litre and an hour's parking at the store costing a further €10, it was not an attractive option, even before the community tax charge, levelled on all car journeys, was taken into account. 'Not for me,' she thought thankfully.

How much better society was managed now. All those superstore sites had been turned into retirement homes, satellite university campuses, local museums, technology learning centres and even school playing fields. As the changes happened there was universal rejoicing – because it allowed families like theirs to shop exactly where they lived, in their own communities, and feel that they belonged there and that in a real sense these local shops, even if they were owned by far-flung multinationals, were owned by them. And how easy the whole process was. Of course, the shops all opened all day every day, which was just as well, given the round-the-clock working hours that were now so common among their friends. Just as the schools were occupied all the year round from 6 am to nearly midnight, so the shops were sometimes far more crowded late at night than in the middle of the day. We have a 24-hour society, people said to each other – and whether they liked it or not that's just what it was.

Of course, the family all had their own account in all the local shops; cash had vanished many years ago, as well as those fraud-prone credit cards that had caused so many individual grief stories over the years. Shopping had become a truly individual and richly varied pursuit. On two or three days a week Patrick and Debbie allowed their children to choose their own meals – within certain parameters, which everyone knew from an early age. There was meat at most once a week, but an amazing range of locally grown fruit and vegetables. The boys particularly liked English apples, and the rebirth of the apple industry meant there was enormous variety available, for home consumption as well as export. The family had its own little routines as far as meals were concerned. On at least three evenings they all ate together, and on these occasions Debbie usually chose the meal herself for everyone – she knew what they liked, and they quite liked the fact that now and again she would do the deciding and they didn't have to go through their own daily ordering ritual. It was social changes such as the reinstatement of the family meal that had made Britain such a different country over the past 10 years. According to the New Delhi-sponsored world survey, Britain now had the most family-friendly practices and happiest children quotients in the post-industrial world. Was it quality local food shopping that had caused this, or were the aspirations so clear to the former supermarket owners that they knew what they had to do to compete? It was hard to say.

Something else that had changed for the better was the service. Debbie's mother always remarked on how wonderful it was when she came to stay with them. At one time it seemed that the universally adopted and highly effective hand-held terminals, which listed everything you bought, checked the items out, and then paid the bill straight from your bank account, would result in the shopping experience being no more enjoyable or personal than in the traditional old out-of-town superstore, with its weary lines of sad-looking shoppers, lack of any sensible information or guidance, noisy metal trolleys, predictable promotional offers, and drab anonymity. People were worried that these new engagingly presented, highly modern local stores might be just as impersonal as the old model. After all there would not be any assistants to pass the time of day with, would there? But that's not what happened – quite the reverse in fact. Because it became clear to all where the new battle for the consumer was going to be fought, all the new entrants set out to innovate in as many ways as they could to surprise and delight the returning customers. The core of the competitive offer became the personality of the shop owners. They had to know a lot about food, recipes, ingredients, food provenance and brands, but most of all they had to know their customers. Now wasn't that a change? Debbie remembered hearing from her old grandmother how in the 1950s, three-quarters of a century ago, there had been a company owned by a family called Sainsbury, and in their shops there had been learned old gentlemen in long white coats and crisp white hats, and they were always to be found cutting bacon, or slicing butter and cheese for the customers, whose names they always knew and whom they treated with the utmost deference. And when they weren't doing this they were washing their hands. How quaint.

It was, she thought, almost as if we had in some strange way returned to these ancient days, even if the new shop owners didn't always wear crisp white coats and hats. They certainly knew what the customers wanted and were always ready to provide the necessary guidance. Since quite a lot of the time they were dealing with (half-grown-up) children who thought they were adults already, or adults who had big ideas but little background knowledge of anything to do with food, they could be worth their weight in gold. Often the phrase would be heard as the shopper left the store 'Well, what a real pleasure it is to shop here', and sometimes the less-informed shopper would comment 'Saved my life – what a lot that manager knows.' That was the difference from the old-style self-service experience – there really was a lot of learning and knowledge vested in these store managers and, as the years passed, they transmitted this knowledge to the customers. Of course, they all had at least one university degree. This eventually began to change the entire food culture of Britain. The old determinants, US-style branded fast-food joints everywhere, and two curry restaurants on every British high street, gave way to lots – several thousand – of individually managed, vibrant local shops. Their pervasive influence became so powerful that in time it affected the eating attitudes of the British nation. It was true to say that perhaps for the first time the British were becoming truly engaged with their food – as their neighbours across the Channel had been since time immemorial. After all, what was the point in 'going out to eat' if the quality of what you were getting didn't match the materials, natural or cooked, that you were offered in your choice of local food store? It was almost a revolution.

Of course, not everyone did what Debbie did, and the families who had two full-time workers might not choose to spend the time that Debbie and her family did in making their shopping experience so informative and rewarding. Internet food shopping had certainly improved vastly from the early days. Now there were many more options, collection where you wanted, delivery as and when you wanted it, no errors or short sales obviously, and sale or return on everything you bought. Even with the internet, the grocery providers – of which there were now many more, and lots of them locally situated – were increasingly being asked to provide much more information and guidance about the order, both before it was delivered and alongside delivery. You couldn't get away with any old driver or delivery person. Everyone was now offering face-to-face personal guidance as part of the delivery offer, and it was usually the calibre of this personal service on the spot that could make the difference in choosing whether to maintain or change the provider.

Another recent big change had been the one that the brand owners had been making. Debbie had grown up in a world where in some categories she had favourite or trusted brands that she would buy, come what may, wherever she shopped. She noticed as the years passed that in some outlets the supply of one brand after another were gradually dying out and being replaced by the store owner's own. These were not at all bad, and of course they usually came with the retailer's confident endorsement and even sometimes at quite a cost saving. But Debbie didn't like the trend, and she felt that to some extent she was being dictated to by the shopkeeper. And then one day she noticed an entirely new shop with a different name – it was called Brands Only, and underneath it said 'Here you can trust the quality.' Luckily she had one of these new stores only a quarter of a mile away, so she could patronize it whenever she felt like it – which was quite often. She liked the choice, the variety and the names she knew. She felt it made the shopping experience as a whole that much richer and more enjoyable. She wondered if these brands-only shops might grow, but she wasn't sure.

Well, looking back, she thought the service was a lot better than when she had been a little girl and been driven to the big Tesco Extra with her own parents. The food quality, the range, the information and the whole quality of the shopping experience – yes, they were looking up as well. But what about the prices? Patrick was always chiding her gently that she didn't know all the prices of the items she bought, which he didn't think was good enough. They also both knew that food volumes sold had dropped very fast, with much less meat being produced and eaten, much less carbohydrates, endangered species like Coca-Cola, the famous but now seemingly infamous drink from the early years of the century, vanishing from the shelves, and healthy programmes universally adopted so that now there were as many underweight Britons as there were overweight, and obesity had virtually vanished from the map. These important changes meant we were enjoying a much better standard of living and were making an approach to the national and international sustainability targets that were now within sight. All this was 'a good thing', certainly, but it had brought with it a steady and now quite rapid increase in food prices and in family food budgets. There was talk that the big retailers – really only half a dozen in the world now that mattered, only one of which was a British company and one a US company – had changed their strategies once and for all. Since there were no more big markets to penetrate and since food volumes in the developed markets were in decline, they had, as a group, elected to look for margin growth. This was the reason for the change and the higher prices. Debbie knew that with some careful management she could afford the increases. Though the country had been successful in reducing the ranks of the genuinely poor, she realized there would be others who would begin to feel the pinch and who might, even given the reduction in size of families overall, have a tougher time than she did in making ends meet. This would probably mean that the European discounters like Aldi and Lidl, which had made big inroads in the developing markets of the world, would have another go at entering Britain, where they had failed so often. Debbie didn't think much of these stores, but if prices really shot up everyone would have to give them a second thought, wouldn't they?

In our lifetime, we have seen food shopping completely transformed. Even in the last 10 years, the number of ways we can shop, and the different demands we place on supermarkets and their suppliers, has developed continuously. Change is the only constant, and anyone competing in the grocery market has to change too; those that do not, or that do not adapt fast enough, fall behind. We do not know how tastes, habits and preferences will alter in the years ahead. What we do know is that any provider will have to be exceptionally alert and fast-moving to stay ahead of the game. The market in the UK, and in most other developed countries, is extremely competitive. In the period we describe here, the first 10 years of the 21st century, we have seen well-known high street names disappear and others falter. A few winners have emerged, a few players look shaky, and others seem strong and promising. We analyse these successes and failures, and try to draw some patterns from the flow of events.

About the book

The first chapter tells the continuing story of Britain's undoubted winner, Tesco, dominant in its home market and increasingly confident and successful abroad. The second looks at Asda: owned by Wal-Mart, the biggest retailer in the world, Asda has some unbeatable advantages, and is beginning to flex the muscle that its giant parent provides.

Then we move on to the question mark that is Sainsbury's: once the clear market leader, with an unrivalled reputation for quality, it lost its way and then moved up from the worst stage, but is not yet in perfect health. In the fourth chapter, we examine perhaps the most seismic change in British retailing in the last 10 years: the emergence of Morrisons from its northern ghetto – a very well-run and profitable place, but restricted – to transform itself through a takeover of Safeway into the fourth big player. It has had difficulties on the way, but is overcoming them now and galloping along at an industry-leading pace. We then describe Waitrose, for years an established favourite of the middle classes for its high-quality products. With the backing of its parent company, John Lewis, Waitrose is emerging from its small south-east base, becoming a potential future challenger.

Chapter 6 on the second tier analyses the retailers that are left: again, we will see some strong performers that may break out of their relatively small shares with differentiated and well-delivered offers – the discounters – and the weaker brethren that struggle along.

The next two chapters examine the markets in Europe, a different place from 10 years ago, and the United States, still dominated by the colossus Wal-Mart. These provide contrasting examples of market regulation and development. We move then to internet shopping, where again Tesco is a clear leader, but where we have a new challenger, the internet-only Ocado. Internet shopping is now well established, but it is by no means clear how the online grocery market will develop.

Then, as not everyone loves supermarkets, and there are problems that concern us all, we examine climate change, and we look at the ways the supermarket groups have responded to public anxieties. Finally, we draw together any patterns we can discern in the kaleidoscope of food retailing and draw some conclusions, about both what has happened and what we believe may happen in the future.

Tesco
The story of a great decade

01

'Transformation' is an overused word. Few stories purporting to describe transformational effect merit the description. One that does is the development of the Tesco business over 30 years, and at an accelerated level for the past decade. There are few more exciting retail journeys; but of the small but significant clutch that have happened in Napoleon's 'nation of shopkeepers' (Marks and Spencer, John Lewis, Sainsbury's) the development of Tesco ranks with the very best of them. How and why it happened deserve close analysis.

Tesco was founded in the 1930s by Jack Cohen in East London's back streets, and its first 40 years were little more than Cohen's own vibrant but harum-scarum life story. He bequeathed to his successors a wayward collection of scruffy stores, a company with no policy (he and his closest aides spent their time noisily and incoherently arguing about what to do next, but Jack always had his own way) and a level of inattention to financial results that had Tesco sailing too close to the wind for shareholder confidence. Any pretensions to governance were non-existent (its boardroom was affectionately known down the line as 'the snake pit'), and Jack refused to consider retirement. When finally forced to, Cohen hand-picked his successor from the playing fields of Malvern College, Tesco's first-ever management trainee, Ian (later Lord) MacLaurin. MacLaurin was destined to lead the company to safety and a radically enhanced reputation over two decades from its rebirth as a serious competitor in 1978. By any measures MacLaurin's tenure was a success, and by the mid-1990s Tesco had displaced Sainsbury's as UK market leader. Ten years earlier, such an outcome would have seemed unlikely, as Sainsbury's brand and fortress-like command of the British food landscape were viewed by the world as simply impregnable.

However, MacLaurin's lasting achievement was to give Tesco an operating board and top-level management team full of confidence; a trading record that delivered steady growth; and finally and most significantly Sir Terry Leahy as CEO. The appointment of the 39-year-old ex-Liverpool business graduate may have surprised the market, but he was in turn scheduled to take Tesco forward at a spanking pace that has put MacLaurin's own substantial achievement over the 20 previous years somewhat in the shade. Not many companies have just two leaders over a period of 32 years and still counting. Still fewer deliver strategic success on the scale these two have given Tesco.

Leahy had arrived at a critical juncture. Tesco's platform as UK leader had been hard won, through organic growth and single-minded pursuit of the out-of-town superstore programme, a process countenanced and perhaps encouraged by the British Conservative government of the 1980s. The British market still looked like a dogfight, and there was a strong feeling that the Tesco renaissance had run its course and normal business trading would resume. There were four high-level contenders, and each had strong double-figure market shares and vied for leadership. Three – Tesco, Sainsbury's and Safeway – were British; the fourth, Asda, by 1999 was a subsidiary of the massive US Wal-Mart corporation. Somewhat smaller but just as competent was Ken Morrison's brilliant Bradford-based firm, and then there were the two well-placed niche players, Waitrose (John Lewis) and Marks and Spencer, each contributing to a competitive and unusually diversified free market constellation. Nonetheless, successive governments from the 1990s onwards disliked the competitive structure and the apparent hold that supermarkets had on British life. So did elements of Britain's vocal chattering classes. Government regularly investigated the industry's approach, using the Competition Commission for the task. It repeatedly found there was little or no case to answer.

The first two phases of Tesco life – swashbuckling anarchy under Cohen and his close family, and MacLaurin's ship-steadying ascent to UK market leadership – have now been followed by an emphatic third stage under Leahy, which we can perhaps call the emergence of global brand strategy for Tesco. Tesco has few peers today in world retailing and, while it is not yet a global leader, those that are still ahead of it – including the massive Wal-Mart – are fully aware of the force that Tesco has become.

Box 1.1 Sir Terry Leahy retires

The announcement of his retirement, at 55, surprised the market. However, Terry Leahy is nothing if not his own man. Understated, highly intelligent, with many diverse interests. It should perhaps be no surprise that after 14 hard years Leahy, as a leader with an enviable list of business achievements, should decide that the time was right to pass on the Tesco baton to Philip Clarke.

Tesco has had a handful of leaders, and only two in the past three and a half decades. When Leahy assumed the CEO role, the company was already the UK market leader. Leahy's arrival signalled the immediate pressing of the accelerator pedal. Since then, the pace of growth, as well as the range of achievement, has been remarkable. Dominance in the home market is a reality, where Tesco's 30 per cent share now dwarfs all others. Extension to Europe and Asia, with rapid penetration of the brand followed. Latterly, three of the world's largest economies are being tackled simultaneously. New sectors, such as financial services, clothing and entertainment, prove that Tesco has a large and growing presence. In areas such as the loyalty card, followed by internet retailing, Tesco – inspired by Leahy's innovative drive – have set world-beating standards. In all cases, it has been the unwaivering focus on the customer that has characterized Tesco's presence and Leahy's strategy.

The numbers tell their own story. Tesco was a medium-sized UK retailer with a market cap of £4bn and today is the world's third largest, with the marked cap almost eight times the 1997 level. Revenue has quadrupled over the same period and annual growth is running at 10 per cent year on year. But great companies are known for their people and their brands, and it is in these key respects that Leahy will want most to be remembered. The Tesco brand, under a range of fascias, is now present in Asia, the Americas and Europe, and has taken a leadership role in markets as diverse as banking and clothing as well as food. No British company can boast as big a transformation in world markets over this comparatively short time. Only by selecting and motivating a powerful and high-performing team can such a record be attained, and it is in this respect that Leahy's period of leadership has been so notable.

Not that Tesco has not lost people. Inevitably they have had to do so and a wide range of British companies, not all of them in retailing, now feature ex-Tesco managers as their leaders. We can expect this to continue. Around him Leahy built and encouraged a high-performance group, who were immensely engaged, thoroughly well rewarded, and challenged through a demanding set of goals. Philip Clarke, hitherto a team member, now takes over leadership of this powerful group and will want to retain its performance level as well as growing its range of achievement.

The job at Tesco begins and ends at home in Britain, and Leahy and his team know this is an ever-present reality. In the core UK-based food business, the new

Box 1.1 continued

team embarked on a programme of aggressive market share growth, continuing but then revitalizing the progress that had first established leadership in 1995. Tesco was prepared to innovate, and it looked for and found new sources of growth, such as the reintroduction of smaller stores to British high streets. Over a 10-year period, a modest but not noticeably secure share advantage against Sainsbury's was converted into a market share now double that of the former leader – and Sainsbury's has now lost second position in the market to Asda. Indeed Tesco holds a share almost equivalent to that of Asda and Sainsbury's added together. 'Dominance' is a difficult word to define in business, but consistently taking business of almost twice that of your two nearest rivals in a competitive market can surely be called domination, much as Tesco itself may dislike the term. Meanwhile Tesco has been able to convert revenue advantage into appreciably higher margins and profit levels, setting and matching the best in the industry. (Of course, as we will see when we look at the range of Tesco's global and product group ambitions, this is something that it simply *has* to do.) More importantly, growth in food sales has provided the funds to deliver a big range of innovatory moves. One of the most imaginative was also one of the earliest and bravest, namely the investment in Clubcard, and the consequent, unique capacity that Tesco has enjoyed vis-à-vis all its competitors of attracting, understanding and ensuring the enduring loyalty of a growing number of consumers. Of the components of business success in British food retailing over a decade, it is clear that the Clubcard-based loyalty programme has probably played the most crucial role. It is no accident that Tesco's core purpose today is stated as 'creating value for customers to earn their lifetime loyalty'. Of the weapons that it has in its arsenal to deliver this, Clubcard must be most prominent, and unsurprisingly too we now find Clubcard playing an increasing role in Tesco's worldwide business.

Other significant components drive innovation and fuel rapid share growth. Tesco was quick to identify its consumer appeal as inclusive or 'classless' – something that had eluded both Sainsbury's (regarded from time immemorial and even today as the middle-class shopper's venue) and Asda, which relentlessly but successfully pursued less well-off shoppers. Until it acquired Safeway, so did its northern rival Morrisons, another clearly positioned and winning company. With Waitrose and M&S inevitably focused on higher-price shopping and the limited-range discounters seemingly unable to make headway in the apparently hostile British market, Tesco was increasingly able to occupy the market's higher 'middle ground'. As time passed it set out deliberately to do this, providing the food ranges to satisfy all tastes and all pockets. The differences were becoming significant, from Tesco Value and later Discount lines catering for those seeking low prices to Tesco Finest, which sold unequivocally higher-quality items at higher prices and put Tesco in a league very different from anywhere it had tried to be before. It was a clear, clever strategy; gradually the differentiation became well understood by

Box 1.1 continued

consumers, and the process has been increasingly imitated and adopted by all competitors, so that now it is an industry norm. In 2009, as the severe UK recession started to bite, Tesco was under huge pressure as the overall leader, and decided to take the process a stage further. Recognizing from research that being price-competitive was going to matter much more, it introduced a new range of individually named 'Discount' brands. Tesco claims a third of its customers are now buying something from this range every time they shop. Perhaps equally importantly, it succeeded not for the first time in the UK in stunting the emergent aspirations of the powerful European discounters (Aldi and Lidl) just when it seemed as if they might at last have the bit between their teeth and were beginning, prematurely it now appears, to trumpet their progress.

Every little helps

For many years Tesco has adopted and has persisted with the somewhat anecdotal 'Every little helps' as the umbrella descriptor for its brand offer. This has certainly allowed Tesco to adopt, under this useful and comprehensive brand banner, wide and regular improvements in different sectors. No doubt it makes its appeal as inclusive and classless reassurance. However, the impression exists that mass advertising of the brand may be less important to retail winners than it is in other fields, and it is questionable whether 'Every little helps' has enough cutting edge and novelty to carry the business through many more years. Tesco has a major challenge to keep its UK brand and stores firmly at the front; there are competitors of all shapes and sizes waiting for it to start sitting on its laurels, and commentators regularly watch the shortest-term results to look for the slightest level of slippage. But, at the end of the day, Tesco has been able to create a reputation as a down-to-earth provider to all kinds of British shoppers, and the approach has been one that, once adopted, has been pursued with praiseworthy consistency. Certainly, as the company has begun to expand from a strong food base into new markets, which Tesco is never slow to do, the slogan 'Every little helps' has been an enviably adaptable vehicle to announce these Tesco innovations. As with all well-known claims, the trick will be to know when its time has finally run its course and how best to replace it.

Building brand differentiation has been accompanied by deliberate, sometimes adventurous moves to broaden the range of retailing formats trading under the Tesco name. Again, this is something the market leader has to do and, in the past 10 years, nobody has got anywhere near Tesco's performance in this regard. Property management has played its part, but the capability to reoccupy the town high streets has delivered massive and unexpected brand visibility. Overall, Tesco has been able to increase selling space by a steady 6 per cent per annum, and it now has four defined channels, adding in total to around 30 million square feet of space nationally. The majority is divided between 450 superstores and around 180 larger Extra stores; these two account for 80 per cent of selling space. Simultaneously Tesco made an alert and decisive return to the local high street, opening up more than 1,000 Express-format smaller sites and something approaching 200 Metro stores in city locations. Many of these stores provide an important service to the time-poor, since they have extended hours, often staying open until 10 or 11 pm, and 24-hour trading is not unusual in major population centres.

While high street trading margins from Express and Metro stores are significantly lower, the volume has hugely boosted Tesco's scale advantage and widened the competitive gap to such an extent that, almost without exception, its competitors have announced an intention of matching its high street strategy (how they will do it is another matter perhaps). Tesco can certainly claim to have assisted some effective rebirth in local food shopping, which had been dying a not-too-slow death in the hands of an independent trade that sadly had shown little realistic will to maintain its existence.

Online selling

Tesco was an early investor in online grocery retailing and, by moving early and learning the ropes, it managed to find an elegantly simple, low-cost model where others had been more ambitious and had failed. With growth now running at about 20 per cent year on year, and good levels of profitability being shown from the UK online business, the claim in the 2009/10 annual report to run the world's best grocery online operations may be justified. In 2007 Tesco further widened its brand availability by launching a catalogue company – Tesco Direct. There are now 12,500 products online, and recent results show 1.5 million customers ordering through this route. These moves combine to make the Tesco home market position in food difficult to attack – unless it makes some big errors or competitors can produce a major innovation. What is clear is that the British leadership team in Tesco understand their responsibility to recognize market initiatives and gain realistic presence.

In summary therefore Tesco can look to a decade of high achievement in its core home market, sustained through the recent recession. Leahy and his executive team knew they had the most to lose when the worldwide recession bit rapidly, and the requirement to keep the home performance secure was the overriding critical prerequisite. The strategy was protected, not without anxieties, but reliably, and having done this Tesco can now move on. With one in eight UK purchases now being made at Tesco, it is starting to leave its food supermarket heritage behind, although for years to come it must fund developments. Tesco's consistent capacity to find innovative ways of building market share is impressive – but it must also become inevitable. Without the security of a consistently nurtured and buttressed home market position, it would be impossible for the company to tackle a range of assignments, in adjacent markets at home but more significantly in the international food markets where it has now planted many important flags. Britain is now becoming Tesco's 'cash cow'. This is not a disparaging description. The United States has been this for Procter & Gamble for 50 years. The Tesco position has been hard won, against committed competitors, including one former dominant leader (Sainsbury's) and the major subsidiary of the world's largest business (Asda). In most cases it is only because Tesco has grabbed first-mover advantage that it has built strong shares. Tesco achieved its UK pre-eminence by consistently offering the market the most comprehensive consumer offer, and if it were to stop doing so confidence would quickly collapse and its capacity to extract significant profit levels from the home base would be threatened. The seed capital for expansion would dry up. However, the intrinsic security of Tesco's current position must be recognized – a trading margin of approaching 6 per cent on sales of approximately £40 billion means that its net return is now ahead of the collective return of its next four competitors. This is the result of a determined first-mover advantage in the years of Leahy's stewardship and earlier. The rewards of building on the platform he was offered in the late 1990s are now being harvested.

Diversification

Another of Tesco's key objectives has been to diversify out of food into new markets where it believes it has an equivalently strong consumer offer. Here too it has been able to outperform the majority of the competition over several years. Non-food sales are growing at 6 per cent per annum and have doubled in five years to a revenue of £12.5 billion or 20 per cent of overall group business. A sign of Tesco commitment to non-food growth is its non-food-only Homeplus stores, which with the contribution from Tesco Direct make the new lines more widely available than would relying on its bigger stores alone to generate the user base. While there is serious competition from its major rivals – Asda in particular is thrusting ahead – in widening the non-food offer Tesco's capacity to innovate and to take on major new business sectors remains overall best in class and not just in a UK context. None of its global competitors, including US Wal-Mart, can point to a more comprehensively achieved group of targets.

So today we find the Tesco brand represented in places as diverse as electrical goods, games, entertainment, gardening and pharmacy. In 2009 the company built a meaningful share of the market for television sets, using an own-brand Technika to achieve this. This too may be a sign of the times. The company appears to be finding a formula with which it can build parent-brand growth, using a range of good-value sub-brands to tackle specific sectors. Of course, this is a delicate process. If you get too clever and tactical you can hurt the main brand, and if you make the wrong choices the whole enterprise loses reputation. Against some severe local and sector opposition, Tesco successfully fought strong opposition and gained control of Dobbies Garden Centres, occupying another divergent sector. (Resolution under pressure is another Tesco characteristic.) Of course, the non-food 'staples' like clothing are destined to play a significant part in Tesco's worldwide portfolio and already appear in its assortment in eastern European and Asian markets. Tesco already claims market leadership in clothing in Hungary and the Czech Republic. The company regards clothing as a market equivalent in size to food, but one where a small share means there is the potential to build it conceivably to food levels. This shows the scale of the opportunity – one of which Asda too is fully cognizant. So far in this sector it is Asda that has built the stronger brand, and no doubt this is one reason for Tesco choosing a new leader for its clothing division, announced in early 2010.

Building brand growth in non-foods is key as they extend their brand into world markets. Tesco is trying the idea of non-food-only stores in Edinburgh and Nottingham (Homeplus). It is clear that web sales are intended to play an increasingly important role in the future and that the company is looking for imaginative ways of integrating the in-store and online offer. For example, Tesco makes its direct merchandise collectable at a reduced price in-store. The overall web statistics are impressive – one and a half million web visits each week, 12,500 products stocked online, and nearly 12 million Direct catalogues distributed annually.

Sourcing

Sourcing will play a key role in Tesco being a non-food winner in years to come. Wal-Mart has shown the way and at scale, particularly in China, but Tesco has been quick to follow. A major international sourcing office exists in Hong Kong, and Tesco has created worldwide sourcing hubs in China, India, Turkey and smaller Asian markets. The process model that Tesco and Wal-Mart are both using – source at lowest cost wherever it can be found and build low-price brands in many new sectors, eg Cherokee in clothing and Technika in TV sets – shows the likely course of market development for years to come across the developed world. There will be negative commentary in the United States as well as in the UK on the growing market 'clout' that these two companies can carry with Asian-sourced materials. Consumers will be asked to vote with their boots on whether they appreciate the new brand ranges and the new low-price floors that are created. So far their verdict on, say, the £5 shirt has been clear and positive.

International strategy

If breadth of offer and non-food growth have been features of the Leahy tenure, it is certainly his international strategy that we regard as his biggest contribution to long-term growth and reputation at Tesco. He inherited a bare cupboard from his predecessors – a half-hearted venture to acquire Catteau in northern France, which was summarily closed before the new strategy took shape – and this is where the new leader made an instant difference. It was just as well. Carrefour had had a 20-year start, and Wal-Mart was hungry for acquisitions in major markets. A thinking chief executive in a global – or in the Tesco case potentially global – enterprise can exercise major influence if the chosen strategies show long-term coherence and begin to work. Leahy has been particularly sure-footed, viewed against absolute standards or against his competitors. From a standing start in the late 1990s Tesco now has a strong presence in eastern Europe, with country leadership positions. Going to the east was an inspired choice. There was big potential there, not much of it had yet been tackled and there was a series of moderate-sized markets where Tesco's new overseas people, especially those on the ground locally, could learn how to run a profitable business and do so quickly. Then they could move with increased confidence to fry some bigger fish. Equally meaningful was the choice shortly later of the Asia Pacific region, which was bound to be critical to a world portfolio in the years ahead. Again Tesco made some judicious choices in discrete markets where they could do well. Today Tesco is leading in Thailand and South Korea. Both these radical ventures were devised and implemented at speed. Nearer home, Ireland has become a strong Tesco market. Few companies have managed this process with such immediate assurance.

Having established these strong footholds, Tesco then elected, against many expectations perhaps, to reject all thought of consolidating its gains, to put the corporate foot down, and with a vengeance. In the second half of the last decade it made three momentous and immense strategic decisions that will change the whole face of the company. Previously, international expansion had not taken the company into a market that was more significant than the UK. Now it entered China and later India via joint ventures and, boldest of all, sent Tim Mason, widely regarded as Leahy's chief assistant, to the western United States to set up a new start-up company, to be known as Fresh & Easy. Turkey was soon to follow. By any standards this is an aggressive expansionist strategy, which might, were it not for the previous successful entries, be called 'going for broke'. The board know this for certain and, there is no question, there are the most substantial operational, financial and reputational risks attached. These latest three or four moves will be the biggest test by far of the depth of Terry Leahy's company's learning abilities. In a sense we feel that Leahy, with a positive set of experiences in Europe and Asia Pacific behind him, *has* decided to 'go for broke' – realizing perhaps that the company's best chance of playing a leading global role in food and related retailing was happening right now and that he was a little way behind rather than ahead of the other big players.

He had either to move decisively or to watch others, notably Wal-Mart but also Carrefour and Metro from Europe and soon-to-appear Asian entrants, take the global positions that were becoming available. Well, we know what happened. Nobody can accuse Tesco or its board of sitting on the fence.

Going local

So much for international strategy. It is capacity to make the operating process work on the ground that will spell success or failure. Many consumer businesses have aspired to deliver the maxim 'Think global, act local'. Tesco believes this passionately as a part of its DNA and practises what it preaches. Local cultures, customers and regulations require local response and on-the-spot leadership. From the outset, this is what Tesco has set out to create. Flexibility of approach has been needed, since the markets it occupies, starting very quickly one after the other, span a huge range of cultures and stages of development. Tesco has been willing to work on and establish important local brands, and has also recognized that an open-minded approach to multi-format options is the most likely way to win market leadership – thus the recent innovative development of Chinese shopping malls. Finally, Tesco understands that international development is not a short-term goal but will take years (decades even) to get right and that quick wins – albeit they have managed one or two – are improbable, especially in the BRIC (Brazil, Russia, India, China) markets or the United States. So now, a mere 10 years from the company's early international forays, the world recognizes Tesco as a genuine world player: a company with a strategy it defends and to which it has adhered successfully, and one that can now begin to regard its set of skills as an asset created in many places and therefore transferable between markets. Unilever did this successfully in maybe 30 years. If Tesco can do it, then that will be a big feather in its cap.

In China, Tesco is developing multi-level shopping centres and, having begun trading in three, is establishing 14 more sites. The market is modestly self-funding. In India, Tesco unusually chose to enter the market via cash and carry, and has an exclusive franchise agreement with the retail arm of the powerful Tata group. Fifty Star Bazaar hypermarkets are expected to exist in five years. Finally there is the United States, where the Fresh & Easy chain, modelled on the

Express convenience concept, now has 150-plus stores. The concept has been imaginatively and thoroughly re-engineered to give it distinctiveness and future relevance for US needs. Thus there are local kitchens for the Californian market, and the stores are as unlike conventional US supermarkets as it is possible to imagine. Without question, economic conditions in the United States badly hurt Tesco's forward estimates of growth and store development. Equally, there have been adjustments to the range, style and ambience of the stores. Understandably, Tesco is proceeding with caution and has deliberately slowed the pace of store extension, while financial results – badly affected by the weak pound/US dollar ratio – are behind plan. This has made analysts jittery. Many believe Tesco's novel approach and store format indicate that it lacks a winning formula for the United States. However, the moves made could be regarded as prudent, and the store and range offer relevant, differentiated and potentially a good weapon for future space-constrained urban US locations. While it has good competitors in the market – eg Trader Joe's and Wal-Mart's Marketside – Tesco's approach has consumer appeal and is on track to succeed in the years ahead.

Now that critical mass exists, the level of return from the international business has become significant to the group result, and enables Tesco once and for all to distance itself from its British competition, which – except for Wal-Mart/Asda – are indefinitely confined to a hard-pressed UK economic home base. Overseas space now accounts for 60 per cent of the Tesco total, 20 per cent of current trading profit is delivered there, several markets are now doing better than breaking even, and five of them are places where Tesco claims to be market leader. Cash return on investment (CROI) has risen steadily and is now a shade below 13 per cent, an attractive investor return, given that it has been achieved quickly. Two final points are worth making on international Tesco. The loyalty card scheme, with its competitive edge in providing consumer guidance, is a critical component of Tesco customer strategy. Tesco has now established loyalty card schemes in four markets, including two where it leads overall (Ireland and Korea), and has pilot-tested in four more, ie numerically more than half the markets where the company is present. This makes sense; it shows the company appreciates the learning advantage Clubcard brings and, importantly, shows the company has the operational skill to make Clubcard operational away from home. Nothing it could do quickly should make investors more confident of future global success.

The Tesco brand is an emerging geographic force across the triad. UK sales are over £40 billion, but already Europe is over £10 billion, while Asia accounts for £7.6 billion. Sales growth contribution was a handsome 20 per cent or more in all three areas in 2009. For the moment, the US contribution is minor and returns are negative. Given this pattern, what kind of judgement should we make on Tesco global expansion? That it has manifest and high-level risk must be conceded (this will be examined later in the chapter). That it is unusually bold and by market standards has proceeded at a pace unmatched by others is accurate. That it has moved quickly from tackling second-level markets to addressing the very biggest (simultaneously) is unusual and striking. But, lastly, that Tesco exhibits a powerful and widespread capacity to learn and a consistent approach to worldwide business strategy is a factor to offset the worst of these anxieties. Its track record is simply second to none for global growth.

A newly framed core objective for Tesco, but scarcely a novelty in terms of its business approach over the decade, is that of 'following customers into retailing services'. Tesco leadership had long identified opportunities in its home market where it has been obvious to the world at large that in important markets the customer was nowhere near the core of many industry approaches to business. In some sectors, well known to the retailer, such as banking and financial services, it even seemed to Tesco that the customer was treated as a painful inconvenience between the smooth reconciliation of production and a strong set of accounts. Naturally Tesco has been keen to expand its banking interests, and while it has adopted a careful, step-by-step approach to growth there is no doubt it sees financial services as juicy pickings and, given the recent recession as well as the long-term industry lack of interest in the consumer, this view must have strengthened: hence the establishment of retail services as core objective number four and its designation as a key future profit target with specified high-level board leadership.

Retail services

Today, if we look at any sizeable Tesco store with the inevitable checkout feature of the Tesco Personal Finance brand, the move to financial services looks a thoroughly natural one. Any new businesses of the company require immediate expression of consumer value and the capacity to express the offer, in-store or online, in direct, uncomplicated terms. The Tesco bank, of which Tesco has now moved to full ownership, has seen a steady development process over 12 years and now has 6 million customers and 28 discrete products. Tesco has finally arrived as a key operator in consumer banking, and one has the feeling that, even without the many forces of unwanted industry disturbance around, British banking will never be quite the same again. With the uncertain and apparently uncoordinated approach by existing banks to providing consumers with usable personal information, financial services may become an exceptional growth area for Tesco in the years ahead. The key weapons are transferable and unparalleled consumer insights and, through time, a capacity to cut costs and improve margins through efficient scale operation. The issue will be whether the Tesco brand can progressively emerge as a trusted financial services provider at the expense of long-established but currently highly unpopular brands. Tesco's timing in banking has been fortunate, and the fact that it is untarnished by the profligacy and intransigence of its competitors will no doubt work to its advantage in creating an inclusive consumer offer.

A second component of the new retailing services division is Tesco. com, now a core element in the trading model. Online grocery retailing was begun early, has been taken further by Tesco than by its competitors, and is now supplemented by having Tesco Direct alongside it as an online non-food provider. A third element is the telecoms entry, via the 40 new Tesco in-store phone shops, a number planned to rise to 100 by the year-end 2010. Tesco has been able to make a good-value offer in this new growth market and is showing competitive levels of growth, especially in prepay mobiles. Its approach appears to be to accept the normal market trading approach, but modestly improve on this with the terms of its 12-month consumer contract. The final element in retailing services is Dunnhumby, the market research company behind Clubcard and majority owned by Tesco. It is the smallest in revenue by some way compared to the others, but important across the business and to future worldwide Tesco success. The company has been imaginative in allowing Dunnhumby to sell a proportion of its expertise – no doubt the bits that Tesco regards as less than proprietorially significant – to Tesco's own retail competitors, eg Kroger in the United States.

Today retail services total revenue is under £1 billion, but a solid level of operating profit – over £200 million – derives from the four sub-brand areas. No doubt this can grow and at a great deal faster rate in the UK than food, or even than some non-food markets. Tesco is setting highly ambitious goals and, if we look at core competences, current market share (low) and competitive skill sets (poor), it is probably right so to do. Delivering revenues of £5 billion and profits of £1 billion, which we understand is the proposed plan, will represent major success. At this level of return Tesco would bring to the table profits above those made today in the core market by any UK food retailer competitor, so the scale of the task addressing Leahy's leadership team should not be underestimated.

Corporate social responsibility

Another key goal is perhaps Tesco's most surprising, especially to those of us who recall ancient Tesco history, its wayward antecedents and its entire lack of concern with community issues. That was then and now is different. Today the same company elects to 'put the community at the heart of what we do', an unequivocally expressed proposition. Responsible behaviour is the overriding stated policy. Each Tesco country has its own community plan, which it must ensure is delivered, and local components of the plans will vary. There are five core commitments: active local community support; buying and selling products responsibly; care for the environment; giving customers healthy choices; and creating good jobs and careers.

The company would appear to have had success in making the initiatives work at all levels across the company and in a range of markets. Thus community champions exist in six countries to work with local schools, charities and services to support the causes that matter most to local customers. To ensure awareness of the environmental task, green energy champions have been appointed in nine markets. The responsibility agenda is certainly being actively pursued at operating levels in stores and depots. There has been a big step change in the Tesco attitude to climate change and environmental responsibility, and this is evident from many of the 'extramural' activities that company leadership undertake on a visible basis and at a considerable cost in time to themselves (see Chapter 11).

The Tesco corporate responsibility report sets out comprehensively the Tesco record in delivering against its five worldwide community targets. It is a document stuffed with detailed and practical information showing where progress is being made. An attractive feature of the document apart from its breadth and level of detail on a growing but diverse worldwide business is its refreshing honesty. There is recognition that the company, and the environment in which it operates, is engaged in a number of important but recently agreed journeys. Some have shown progress quickly, while others are a lot more challenging. This is reflected both in the transparency about progress made or not made and also in the occasional bullets of criticism that are happily included from outside sources (lots of 'must-do-betters'). You get a strong sensation from the corporate responsibility report 2009 that Tesco really believes that the achievement of its five targets will be as important to ultimate corporate success as the business performance targets we have been discussing above. This is surely a sign of board and management cohesion in the company and reflects confidence that the leadership team has a degree of unity in framing winning long-term strategies.

Future performance

We now move to review uncertainties and risks, to consider the important current and future issues driving performance for Tesco, and finally to try to provide a profile of the company, outlining its strengths and suggesting one possible view of its future.

At its simplest we can use the same frame of reference for companies as we do for individuals. Great companies, with predictable and positive behaviour patterns, come in time to be regarded in the way we regard personal friends – we can rely on them and have deep-rooted trust and confidence in them. Few businesses achieve this, but when they do they have a priceless asset in their armoury. In the later years of the 20th century, IBM and P&G probably achieved it, and in the last decade Google, Apple, Amazon and Tesco's competitor Wal-Mart might all be contenders. One interesting aspect of this classification is that it took decades for companies to achieve this status, but more recently in our information-laden world they seem to get there much faster. Is Tesco in this category yet, for if it is then its outlook truly is a bright one. To try to answer the question we identify a quite brief list of crucial issues that are determining and will decide whether in future Tesco can meet the highest standards of world business – not just as a retailer, but as a company as a whole. The issues are: 1) diversification; 2) capital funding; 3) business performance; 4) ethical risks, notably but not exclusively in the supply chain; 5) people capabilities; and 6) regulatory/UK governmental matters. We now examine these in order.

There are several ways in which it is correct to see Tesco as a 'stretched' business. First impressions are instructive. When you enter its doors the impression is of a determined, energetic and thoroughly occupied team. While the culture is collegiate, there's little time for small talk, and you feel there's a shortage of dilettantes on board ship. You might see the same in the stores – Tesco people do not hang about. They know their job is to give the customer a great time but, if that has to happen at the expense of the home team chasing hard, so be it. Stretch expresses itself in many ways. Tesco has been the first to extend its brand ranges from Finest on the one hand to its Discount brands on the other. Channels show similar breadth, from the Extra superstore to some tiny Express convenience stores. Online and Direct are further customer channels. The food (and for that matter non-food) offer is complex. Tesco needs this complexity to deliver a dominant UK market share, which it needs in turn to fund a global business. You can see this as a sensible integrated process, but it's already several levels of complexity beyond that of their direct UK-based competitors.

Add product group stretch – banking, telecoms, clothing, hard goods, entertainment – and much more inevitably to come. The range dwarfs that of any of the manufacturing companies or even erstwhile conglomerates. Tesco people have to cover a wide range of industrial practice. Finally, as if these two levels of complexity were not enough to satisfy one company's vaulting ambitions, you now add the acquisition of major geographies, including the biggest of all, world markets (China, India, the United States, Turkey, approaching 40 per cent of the world population, ie 3 billion people), all added in the space of about three years. Surely, the commentator says, you can't be serious. Can anyone do all this? Who can run this fast all the time? Well, says Tesco, we can. But stretched – mightily so – it surely is, by any objective measure you care to take.

The second big issue, closely related, is funding. Capital expenditure has doubled over five years, and splits four ways, namely the UK (the most at 50 per cent of the total), Asia, Europe and the United States. Budget expenditure is forecast to reduce in 2009/10, and specifically UK capital is forecast to reduce sharply: is this a sign of financial constraint operating? Tesco manages its property funding imaginatively and has real UK-based competitive advantage, not popular with everybody but real nonetheless, here. It has a strong balance sheet, historically well able to support investment in all parts of the strategy. Its process controls, set out in the corporate governance sections of the annual report, are clear, comprehensive, actionable by company CEOs and covered by strong audit measures. Nonetheless the range of demand, from major and certainly less predictable new requirements (eg the BRIC markets, the United States and financial services), means that historical efficiency may no longer be so good a guide. At the end of the day the question will be whether the company has made adequate allowance for funding needs to enable the fast growth that is forecast, eg in China, the United States and retailing services, to take place. Since Tesco starts today a long way behind the leaders in all three of these areas, there is not much room for 'slack' if it turns out to be wrong in any one of them. But the core process is a strong one.

Business performance is a key issue for Tesco. The record is very strong, and points now to 20 years of delivered plan. Not many companies to our knowledge match this, and when they do they sing and dance about it in ways that understated Tesco avoids. The UK has been the permanent base, but there have been high-quality performances in European and Asian markets, and rapid moves already to market leadership in both continents. In the non-food areas and new sectors, including financial services, Tesco may indeed be able to surpass some of its targets, since it will not be competing with companies with the calibre and experience of, for example, Wal-Mart or Asda. The culture is one where high performance is a watchword and, once ingrained, it is hard to eliminate. One must view this as one issue on which Tesco is emphatically ahead of the game, whether it be its own plans or the level of competition it faces.

Supply chain and related ethical risks are clearly an issue, with the degree of food market dominance that Tesco holds, and has held, for many years. That the company appreciates this can be seen from the lengthy review of these risks on page 30 of its 2009/10 annual report. It is inevitable that any really big company gets 'slated' with the accusation of abuse of market power; Tesco is no exception today, as the UK's Sainsbury's was not in the 1980s and as the United States' Wal-Mart is not today either. Much of the comment in Britain emanates from a public deeply unaware of the business case that Tesco can fairly make, and equally ignorant of the corporate responsibility processes that it follows. From bullying farmers to denuding high streets of independent traders, the complaints are vociferous and endless. Some critics have to be taken more seriously. Tesco has been accused – by War on Want – of a disturbing ignorance of its own supply chain. Commentators who should be well informed, and often are, mean that Tesco has real issues to defend here.

As a principle, and however unfair it may seem, with market dominance comes the concomitant obligation to behave with a more developed sense of responsibility than others involved. We have a strong sense that, at a strategic level, Tesco understands this well, whether it be among the 'operating group' – led ultimately by the CEO himself – or by those handling corporate governance, such as board member Lucy Neville-Rolfe. It is less clear that 'down the line', for example in overseas sourcing or among the product buyers at Cheshunt, the same attitudes persist. There may be a need for greater vigilance here, and certainly it will not help Tesco's worldwide reputation if, for example, it becomes associated with the view that the UK farming industry is dying on its feet because of the tough conditions it has to endure given Tesco buying policies. The farming lobby is well versed in negotiating tactics, but Tesco will have to recognize that the public see the farmer as the underdog in the process and it will have to convince the public at large of the merits of its case.

The fifth issue is human performance: how capable is the team that David Reid as chairman and Terry Leahy as CEO have assembled to deal with the huge and complex challenges that we itemized under the first issue reviewed above, namely diversification? Nowhere, we believe, does the company emerge with greater credit and inbuilt resolve than it does when one addresses human capabilities.

The work that MacLaurin's leadership did in establishing basic coherence of process and teamwork by the mid-1990s has been recognized. Nonetheless, as Tesco set out on its global adventure and began the new drives into non-food, internet trading and financial services, its competences were deep in winning the consumer's vote in food stores but, frankly, not much else. The board's pride and joy had been the capability of a range of school leavers who became deeply experienced in successful store operation and grew into positions of major business responsibility. Years ago, Terry Leahy said, 'Yes, we recruit graduates, but they start later and they often can't catch up.' The transformation achieved over a 10-year period has been, by any measures, enormous. Tesco starts with its board appropriate for the major global competitor it has become. There is relevant experience and continuity, but perhaps above all a demanding and open process.

It's at the next level that dramatic change has occurred. Again, it is with admirable completeness documented in pages 50–64 of the 2009/10 annual report. Far from obfuscating top management remuneration, Tesco accepts and even enjoys full disclosure of its policies and actions in considerable detail. Leahy has succeeded in building a team of eight executive directors that would be the envy of many international companies. Like him, all eight are in their mid-40s to mid-50s and have had a minimum of 10 years in the business, and the majority have had 10 or more years as board members. This is an experienced team with a strong record, which has also shown a genuine capacity to extend its competences as the business has grown in complexity. Several could no doubt have been seen as potential successors to the CEO, though until recently there appeared little likelihood of Leahy relinquishing his responsibilities. Great companies need great and continuous leadership, and this Tesco has enjoyed. Leahy's retirement took the UK market by surprise. Continuity at CEO level is held by his direct-report team – without question many could have jumped ship in recent years and could do in the future. It is a tribute to blue-chip reward policies and to an underlying teamwork culture, but no doubt most of all to the fact that, more than most, Tesco has an enduring winning record. Not many players still in top form elect to leave Real Madrid or Manchester United. If management capability is a Tesco issue, it is one to which it responds with élan.

A final issue for Tesco, not one mentioned specifically in company documents, is its reliance on the UK for growth, people and funding. A UK advantage in past years has been its free market nature. Unlike the case in other big European economies, growth has never been capped by regulation, nor have the many national and local planning constraints been particularly arduous. That Tesco can operate with success from a core base in the UK is, given its record, not in doubt. What is today less secure is the UK economic environment, following the 2008 recession, and the resultant ability of business to operate in a market with growing constraint, consumer uncertainty and probably higher future corporate taxation. Of course, nobody will admit to anxiety about the capacity of the UK economy to recover, and perhaps for this reason it is not formally recorded in Tesco's business report, but the realities of high debt repayments stretching over several years cannot be avoided. In this context the failures of UK-based secondary schools' education, an area on which both Leahy and Neville-Rolfe have commented openly, must be a significant headache for a company leadership needing constantly to reinvent and rejuvenate against world-class standards.

Allied to this it is worth noting that the UK supermarket industry, despite or perhaps as a direct result of its overall positive results, has been subject to regular UK government investigation, some of which appears to be continuing. The last major enquiry, operated on behalf of government by the UK's Competition Commission, produced its findings in 2005 and gave the industry a virtually clean bill of health. A summary of the situation from the Tesco viewpoint might be that it has often seemed to be operating in a surprisingly hostile environment. Tesco's advantage is that year-on-year growth, particularly overseas, has made big strides, rendering the company more immune from at least the less constructive elements of investigation. Its presence in world markets is therefore an increasingly prized or necessary asset.

The conclusion

Tesco is not just by a huge margin the UK's best retail company, but a contender for being the world's most innovative and certainly ambitious retailer. (It does not have it all its own way: see Box 1.2.)

Box 1.2 Are you satisfied with your grocery shopping?

Two separate and recent studies tell us all we need to know about consumers' rating of their food shopping experiences. The Consumers' Association publishes *Which?* and in February 2010 published its findings: 'Supermarkets – are you left satisfied?' Simultaneously the National Customer Satisfaction Index measured satisfaction with supermarkets against department stores, electrical and petrol retailers and e-commerce. The Index found that there was a slight decline in overall approval of supermarkets (73 per cent) and confirmed that the supermarket overall was the lowest-scoring retail industry for both service quality and price. Specifically the Index showed that Waitrose (up 4 per cent to 85 per cent) and Asda (also up 4 per cent to 79 per cent) were the biggest winners, with Morrisons edging upwards to 77 per cent, ahead of Sainsbury's and Tesco, unchanged at 73 and 72 per cent respectively. Other major competitors and smaller supermarkets were rated significantly lower than the five majors listed above.

The *Which?* study questioned 13,000 Consumers' Association members in considerable detail, and its findings are consistent with the National Customer Satisfaction Index conclusions listed above, an encouraging confirmation for both organizations of the accuracy of their respective responses. Eighty-one per cent of *Which?* respondents stated that product quality was the important criterion in their choice of supermarket. Waitrose dominated positive replies where *Which?* users

Box 1.2 continued

were concerned, perhaps not entirely surprisingly given the demographics of the audience. Nevertheless the margin of difference between Waitrose in first place, with 79 per cent being positive, and second place occupied by Marks and Spencer at 64 per cent was huge and confirms findings elsewhere in our book that Waitrose has found ways to leave competitive offers – including those of M&S – in the shade recently. Shopping at Waitrose was described as 'a pleasure', and comments on its uncluttered appearance and wide aisles were many. Service, quality and punctuality were all given the highest ratings (five stars), and only price (two stars) was found wanting, again unsurprisingly. Waitrose shoppers are not there for the bargain prices. Online Waitrose matched the store ratings, showing that this company is genuinely capable of building a strong retail brand in more than one distribution channel.

Marks and Spencer aspires to satisfy the same audience but is not quite bringing it off. Shopping there is likely to be of the 'top-up' variety. 'It's too expensive to do a main shop there' is a frequent comment. Where Waitrose gains five stars for quality, M&S does well (four stars), but there is a perceived difference. Without question, for the time being the limited M&S range is a handicap, and the stated strategy to extend the brand list is no doubt intended to deal with this deficiency. Overall, M&S has not moved forward since the heady days of the 1980s when its new food offers and particularly its ready meals were the talk of the chattering-class dining tables. Prices are high, but you get what you pay for, and the quality is still seen as excellent. There is a good base here for future development, if the sites can accommodate the company's range of aspirations.

The big surprise in the *Which?* study must be the relatively high ratings given to the two hard discounters, Aldi and Lidl, which have modest market shares. They are jointly in third place at 61 per cent and are accorded five-star ratings for their prices. 'They have good deals' and 'I am happy with their value for money' are typical responses. Significantly, too, Aldi and Lidl match the mainstream supermarkets in their perceived food quality ratings, ie they all achieve three stars, no more and no less. There are few meaningful differences between the big four companies, although Morrisons does have a lead against the others and, at least for *Which?* users, whose loyalties to Sainsbury's have been long established, Sainsbury's too leaves both Tesco and Asda a long way behind in the respective overall ratings, which are as follows: Sainsbury's 58 per cent, Morrisons 56 per cent, Tesco 49 per cent and Asda also 49 per cent. Bringing up the rear are the Co-op (45 per cent) and the third hard discounter, Netto, which at 41 per cent can't match its discounter competitors.

There is not much good news in the *Which?* results for the market leader Tesco nor for its nearest competitor, Asda, although they may jointly feel that this is not their target audience. Not only do they as expected lag behind Waitrose and Marks and Spencer on the quality dimensions, and Aldi and Lidl on price perceptions, but

Box 1.2 continued

there are signs that Morrisons is proving an attractive and relevant competitor with good ratings for service and price. Meanwhile Sainsbury's has not fallen behind with this audience, and indeed the ratings of its online service are on some measures better than those of its big rival Tesco.

The composite picture suggests that the UK consumer is pretty much spoilt for choice, as perhaps we might have expected from other sources. The respondents as a whole showed this in the inconsistency of some of their overall viewpoints. On the one hand, two-thirds of the group replying said they liked to be able to buy everything under one roof, and 72 per cent had bought homewares in a supermarket in the past six months. However, about half the group thought supermarkets should stick to selling food.

Britain may have too many denuded high streets and lament the demise of the range of local shops catering for everyday food needs in its towns and villages, but there is little sign in shopper behaviour that there is much real anxiety about the position, nor do studies like the National Customer Satisfaction Index or the *Which?* report suggest anything other than consistently good ratings for the quality, service or prices on offer.

Tesco is a company that Britain should be proud to host, one that developed from entrepreneurial but chaotic beginnings to achieve market leadership in the UK by the mid-1990s, displacing in the process a business (Sainsbury's) that had itself over more than a century stood for high-quality food retailing and given the UK market its very first genuine supermarket in the post-Second World War years. The 21st century has seen Tesco stepping up the pace markedly, broadening the range of its UK offer into many new categories, and simultaneously achieving what could be lasting domination of the British food market. Additionally Tesco had decided its future was now to be global and entered the markets of eastern Europe and Asia Pacific with considerable and in some cases rapid success. Having started to secure a worthwhile international portfolio, the company once again raised the pace, opening four new ventures in the major markets of the United States, China, India and Turkey, all of which, though still showing modest revenues for Tesco, are being pursued with innovative strategies and high management determination. Most important of all perhaps has been the maturing of this fine company into a brilliantly led and managed enterprise, with business process, corporate culture, management talent and top-level leadership that set great standards and must be the envy of many well-run companies. Confronted at the end of the decade by a damaging worldwide recession in all its markets, Tesco surmounted the challenge and has emerged, in the words of the leader, 'with our strategy intact'. These are the reasons we subtitle the Tesco chapter in our book as 'The story of a great decade'.

Asda

02

Thrift is a requirement in an orderly society.
JOHN D ROCKEFELLER

Is Asda a lucky company? This may seem an odd question to ask about Britain's second biggest retailer. Anyway, as everyone knows, the best companies make their own luck, and no doubt Asda will say it has had to make its own luck. In its 50-year history, there have been times when things have gone well. One such time was the early 1980s, when the Leeds-based company was uniquely go-ahead where manufacturer-led promotions were concerned, apparently happy to run Persil promotions at a net margin of 1p a unit, something nobody else would have countenanced. Of course, it moved terrific volumes once the world got to know what was happening. But it was cyclical, and there were other times when its leadership appeared to lose its way, as the years just before the Norman/Leighton revival took place showed. Somehow, when this has happened, at the key moment significant change *has* been engineered from somewhere, and the business has been able to take off once again down its now well-trodden path to deliver best-value products to British consumers. Such on the whole has been the experience of the past decade, at the beginning of which the most momentous change of all in Asda's 50-year life occurred. The Leeds-based retailer, already regarded by the stock market as 'in play' and seemingly certain to be acquired by Geoffrey Mulcahy's hungry UK-based Kingfisher plc, found itself spirited away right from under Kingfisher's nose by the powerful US Wal-Mart company. Initially it was not clear how this might affect Asda's fortunes, although there were obvious signs that the Asda leadership was not an unhappy seller. The move attracted huge public attention, and Wal-Mart's worldwide CEO was seen being interviewed at 10 Downing Street by an apparently eager Tony Blair, who might have seen a new and powerful economic ally arriving. Wal-Mart had purchased Asda for what must have seemed to Bentonville's hard-nosed buyers like little more than small change, and there was a feeling that they were capable of turning the British market upside down – supercentres on the Yorkshire moors or the Welsh valleys perhaps – hence the political interest. Could Mr Blair and Wal-Mart's Mr Scott use rock-bottom prices to help each of their respective constituencies? Asda had fallen to Wal-Mart early in the US company's foray into international waters, so there was not much of an established pattern to which the new owner or the European subsidiary could turn as a model for their future development. As it happens, Wal-Mart had been lucky enough to do the deal, waved on by Asda's board, at a time when the good times had been rolling in Leeds, while in Mr Blair's Britain they were starting to roll in the country as a whole. In the background, quietly but purposefully, Tesco had been flexing its share muscle under its new understated leader, while arch-rival Sainsbury's acute troubles were becoming more and more visible. While this had been going on, Asda's well-equipped leadership team, with Archie Norman as chairman – his era at Asda is still referred to engagingly as the Norman Conquests – and experienced Mars-trained operator Allan Leighton, had been returning the British company to its historic and consistent low-price/low-cost strategy with considerable success. It was Wal-Mart's great good fortune to inherit the company at a stage when this strategy, not in any sense a new one, had become well established once again. The strategy was working; there was springtime abroad in the air. It was Asda's own good fortune to discover a new parent, itself fully convinced of the intrinsic merits of Asda's 'best value' approach – 'We couldn't have done better ourselves', they were probably saying. Had not Wal-Mart been born and nurtured to US maturity pursuing an identical approach, driven first by founder Sam Walton and then by his successors? How often do acquisitions like this take place? Truly, it must have looked like a marriage made in heaven. The first portents were undeniably good, and so, on the whole, for the months and years ahead, they turned out to be. Within sensible limits, all *has* been for the best in the best of all possible worlds. Now, 10 years later, the buyer remains very happy, and the new progeny has adapted its behaviour to provide the soundest of returns, ranking right at the top of Wal-Mart's worldwide portfolio and able to offer on its own account relevant learning and development experience to be adopted across the now much wider Wal-Mart world. So, yes, we can conclude, today as at many times in its past, this is still a lucky company.

The essential congruence between Asda's UK strategy and Wal-Mart's long-established approach – 'lowest price always' was the way Sam Walton most often chose to describe it – must therefore be the fundamental reason for Asda's continuing success in Britain. Nobody can pretend that it has lacked competition, either in the market as a whole or indeed in its own chosen low-price segment. Specific and from time to time successful (Kwik Save) and less successful (Somerfield) low-price operators have come and gone. Just next door to its own Yorkshire home was and is Ken Morrison's Bradford base, and for many years Ken's formidable powerhouse business gave Asda, and indeed everyone else, a run for its money. Then Morrisons' ultimately successful acquisition of upmarket Safeway demanded that a new strategy emerge for this now much larger and very disparate company. Effort upon effort to gain a meaningful foothold has been made by the European hard-discounter fraternity, and the current recession has seen both Aldi and more significantly Lidl on the march once again, determined to increase their store presence across the land, which they have achieved. But still in Britain it remains difficult to establish hard discounting with the panache that has attended this format in most parts of continental Europe. (This time, after an initial flutter, they seem to have failed – again.) The mainstream competition, Tesco and to a lesser extent Sainsbury's, have been anxious to ensure that their own low-price credentials are not forgotten, and they are resolute in fighting their own corner. Both through specific value ranges in their portfolios and also from time to time (in Tesco's case at least) through head-on challenge to Asda's 'lowest price in the market' position, these competitors are simply not prepared to give Asda's low-price promise free rein. Confronted by all this noise, quietly when it could, but raising its own voice to signal determination when it needed to, Asda has pursued the most consistent of approaches protecting its core promise, latterly called 'affordability', with a level of consistent and exemplary resolution. Importantly, therefore, it has shown its competitors, actual and potential, where it stands and where its own lines will be drawn, today and in future. Consistency is a simple virtue. The Asda leadership recognize it and stick rigidly to their low-price heartland.

Andy Bond, Asda's latest and thoroughly well-versed CEO (who stood down as CEO midway through 2010), used striking words about the relevance of pricing as an element of market 'management' and what it meant to his team and to confidence in the Asda business culture. 'Being the UK's best-value retailer is what comes first and foremost', he said. 'It's pervasive, cultural, the heart and soul of our company; it creates a virtuous circle, a set of systemic beliefs.' These are not points of view dreamt up ahead of an interview, or even to feature in this or any single year's annual report. You can sense the absolute degree of determination to hold the position it wants to occupy in the British market from the firm way he talks about the task. His may be expressions of an essentially very simple intention or idea certainly, but as we all know strategies should in the end be simple. The price position tenet applies in the beliefs of the Asda and Wal-Mart leadership teams, even in markets intrinsically affluent and even in periods when prevailing economic conditions are more relaxed than they are now, or are likely to be in the UK for some time to come. Where food is concerned, this company has a firm belief that low price will be a main determinant of food buying for a majority of buyers now and probably for ever, and it is building its business on this unalterable premise. For 11 astonishing consecutive years in this highly competitive UK market, Asda has been formally awarded the title of the UK's lowest-price retail chain.

Perhaps it is now time to abandon the notion that it is a competition and begin to recognize what looks like a permanent market axiom or reality. Time and time again down the years, Asda price has earned its spurs in the market and, if its present UK or US owners have anything to do with it, it is not going to go away any time soon. Box 2.1 tells one story of how it comes to life, for which we are indebted to Elizabeth Rigby, retail correspondent of the *Financial Times*.

Box 2.1 Supermarket price warriors never taste defeat

It was the height of last summer when a food buyer at Asda House in Leeds hatched a plan to offer customers a £1 frozen pizza. With the cheapest pizzas retailing at the time for about £1.49, the price cut was a drastic one. Even so, Asda did find a supplier that thought it was possible.

Northern Foods, a big supplier to Marks and Spencer, struck a deal with Britain's second largest supermarket to slash the price of one of its pizza lines in return for two draws: first, the promise of a big rise in sales volumes to help offset the cut in prices; second, an agreement from the retailer to keep the product simple.

By offering just two types at this price – shoppers were limited to cheese and tomato or pepperoni – the manufacturer made the numbers stack up by dedicating nearly an entire factory in Ireland to producing what is, in effect, one product.

'The cheese and tomato version goes down the production line and, when we want to do a batch of pepperoni pizzas, we switch on the sausage machine and it puts on five slices of meat or whatever,' explains Stefan Barden, Northern Food's chief executive.

Box 2.1 continued

With big volumes at low cost, they flew off the shelves, leaving the pizza maker and the supermarket with some profit while also giving customers a slice of Italy for a lot less cash.

But win–win situations in supply agreements between retailers and suppliers are few and far between.

Relations between the two are typically combative rather than convivial. In the highly competitive British retail market, supermarkets are constantly trying to drive better deals from their suppliers – all the more so in the teeth of the downturn. 'There is pressure to push the costs back down the supply chain,' says one manufacturer who asked not to be named.

'You have to think of it as the converters [companies that take ingredients and produce ready meals, sandwiches, cakes and so on], the ingredient suppliers and the farmers themselves. A converter will buy from the two below them and the pain is felt right down the supply chain when the retailer tries to cut its costs.'

Tesco, the UK's biggest retailer, has been among the highest-profile companies to pile the pressure on suppliers, renegotiating prices and payment terms, making hundreds of non-food suppliers, for example, wait 60 days rather than 30 to be paid.

Its efforts paid off. Last week Tesco announced that it had made savings of £540m in the last financial year, helping it to deliver margins of 6.2 per cent.

Judith McKenna, finance director at Asda, says retailers have an arsenal of weapons they can draw upon to try to cut prices, including painless measures such as avoiding empty lorry trips and cutting packaging.

When it comes to suppliers, the three main levers are to extend payment days (as Tesco did), cut the amount of inventory being held by the retailer to improve its working capital, and to drive down the amount paid for goods.

In recent weeks Asda has brought back e-auctions, having phased out this practice four years ago. Under this system, suppliers must submit their best bid for a contract online in a blind auction in which they have no idea whom they are up against. While the lowest bid might not win, it may be used as a starting point for the negotiations.

Asda says it has only used this on certain commodity products, with just 50 contracts agreed this way out of thousands. But some suppliers are disgruntled.

'They are using these technologies to get lower prices,' complains one food manufacturer. 'You have to submit a bid on an auction, you don't know who else is there and you have to submit a price blind. It is psychological, it concentrates all the information [about what suppliers can offer] on one side.'

The primary producers that support the chain – farmers and ingredient manufacturers – know this only too well. Theirs is a market of supply and demand, but in commodity markets where there is plenty of similar product, they have little room to manoeuvre.

Of course, there is a real sense when you talk to Asda people that they feel this is their moment, here and now in economically pressured Britain, and that, as the truth about the depth and longevity of Britain's economic crisis becomes known to the public at large, more and more customers will start beating their way to the Asda door. Some will do so by choice; some may just feel it would be irresponsible not to. Recent results for the business have been strong, with excellent like-for-like growth year on year, and no doubt Asda's continuing ability to see off challenges to its low-price supremacy from competition has added to its current and tangible confidence. Tesco of course will not give up the battle for one moment, but it too seems to have realized and even accepted the 'marker' price positions Asda will always seek to defend, so, while we can expect continuing price sorties, roll-backs, the usual phenomena such as 'this month's astonishing reductions on hundreds of items' to continue, Tesco's requirement to maintain a consistent level of profit delivery from its dominant UK food market share obviates a more damaging set of price wars. In game theory terms it is not always obvious who actually is blinking first, who needs to or indeed if anyone might have done so. It is not a bad contest. In the red corner we have Britain's dominant, highly successful and highly profitable market leader. In the green there is the challenger, the undisputed number two UK business, one that has held the low-price position consistently for years and has a formidable coach as backer with the deepest pockets in world retailing. If it were ever to come to an out-and-out showdown, one feels Asda might possess the better hand to deal with Armageddon even than mighty Tesco. But Armageddon does not look a probable or appealing scenario to either contender just yet.

Meanwhile, this inherently lucky business spends a lot less time cursing the recession than most do. Footfall in Asda stores was well up in 2009, and composite sales growth for the year stood at more than 6 per cent. Perhaps more surprisingly, Asda was able to record an increased average basket spend, which it attributes in major part to customers from higher-priced stores trading down. Asda has in fact managed to outperform the market for 15 consecutive quarters, encouraging it to claim it might possess a superior operating model than others. It is recording an annual share of just above 17 per cent for the year 2009 and as a result is widening the gap against number three, Sainsbury's, which shows little sign of reinitiating the chase for second place. As a sign of its recognition of how important low prices are now and will be in the future, Asda is again seeking to express its price promise in terms of everyday low pricing (EDLP), differentiating its consumer offer of low pricing from the industry norm in an endeavour to put more clear water between it and the competition. Most UK retailers, encouraged by their major suppliers, still tend to follow the promotional route of high/low pricing, ie prices that change from week to week in response to the manufacturer/retailer promotional activities on the brands in question. (Asda engagingly describes its competitors' promotional price reductions as 'weapons of mass distraction'.) If Asda can achieve this difference and communicate it effectively, it should serve to underline and solidify its low-price advantage and reputation. The Asda price gap versus key competitors widened over 2009 partly as a result of the adoption of EDLP, and it seems the price gap is here to stay.

Price and cost are inevitably closely interlinked, and in the case of the Asda UK business, as with US Wal-Mart, a necessary support for the company's low-price strategy is to secure an equivalent level of cost advantage. EDLP and eliminating promotional 'spikes' are one way in which price and cost are inextricably linked, but the company knows it has to do much more, and in this regard the Wal-Mart shield and umbrella have proved and will continue to provide a major element in the UK company's low-cost strategy. Wal-Mart's reputation as a low-cost operator is of course legendary and will be referred to in Chapter 8. Wal-Mart's four new global merchandising centres are an important element in the company's worldwide sourcing strategy, and the scale advantage that Wal-Mart's size provides means that the UK company can extract major advantage from this new organizational approach. The UK company itself, however, now has a key worldwide role, and is to use its own UK-based global merchandising centre (fashions) to back up the now worldwide George clothing brand, with Asda's innovations being adopted in many global markets (see later in the chapter). The company will look to increase direct sourcing and on a global basis to drive down costs further, cutting out intermediaries in the process. A further move in the UK has been to acquire International Produce Limited (IPL), a dedicated supply partner for Asda's produce business – melons, stone fruit, grapes, apples and citrus fruits – and one of the largest produce importers in the UK. Again, this move has global relevance, and will exploit global scale advantage, since IPL supplies some US as well as Japanese Wal-Mart requirements. The picture is becoming clearer by the day. Asda UK benefits hugely from being an important member of the Wal-Mart family. Wal-Mart has for years looked to exploit cost advantage, notably in its US market, but this is now being converted into a global activity. Chinese sourcing is playing a large part in the process. There seems little doubt not only that Asda will itself benefit significantly from this move, but that it can also hold its own as a provider of increasing scale and cost advantage to other parts of the business. It is hard to imagine that any worldwide competitor has the chance of matching this in terms of effectiveness, and the company is in the process of building an enduring cost advantage in more than one category for the business as a whole.

For many years, Asda took a distinctively different route to building business growth from its US competitors in that it sought to deal exclusively with customers through major-scale 'one-stop' supermarkets and superstores. This was another area where the Asda model was a useful underpinning of its low-price/low-cost strategy, since it was obvious that operating smaller stores, in high streets and with a range of different formats, produced significant diseconomies that Asda did not experience. Asda was therefore able to deliver a higher market share (17 per cent) than Sainsbury's (16 per cent) but from less than half the number of stores. It is clear, indeed inevitable, that Asda has a sustainably higher trading margin. The Asda preference for major one-stop stores was a further philosophical similarity it enjoyed with Wal-Mart, which when it bought Asda was engaged in flat-out extension of its huge supercentre network in the United States. It seemed that the trend in the United States was becoming irreversible as year after year more supercentres opened. Meanwhile, in the UK, the company was inhibited from expanding as much as it wanted to, simply because of the lack of availability of big sites, accompanied – in Wal-Mart's thinking at least – by unnecessarily restrictive national and local planning restrictions. However, as time passed, and on both sides of the Atlantic, subtle changes began to take place. There has been some embryonic return to city centres and to high streets, encouraged by government's increasing anxiety about empty brownfield sites and denuded town centres. In the UK, the market leader pioneered, on an ambitious scale, the opening of smaller high street stores – Tesco Express and Metro – and Sainsbury's was quick to follow with Sainsbury's Local. Asda for the time being remained in its (large) tent. There is a feeling today, with so far limited practical evidence, however, that consumers may be beginning to look for increased local, less car-based shopping, and that communities, in spite of all the difficulties, may be demanding high streets with better, more populated shopping stores. Faced with these trends, Asda UK has finally embarked on a programme of small store openings, late in the day it must be admitted, and still today on quite a small scale (50 stores). It is clear that Asda agonized over the smaller store option, since it had certainly been considering the idea for some years before biting the bullet. No doubt its hope, perhaps expectation, is that, as further consolidation in the UK market takes place and the weaker competitors give up or sell some of their less well-performing outlets, Asda will be in a position to buy these at attractive prices and to make the resulting store a great deal more effective once the Asda (and George, etc) range is introduced. There are signs this is already happening. Asda may feel its growth in the UK is constrained by space and planning policies, and there is no doubt this is the perspective of its free market US parent. Nevertheless, over a five-year period to 2009, its store figure growth looks numerically quite impressive: 10 more supercentres, 30 more superstores, a doubling of the number of smaller stores and the opening of 12 George outlets – by any standards both in numbers and in types of store an ambitious programme over five years and one that looks set to continue in a consolidating market. Andy Bond confirmed that there is no shortage of either innovation or the capital available to support store numbers growth in the business. So, given the strong likelihood in tough economic conditions that more 'superfluous to current needs' stores will become available from the weaker players, it looks as if Asda's challenging programme of store expansion will continue, which should widen the gap against its smaller competitors as well as putting renewed pressure, notably in the non-food sectors, on the leader.

Diversification

The George brand

Over the past decade Asda has been a particularly adept leader in extending its range beyond food, this ambition being assisted by the existence of very large stores within its portfolio, by its increasingly solid reputation for delivering the lowest continuous prices in any markets it enters, and finally and obviously by the encouragement of Wal-Mart, which has made range widening its long-standing hallmark in its US supercentres. Perhaps more surprisingly, Asda has been successful in building an undeniably attractive fashion clothing brand in the process and, since Asda's ability to brand had never in the past matched that of either Sainsbury's or latterly Tesco, this can be seen now as a rapid and market-changing achievement. It was right at the end of the 1980s that the company formed its partnership with famous designer George Davies and introduced its George clothing brand into 65 of its major stores at that time. It was an innovator at the time and has, in this sector, remained ahead of the game from then on. Of course astonishingly low prices are instrumental in driving its clothing market share, but the clever notion of recognizing that competitive prices and designer endorsement could live happily alongside each other was the breakthrough that made the big difference. At the prices they sell at, Asda's clothes might well have been perceived as rubbish. They certainly are not. Today a sensible level of style, fashion and quality is advertised at prices that are often half yesterday's norm bottom-price levels or lower. The George range is big, with more than 2,000 items in it. It has been welcomed effusively by Wal-Mart, which has taken it from the UK into many new markets, including some of the biggest in the world – the United States, Brazil, Mexico and Japan, for example. In the UK, Asda's brand has produced a modest revolution in the mass clothing market, and George now finds itself regularly the volume market leader, ahead of recognized clothing specialists such as Primark and even Marks and Spencer. Few competitors even try to match George prices; men's shirts, for example, start at £4 for a white work shirt, but the more fancy designs cost a bit more, maybe £7. George continues to strike a successful balance between price and quality in new sectors – its school wear, for example, carries a 100-day 'it won't wear out' guarantee. The brand has moved into wedding clothing, and offers to kit out an entire wedding party for £200, which it is claimed is about half the price specialized wedding stores can manage to do it for. The George range must adhere to the sustainability standards that the company has adopted (see below), and sourcing standards from Asia are carefully monitored, for example by George's Bangladesh-based office. This has enabled the company to carry out unannounced factory audits and improve worker standards through having regular and close contact with production processes. Without question, George is behaving in ways that show it is destined to play an increasingly significant part in Asda's as well as Wal-Mart's future. Some of the reasons are obvious. As food has declined as a proportion of household shopping in developed markets in recent decades, clothing and fashion have shown much more resilience, and this now seems likely to be the case for years to come. Competition in clothing markets, while intense and increasingly price- and cost-conscious, does not in the UK at least have quite the same efficient professional manufacturing and sourcing standards as food retailing has enjoyed. Finally, the capability of creating and maintaining a global clothing brand is a more feasible proposition than trying to do the same in food, a task where many have tried and failed to deal with the local components needed for successful food brands. Once created, the global clothing brand can bring to bear the massive cost economies deriving from scale production in lowest-cost markets. So it is little wonder that Asda and Wal-Mart are devoting the priority to George that they have done in the past decade. The overall targets now look clear and have been openly acknowledged. Food leadership for Asda in the UK market may now be conceded privately at least as a lost cause, but there is confidence Asda can become a stronger number two and at least put share pressure on Tesco. Non-food and clothing in particular are quite another matter. Here Asda has boundless confidence and is unequivocally committed to holding the position of leader. Here it feels it has the brands and the resources to do better than Tesco.

Asda Living

Alongside the determined push into clothing behind the George brand, Asda Living is playing a growing and important role in the company's priority for non-food growth. Beginning in 2004, these again large stores carry the entire non-food range and focus on a wide range of general merchandise as well as clothing, more than 20,000 items in a typical Asda Living outlet. The company speaks of these outlet volumes exceeding its expectations, and certainly in recent years new Asda Living stores are taking a higher profile among the new store openings undertaken. By now there are 20 stores in this category open.

Online selling

Online selling is another area that has assumed a lot more importance in the past few years. In the UK, Tesco has played the leading role and Tesco.com has been an online retailing model that the world has envied and in many cases copied. While it may not have been the innovator therefore, Asda with parent backing is now fully aware of online's significant potential for the future. Certainly while it may have been slow out of the blocks the online business is now growing fast and the company claims to have something approaching 100 per cent national coverage, an important criterion for Asda, which has many fewer stores on the ground than either Tesco or Sainsbury's. Asda is now the second biggest online retailer in the UK, and believes it is gaining share in the online market. The George online display shows Asda at its very best – clearly presented items in mainstream categories that customers wear every day, and at hugely attractive prices, in many cases miles below what any specialist clothing shop might be offering. Asda, like Tesco before it, has adopted the low-cost shopping picking centre approach to sourcing, and having opened its first such centre in Morley in 2009 it intends to open more and to locate them in parts of the country not well served by its stores. Asda Direct and George.com will play complementary roles, and the in-store collect service is now in place, encouraging customers to collect their purchases from a store near them, a lower-cost option than home delivery, which is also available. Keeping their costs low and maintaining the lowest prices should help the company steadily increase its online share, and there is an air of confidence about its ability to do this in the years ahead. Again it is likely to be in clothing that the potential gains will be the greatest.

Sustainability

Sustainability has become an important feature of the Asda business in the last five years. (This topic will be dealt with primarily in Chapter 8 and also Chapter 11.) It was after all worldwide CEO Lee Scott's Sustainability 360 speech in 2006 that charted the new direction Wal-Mart as a business was to take, but the UK subsidiary has become a rapid and apparently committed leader in adopting the new requirements. Alongside people – customers and colleagues – and prices, Asda will now list a third critical 'p', namely planet, providing a better future by seeking to reduce its global impacts. It continues: 'Everyone should be able to purchase products that respect the environment and that are ethically and sustainably sourced. The product range as a whole needs to be both affordable and sustainable.' Practical steps taken quickly by Asda included the removal of artificial colouring from all its own food and drink brands; it was the first to do this. Distribution revisions helped to make major reductions in road miles in bringing products to store, and in addition Asda points as evidence of the new commitment to its unique Oldham 'timber only' store, to big reductions in energy use in store, and to a major clutch of 'environmental retailer of the year' awards that it won in 2007 and 2008. However, the onset of the recession may be tempering the environmental zeal somewhat, and sustainability may now be forced to take a slightly lower profile. The 2009 formal statement of results notes under major risks that 'we recognise we have a responsibility to minimise the adverse impact of our activities on the environment', and goes on to list three 'aspirational' targets:

1 to be supplied by 100 per cent renewable energy;
2 to create zero waste; and
3 to sell products that sustain our natural environment and resources.

The operating target now reads that 'to protect our lowest cost to operate model, and to act in a responsible way we have set measurable targets and objectives in each of these areas'. One might conclude that, as Asda has achieved a worthwhile degree of change within the company and an enhanced environmental reputation, present economic conditions will demand more single-minded attention to price, cost and resultant volume and that significant further environmental progress may have to await an easing of economic stringency.

At the outset, we described Asda as a lucky company but went on to suggest that companies have to make their own luck. It is in Asda's approach to the human components of the business task that one observes different ways, a behavioural approach, and a set of attitudes that have determined how Asda's various people constituencies interact with the company and how they feel about it and react towards it. In this respect we can say that Asda has plotted its own course and today is in a very different place from that of its sometimes quite harassed US parent.

We begin with the communities that Asda serves. A frequent criticism of supermarkets is that they are vast impersonal emporia situated on the outskirts of population centres, which detract from rather than enhance the communities of which they are, to some degree at least, an important part. Of the major UK operators, Asda can legitimately claim to be the least like the model described. It can claim to have tried to do more to be a welcomed and welcoming community citizen and to be so regarded in the communities where its major stores are. That it has an advantage through having very big stores and therefore having more capacity to act positively in specific localities is true. That its roots are in Yorkshire rather than London or its suburbs probably helps it some more. Finally, because it set out to price low and therefore to be seen to help the underprivileged is an advantage to its customers – affordability is a fine banner to march under in the best or worst of times. Nonetheless Asda enjoys, and has for many years been able to hang on to, a reputation as the store the local community likes to have, and this does the company no harm at all.

A primary reason for being seen in this light in its localities is of course its status in these same communities as an employer, and here again Asda has played its cards with considerable shrewdness and wisdom. Big stores have more impact on employment prospects than smaller ones. The north is a tougher economic background than the south. This is the Asda homeland. We don't see these differences as being attributable to a company that pays more in basic salary or wages. It doesn't, and in this respect it may be likened in some degree at least to its parent, Wal-Mart, which has earned a reputation in its home market for underpaying its store staff wherever possible. However, in this respect, quite unlike the case at Wal-Mart, Asda's employee relations have for years remained a business strength. Asda does not have the inimical anti-union relationships that Wal-Mart is plagued with. Steady annual growth has produced good levels of employee bonus. Asda store managers are given a high degree of individual discretion to vary their approach from the central norm, when there is good reason for so doing. The company recruitment and retention records are outstanding, claimed to be the best in the industry for staff retention, for example, and Asda prides itself on its policies supporting female employment, diversity and anti-ageism – Asda is prone to recruit in the post-retirement cohort, for example.

Successive down-to-earth leaders, certainly including Archie Norman and Allan Leighton and running through to Andy Bond, are viewed as straightforward, down-to-earth business leaders who look for and make sure they get spontaneous interaction and response from the workforce. There is an enormous amount of highly studied (no doubt) informality. Some of the Asda stores look a bit like a fairground and so frequently, and not by accident, does its Leeds headquarters. Dressing down is not just practised, but has an aura of inevitability about it – who would want smart business dress here? 'Team' is certainly an apposite word to describe Asda people, but 'family' would not perhaps be too indulgent a description to apply to them. Sam Walton, Wal-Mart founder, who used the word often to describe his US colleagues, would feel he was at home and would be proud of them.

Following cost and community, we arrive at the third 'c', the customer. How should Asda's performance in this context be viewed? Finally, perhaps, we have arrived at an aspect of the business, and of course it's the crucial component. Here Asda's (not-so-good) fortune is to compete with a market leader (Tesco) that has made attention to the customer not just its watchword but its ultimate goal for many years and in so doing has created a degree of UK dominance that is remarkable to behold. For Asda to be capable of differentiating itself from the market leader is inherently difficult, and the impression, gained from a close study of its leaders over many years, is that it no longer seeks to do so. 'Ploughing one's own furrow' might now be the right way to describe things. Asda knows the market and the competitors it is dealing with; it is competitive, but realistically competitive. Asda's view of the customer is understated, and of course it will say the customer comes first. Of course, this is the key goal. Asda means it, and it will compete resolutely and consistently to prove it means it – it is just that the Asda means to the end is framed differently, and delivered in a different way from that provided by its main competitor. When Andy Bond went on to describe what made his business work, he offered three ideas:

- affordability;
- customer focus; and
- competitiveness.

Not only is this, as you might expect, a very good summarized view of what Asda is, but look at the order in which the three ideas emerge. Affordability comes first. This is what makes Asda (and, by the way, Wal-Mart since the earliest days of Sam Walton) different. Affordability or low price – always – is the Asda way of delivering consumer focus. It is the means to the end, but in Asda it is also the end in itself and, as we saw when we were looking at Asda's consistent approach to pricing. To conclude, therefore, affordability or low price is the way Asda tells the customer 'We care ultimately, and more than anyone else, about you. We will deliver this pledge for you.'

And so to competitiveness, the third key claimed component in the Asda business. Does the foregoing review of the customer suggest to you that this is a competitive business? There is no need to ask, is there? This is a first-class company prepared to set itself thoroughly ambitious targets and to operate with just as much visible and silent commitment as it needs to achieve these. Once again, the cultural links between this seasoned, no-nonsense UK company, with its strong Yorkshire background, and Sam Walton's ruthlessly competitive business, with its mid-western US roots, are easy to identify and make for the highest coherence between the British and US leadership and goals.

The fact that the need for affordable food exists, particularly among less well-off members of the community, has invigorated the Asda team at Leeds and given them a feeling that, while they've been doing well, they can build to an even stronger growth platform over tough times ahead. The last decade has in any case been a good one for the company, with growth regularly beating market levels, and the business grew at more than 6 per cent per annum in each of the difficult years 2008 and 2009. Looking at the decade as a whole, the company can feel it has significantly outperformed a market in which there is high-quality competition. Only in the middle years of the decade did growth seem to slow, and some lack of focus appeared to affect the company's performance. The explanation is not hard to find. This was the period when the British Safeway company became available to purchase. Asda, with Wal-Mart's eager background support, felt it might be in pole position, and there was a view both in Asda House and in Bentonville that the prize might be theirs. After all, the group had the deepest pockets. But it was not to be, and the disappointment in Asda and Wal-Mart could not have been more tangible – this single decision eliminated at one stroke of the legislator's pen any chance Asda had in the near term of getting close to leadership in the UK food retail sector. Shortly after this period Bond himself took over as CEO, and the years that followed have taken on the priority tasks of restoring sound growth to a sound company, with food share moving forward and particularly stimulating advances coming in non-food, and as an accompaniment building business confidence in the company's leadership capabilities.

Everything about Asda suggests a company with the bit firmly between its teeth, firing on all cylinders and with the capacity in many sectors – apart perhaps from food – to lead the market. As suggested already, there is nothing complex about Asda, and it seems to enjoy, as Sam Walton did in his early years in the United States, putting its simple price message in increasingly relevant ways to widening segments of the UK population. While there is no specific target aimed at the better-off shoppers, Asda has been making gains here recently, reflecting the increasing relevance even for better-off families of low-price food, and the espousal of EDLP as a key part of its presentation should help to underline this message. When asked about how the style of the company differed from that of the leader Tesco, the CEO was very clear about his answer – Tesco, he says, is all about process. Tesco has been successful at institutionalizing process in ways that have enabled it in its wide range of UK stores to become both efficient and successful. Asda is more about culture, about feeling it knows in simple and straightforward ways about the directions in which the whole team want to go. If what the CEO was saying is true, it is indeed a meaningful difference – but it is not clear that it is. It is a fact that Asda is a business that is a bit simpler and easier to comprehend and perhaps to drive, whereas Tesco, especially in Britain where it has its heartland, has become, necessarily, a lot more diverse and, it would contend, more inclusive. The two companies have both strong and well-tested business models and can point to many years of consistent trading success. Coexistence therefore is and remains possible.

Asda's own business model has unquestionably gained from the Wal-Mart acquisition of it a decade ago now. Without it, it is doubtful if the company could have made anywhere near the same progress. Present Asda leaders acknowledge this happily – yes, they say, it has been 'a good experience'. In this acquisition, Wal-Mart has done a first-class job in leaving the existing levels of business confidence in its new subsidiary unimpaired and even doing a lot more to help Asda expand. We have noted the high levels of brand and process synergy between the two companies, and there is no doubt this has contributed to making Asda probably Wal-Mart's most successful single purchase. Bond says confidently:

> Wal-Mart has made Asda a better Asda. It's good for us to have a single owner, and it's good to have one who is so naturally well informed. We like the way we can discuss the important long-term decisions, and they

know that this is where they can and should be adding strategic value, as well as capital flexibility to the direction of our UK company.

Asda will – and does – point out that Wal-Mart has itself been on a steep learning curve where running an international business is concerned. Until Asda came along, Wal-Mart had not done well with companies that were out of the North American time zones. Mexico and Canada had worked well, but not much else was turning the corporate lights on. Wal-Mart has itself moved on and become more used to international winning ways now. Bond points to China and India as two big opportunities that it looks as if Wal-Mart is now getting right. But we might think that Asda's leaders might be being a little modest about their own role in the Wal-Mart worldwide coming of age. Back in 1999 when it started, Wal-Mart was a European novice and had very little to offer other than of course its financial muscle to a well-positioned UK company. As acquirer and acquired settled into their new relationship, Asda was able in lots of ways to mark its own card, continuing to produce good operating results, growing share in a tough food market, rapidly developing a leading clothing brand, maintaining fine employee relations and, importantly, providing managers to be placed around the Wal-Mart worldwide business. Most significant of all, Asda was able to continue to adopt the classical Wal-Mart lowest-price/lowest-cost positioning with no inhibition. It wanted to do it anyway, simply because it was best for its own British business. This is the source of the underlying comfort in the relationship, a phenomenon that is quite unusual between US headquarters and invariably smaller UK-based subsidiaries. There is a tangible lack of tension, not obviously leading to any complacency – these two companies are nothing if not results-conscious. But, to summarize the relationship, it looks to the world like one of high and enduring confidence. Wal-Mart feels it made a good acquisition and it did. Asda has gained scale, cost-effectiveness, innovative capability and worldwide brand presence. Asda has shown Wal-Mart how to get the very best from a well-run 'subsidiary' ('partner' might be a better word) that wants to and can do a great deal more for the worldwide business than just producing a growing market share and improving profit returns over a 10-year period. That is Asda's leaders' principal achievement over the past 10 years, and it is one in which they can take legitimate pride. Yes, Asda is a company that has made its own luck.

Sainsbury's

03

He has put down the mighty from their seats.

T he story of Sainsbury's is one of the most remarkable in British retailing. The business has already lasted for almost a century and a half, significant by any worldwide longevity measures. At its Victorian foundation 140 years ago, Sainsbury's was the archetypal family business, starting out as a small store selling fresh butter and eggs. Four generations of Sainsburys were destined to lead this company, six family chairmen, and securely and steadily it marched forward, standing throughout its long life for the best in British food retailing. The family became in the eyes of the public at large a British dynasty, and their company an institution. In the last quarter of the 20th century, and after a century of successful food trading, the Sainsbury family made what seemed at the time the inevitable decision to take the business public. They had ambitious plans, not merely to increase their leadership in Britain but to take their brand and management skills elsewhere in the world. It was a well-timed decision and a phenomenally successful flotation, a visible indication of the veneration that the British population held for the Sainsbury's brand and its inherent quality. It was no surprise then that the public offering was oversubscribed by many times. The public were beginning to feel by then that Sainsbury's could do no wrong and that its skills dwarfed those of its competitors in all-important respects. A decade or so later, in the 1980s, Sainsbury's occupied a position of such apparent impregnability in the British market that there was never any hesitation in answering the question 'Who is Britain's best retailer?' It was always Sainsbury's.

The cash raised from the successful public offering enabled the company, as expected, to raise its sights, and it became one of the earliest international investors among retailers – buying Shaw's in the affluent and go-ahead US New England market. This turned out to be a disappointment for the company, and even in the days when its home business was flying high it was unable to achieve the same performance in New England. At the same time, however, it began extending its offer out of food and into hardware and DIY, moves that would be replicated by others in years to come – but Sainsbury's was first mover. Year after year, Sainsbury's shares moved strongly ahead, making the owners some of the richest people in Britain, but simultaneously creating a cadre of management and staff who were happy with their own regular earnings increases and in some cases share-related bonuses. There were no losers as Sainsbury's extended reach and power while creating one of the first outstanding consumer brands in Britain that became generally respected and then in turn even loved by middle-class British shoppers. Under (Lord) John Sainsbury's determined leadership, the company battened down its lead in the home food market, most notably in the affluent south of the country, where it built a huge share advantage. Even shoppers who did not patronize the leader's shops knew that, though not the cheapest, Sainsbury's was unquestionably the best. It had built a food brand with inherent quality and a Sainsbury's own-label brand that stood out from the pack, making others look second-class.

Each year Sainsbury's share of business in its own brand grew as a percentage of total sales. Food manufacturers as a group rated the Sainsbury's brand as the gold standard. Each year its position grew more and more impregnable. Each year Sainsbury's buyers showed from their confident manner that they were the leaders, that the market would run according to Sainsbury's behaviour patterns and that they set the standards that others would need to follow. For Sainsbury's all was for the best in the best of all possible worlds. Was there anything this powerhouse of an institution could not do? It established the Homebase business in DIY and began to spend heavily to extend its US interests in Shaw's and later in other big east coast retailers. By 1990, as John stepped down, his Sainsbury's juggernaut looked unstoppable. Investors as well as customers revelled in its progress, and the family, retaining a major shareholding throughout the period, was in confident mood. Elsewhere individual Sainsbury family members, as representatives of an institution, had significant influence on British social, cultural and educational life. It was no surprise that even prime minister Margaret Thatcher could be seen pushing her Sainsbury's trolley during her term in office. Why wouldn't she?

But, amazingly, there were some hidden skeletons in the cupboard, and bad times lurked just around the corner. After more than a century, and 20 years after becoming a public company, troubled times lay ahead for the business and its latest family leader, (Lord) David, who had taken over the reins from his cousin John by then. In retrospect, it is astonishing the speed at which the wheels fell off the Sainsbury's machine. The company seemed to move from impregnability to imminent disaster in a matter of a very few years. How could this happen? There were many reasons for the change, but the fact remains that in a decade, through the 1990s, the company moved from British bellwether to a hopelessly demoralized outfit. An incredulous stock market was nonplussed – initially unwilling to believe it was happening and then patently at a loss to understand what had happened. In retrospect, it was the company's growing complacency – many said arrogance – that had blinded it to changing realities in the market taking place all around them. In the last years of chairman Lord John Sainsbury, when it looked as if he was carrying all before him, it now seems he tried to make too much money and pushed the profit-making machine to breaking point. John certainly wanted through the profit record to leave indelible marks of success and confirm how strong his tenure had been. The transition from John to David was always going to be uncomfortable, and it lived up fully to expectations in this respect.

Meanwhile the business had come under sales pressure from – of all unlikely places – Jack Cohen's upstart Tesco and separately from a reorganized Asda, later owned by US behemoth Wal-Mart, which would provide still more cash. Competitively, Sainsbury's always refused to see Tesco as the serious challenge it would become, regarding its growth as an inconvenience to Sainsbury's own aspirations, but still viewing it as 'no contest' in management capability between the two very different companies. Manufacturers had been happy to see Tesco make strides forward because it was so much easier to deal with Tesco buyers, and the ratio of scale moved steadily in favour of MacLaurin's Tesco team through the 1980s, as they bought more out-of-town sites. When two neatly executed acquisitions overnight then removed UK market leadership from Sainsbury's, reality in Stamford Street, Sainsbury's headquarters, finally began to dawn. Then, and sadly, all heart seemed to vanish from this once great company. After all, it was not a position with which it had ever had to deal, and the long-established senior team was lost for a response. As the new century arrived the company had no choice but to draw in its horns, abandon the non-food ventures, exit the US market and even accept a major reappraisal of its iconic own-label brand, with which others were now competing.

Throughout the 1990s Sainsbury's business drifted gently downwards, losing touch with a rampant Tesco, which was determined to grow its brand and its big out-of-town stores, and was establishing a huge lead in the market. Worse was to come. By 2004 Wal-Mart had triumphantly announced that Asda had taken over in second place, and the core mid-market battle was now the preserve of Tesco and Asda, where it had been traditionally a Sainsbury's and Tesco contest. Asda does not look at all likely to lose second place and sometimes even looked capable of getting closer to Tesco, so leaving Sainsbury's far behind in its wake. The biggest company in the world was squaring up to an adversary, Tesco, set to become a British national treasure, and Sainsbury's was being drowned in the crossfire. The 10 years to 2005 are less than affectionately known to later Sainsbury's managers as 'the dark ages'. The last two family leaders must be primarily accountable for the ship hitting the rocks. Thereafter they were succeeded first by Dino Adriano and then as CEO and chairman by Sir Peter Davis, but by then Sainsbury's was irretrievably holed below the waterline, and in the time available neither of the non-family leaders could have any positive influence on the downwards spiral.

We have reviewed the years prior to 2005 as we need to take into account Sainsbury's long and stellar history when concluding where this company stands today. It might now seem correct to view Sainsbury's as another mid-ranking British company and to regard the destructive meanderings of the 20 years up to 2005 as simply a sunk cost, which we can now ignore. What Sainsbury's needed by then was a fresh start, a chance to forget why and how it had lost its bearings, and just how much business as well as reputation it had sacrificed in the process. What it certainly required to begin with was a realistic appraisal of where the British retail food market now stood – so very different from the Sainsbury's experience through most of the company's life, when it had been able to initiate many of the key developments and, if anybody did, to dominate the innovative process. Above all the situation demanded a clear new strategy that would enable it once again to carve out a well-differentiated future role for the company and that could begin to re-establish the once unique Sainsbury's brand to restore confidence in it in the minds of British shoppers. But it was obvious this was a tall order and it would not happen in a hurry. Has Sainsbury's achieved this? How much progress have the last five years produced? While nobody expected overnight success, there was legitimate hope that some trend towards renaissance might by now be clear.

When the troubles had started and Sainsbury's was searching for an authoritative figure to dig it out of the mire, Peter Davis had somewhat surprisingly thrown his hat in the ring, feeling from his previous successful tenure as Sainsbury's marketing director that he knew just what a formidable brand and company it could be. Davis had limited time at his disposal, and he probably underestimated the scale of the task involved in turning round a failing business, which is what it by then was. Davis might not have been aware how little had been achieved for more than a decade while competitors moved sharply ahead. He then moved up to chairman as it became clear to the board that an energetic and probably younger new CEO was needed, but the Davis tenure was by then becoming an unhappy one. There was simply too much to do, and the scale of difference from the original Sainsbury's no doubt had left him gasping in amazement. He eventually left under something of a cloud, with the board questioning his severance terms, and the move to appointing his own successor as well as a new CEO was now even more pressing if the company was not going to fail completely.

The board's choice as CEO fell on Justin King, a young man with solid marketing credentials from Mars and other blue-chip companies and thereafter seven at least relevant years at the 'retail coalface' working for the redoubtable Allan Leighton at Asda. Soon afterwards, Philip Hampton, a highly experienced financial man and company leader, was persuaded to take over the chairman's job. The new pairing looked balanced with a nice combination of marketing and finance skills. King was quick to recognize the scale of the task he was confronting. He could see for himself how his immediate predecessors had made little or no headway in addressing Sainsbury's problems. He knew, as did the entire world, what was different about the company – 135 legendary years of steady march to market dominance as Britain's leading food stores – and to this day this banner still features as the leading element in Sainsbury's current message on its website. That this context still matters to the present team is clear – they took no time in selecting the clarion call they chose to give to signal their forward intentions. In a message to customers and shareholders, but principally perhaps directed to their anxious and disheartened internal team, they decided the core task was simply 'to make Sainsbury's great again'.

Nobody could fault this as lacking in relevance or ambition. Having decided five years ago where they wanted to go, they have persisted – this continues prominently in the annual report five years later. It is now well understood by all concerned so that it requires headline letters only – MSGA. Have they been able to make this happen – quite simply, five years on, are they on track to achieve their stated goal? It is not too early now to make a reasoned assessment. Great companies must either be leaders or at least show they can create a path to reach leadership in a definable time. By this demanding standard and on a strict assessment of their performance the new team have not made it happen yet and indeed they still look some considerable distance from the finish line. They frequently claim to have created a platform for recovery – and as a minimum to have arrested the process of losing ground (market share, reputation and profitability), which had been the norm for this company over the previous 15 years.

To have stopped the rot is in itself an achievement, and it has meant a change of direction in several positive respects. Nonetheless, today's facts still make for pretty sober reading. Sainsbury's is stable in market share terms (16 per cent) but is in third place in a market dominated by Tesco, with Asda holding a solid second place, backed by its now visible determination to make the low-cost offer across Britain its own. Sainsbury's market share is a mere single market share point behind Asda's, but it is worth noting that a point is worth around £1 million in revenue, so is a meaningful level of difference between two companies. From time to time now Sainsbury's can claim to be growing at average market rates – at least in percentage terms. Occasionally its growth is faster than Tesco's, but only very occasionally, and now Tesco is twice the absolute size of Sainsbury's and immensely more profitable into the bargain. In addition, Sainsbury's needs to have on its mind a highly resurgent Morrisons. Morrisons has an exciting fresh food offer and is growing well above the Sainsbury's rate. It must believe that, if it carries on growing, there is a chance of catching Sainsbury's up. Finally, the much smaller but highly innovative Waitrose is snapping increasingly eagerly at Sainsbury's heels and, although not more than a quarter of Sainsbury's in size, it has Sainsbury's top-quality food range in view as the softest volume it can acquire. In terms of sales Sainsbury's has created a platform for growth and is certainly growing its like-for-like volume, but not rapidly enough to make any noticeable change to the overall competitive balance. Finally, although there has been modest sales recovery, none of the improvement in volume has been able to correct Sainsbury's chronically weak trading margins. Despite modest profit increases in each year since 2005, Sainsbury's is having to get by on net margins of about half the level of the top performers (eg Tesco and Morrisons). Summarizing performance over a five- to six-year period, therefore, we might say continuous progress has been made, but that there is a whole lot more to do if the company is ever to become great once again.

Strategy

The importance of strategy in looking at potentially great companies cannot be overstated. Strategy is a vital consideration in establishing recovery and then solid growth. Great companies have clear and winning strategies. Sainsbury's certainly had one for the first 100-plus years of its life and, like all great strategies, it found the simplest of expressions: its maxim was 'Good food costs less at Sainsbury's'. It was the good food element that mattered most, since the company was often happy to get away with prices that were nowhere near the lowest. This is the privilege of a market leader whose quality is not in question. Today Sainsbury's offers five principal new goals, which it claims direct its operations. These are:

1 to sell great food at fair prices;
2 to accelerate non-food growth;
3 to drive growth through new channels – banking, etc;
4 to acquire significant new space;
5 actively to manage its property portfolio.

A new element was added to the 2009 annual report, which appears to mark some change of aspiration, or at least a change of gear: the company now intends to simplify its structure so as to provide good and sustainable returns. It is worth examining these statements of strategic intention by the company. While all five listed overall goals pass the test of relevance and no doubt if success is achieved with all or even most of the headings, the business will certainly emerge a lot stronger, it is the lack of distinctiveness and adequate precision about the listed goals that is worrying. Since Sainsbury's start a long way behind the leaders, it is simply not good enough to trot out standard industry goals and expect competitive advantage at a strategic level to result. There is nothing at all wrong with them as targets, except that any one of the industry leaders could have written them. They all happen to be recognizable areas where Tesco has extracted major advantage over a 10-year period, so its knowledge and ability to move faster are self-evident. It is not clear how Sainsbury's can get itself to a position where it could begin to outperform the market in each of these designated areas. The credibility of its plan would be materially helped if discrete targets or milestones could be quantified, hopefully one day on a competitive basis. How, for example, do customers recognize when they are buying food at a 'fair' price? Does a fair price mean it has to be lower than that of key competitors or higher? We are not informed. This is 'soft' targeting. There is a sad resistance to quantified targets in today's Sainsbury's reporting. The addition of 'simplifying structure to produce better returns' is no doubt highly relevant to Sainsbury's position and to the likelihood of tough trading conditions for the market as a whole as the UK recession and its aftermath begin to bite harder. Given Sainsbury's margins it is clear that it is not operating anywhere near a low-cost-producer level, which shows that there must be opportunity to simplify and make the process more effective. The need for good and sustainable returns is obvious and must be one reason why, despite the level of recovery achieved over five years, it has not produced movement in the share price. To summarize, therefore, Sainsbury's still today seems to lack a clear, definable strategy for competitive advantage. This represents a serious weakness and creates anxiety about the business future.

Under a similar heading, it is worth asking how Sainsbury's now feels it is differentiated, as a business or brand. Great companies know they must not just be good but be good and simultaneously different. Sainsbury's had powerful points of difference for many years, which it summarized in the crudest of terms but with credibility as 'We sell great food'. Sometimes it added some price and cost reassurance, but it was the perceptions as well as the reality that Sainsbury's had the best food that gave consumers unique levels of confidence in shopping there. It was not just advantage but differentiated advantage in an area where customers believed they could discriminate and where they certainly cared. But at Sainsbury's this no longer applies. In the middle market, neither Tesco nor Morrisons will any longer concede an inch to Sainsbury's on perceived food quality. Meanwhile, for the consumer who is more relaxed about price, Waitrose now offers a new gold standard, a level Sainsbury's cannot pretend it tries any longer to reach. The same comments could be made about Marks and Spencer, which is also looking for a high-ground position as the best-quality food producer in the market. The quality high ground is now a thickly populated sector, given that in volume terms it accounts for rather less than 10 per cent of the market. The big changes have been in the customer's diminished perceptions of the Sainsbury's brand. Its heritage was profoundly appreciated for many years and is still alluded to in company reports. But today those perceptions have largely disappeared, at least for the mass of the shopping population. *Which?* readers, for example, a group seeking quality if ever there was one, prefer Waitrose by a big margin and rank Tesco and Morrisons as just as good as Sainsbury's. There is a core group of loyal Sainsbury's shoppers who are still 'in the fold', and there is no doubt this segment's beliefs are more positive than they were five years ago, but so there are today in all the competitors' shops. We are talking here about a level of trust, an attribute that a very few brands are able to command and an even smaller number can hold on to indefinitely. Sainsbury's was one of those brands, and it hung on for longer than most. Trust takes years to establish and, as short a time as 20 years ago, trust in the Sainsbury's food product was deep-rooted and seemed irreversible. In Sainsbury's search for renewed greatness, there is no single action that would set it on course faster or more firmly than a renewal of perceptions and trust in the 'best in class' characteristics of the Sainsbury's food brand. Objectively, there is not much sign of this happening, and equally there is little sign of any meaningful approach to creating differentiated advantage for the brand in other ways. Taken alongside the need for a statement of competitive strategy, this lack of brand differentiation is an issue urgently requiring a company response. Is one going to emerge?

The company states its enduring values under five headings, as follows:

1 healthy, safe, fresh, tasty food;
2 sourcing with integrity;
3 respect for the environment;
4 making a positive difference to communities;
5 being a great place to work.

The company statement continues: 'these are the values that direct all our activities, and define the differences from our competitors'. Here we can identify at least a desire for differentiation, but again there are no specified or measurable goals. The picture one gets is of a business that for too many years lost its way and is now trying, with some sensible statements of purpose, to find its way back. However, enumerating a set of goals that could have been set by its competitors will not change Sainsbury's fortunes, especially when these same competitors are well on the way to achieving their own similar and stated goals. The Sainsbury's values statement lists strong and worthwhile values for a good company to have; they do not constitute, on their own, a sufficient platform on which to build any kind of path to greatness.

Are there other areas where we can see differentiated progress? Sainsbury's has several new and attractive promotional approaches. Some of the recent ones noted during the recession, such as 'Feed your family for a fiver' and 'Love your leftovers', show genuine imagination. Perhaps more enduringly the company has solidly maintained a return to its traditionally highly stylish presentation of its food offer, including Sainsbury's renowned recipes, and in doing so has re-established a tone of voice with an ambassador in Jamie Oliver who has certainly brought back much-needed warmth and authority to its communications. This is one of the areas where it is possible once again to see a link to the Sainsbury's of old, and the combination of warmth, knowledge and authority must be making some worthwhile contribution to the restoration of the brand's values. This is an important step in the right direction, and the company's marketing leadership deserve credit for recognizing this and delivering it consistently through a range of media for several years now. It is not their fault that in the interim the market became a lot more competitive and the attribute 'warmth' is one that others – such as Asda or Morrisons – might now lay claim to. The fact is that this is something that was and is a visible part of the Sainsbury's heritage and, if it can be given more specific cutting edge in the company's strategy, it could still be one of the important weapons in its future. However, it will be aware of Waitrose sitting on its right flank, with similar high-style credentials.

During the dark years, nothing was more detrimental to Sainsbury's poor performance than the appalling state of its sourcing and supply chain arrangements. Since this had been a historical strength of the business for many years, the position reached by the late 1990s was inexplicable. So devastating had the failures become that during the period of Peter Davis's leadership he was forced to turn to the consultants Accenture to resolve the company's stock problems. These had become so desperate that Sainsbury's personnel themselves often had little idea of what it had, or was about to have, in stock on its own shelves – invariably less than was needed. Accenture arrived, pitched its expensive tents and stayed for a long time, entrusted not just with the need to resolve the basic supply process, but also to make sure that the measures would be internally implemented in a secure and effective way. Eventually the issues were resolved but at enormous cost and not without considerable damage to internal business confidence. Today Sainsbury's supply chain is at least coherent, but the strong impression persists that it is not yet anywhere near a competitive weapon, and it is clear that certainly Tesco and Asda and probably Morrisons are all operating in much more established and cost-effective ways. This is an area where Wal-Mart in particular has set very high standards and has used its scale to drive down costs and push up effectiveness across its company and probably also across the entire industry as a consequence. Sainsbury's search for simplification of structures and a better inherent process suggests that it now sees this as a highly relevant opportunity or indeed a requirement. However, this is also simply Sainsbury's playing catch-up given the cost and process advantage that Tesco and Wal-Mart now focus on internationally, and the quantified targets that each of them has been setting for its internal sourcing teams and outside suppliers for many years. A conclusion is that the supply chain probably offers Sainsbury's real process and cost advantage in the period ahead. It is unlikely that improvements will narrow the gap much against companies with worldwide and major scale advantages, but of course that is no reason for not embarking on the task quickly.

Sainsbury's now identifies a big opportunity for the company to widen its offer outside food. In fact it was, with Homebase, 20 years ago, one of the first supermarkets to make a substantial move outside food. Today, although Sainsbury's is no longer in the lead, expansion into non-food represents the chance for faster growth than food, and Sainsbury's has been building experience in areas as far apart as clothing – where it appears quite pleased with the progress made by its Tu brand – and banking, where Sainsbury's bank has existed for most of 10 years. These new growth areas are certainly activities where Sainsbury's must achieve growth and also produce margins that can begin to close the gap between the company and the industry's food margins. So far, it is others that have been taking the lead – Asda in clothing and Tesco in banking and financial services. These are predominantly new ventures for the company, therefore, and – to take one key target – it is unproven whether a collection of new 'big box' stores selling clothes can be turned into a winner for Sainsbury's in today's immensely tough fashion clothing market, where regular casualties abound. Market entry into clothing now is a lot more demanding given recent market experience than it was when Asda started with George many years back.

At any rate Sainsbury's appears committed now to driving more growth through additional space, and this represents a positive change against its existing plan – it is looking for 15 per cent new space vis-à-vis the existing target of 10 per cent. This gives the company a better chance to compete than it has had hitherto. What it needs to decide is where the quickest wins can be obtained given the many choices it has available. In-home shopping is a further opportunity where the company is now reasonably placed, as is internet shopping. Nectar's multi-company loyalty card has given the company a stake in the loyalty card market, but it is clear that the level of learning and consumer advantage from Nectar is minute compared to that of Clubcard. If we assess this range of extension options and recognize that Sainsbury's will want to move quickly now to establish what looks most promising, it is clear that it will be faced with some very difficult choices. Not all of these openings can be serviced at the same time, and in many of them the company will probably need to recruit the best-quality new leadership to drive innovative programmes forward. This is going to make the process of selection very important, and it will be critical to results and to Sainsbury's own confidence that the selection process works quickly and well. The first one or two areas chosen must be made to move forward quickly and positively. It will also be imperative that the company does not divert resources from the key task of strengthening the core food business. Rather it must ensure that the brand and business mix that emerges from new ventures has a synergistic effect and that it makes the resulting portfolio for Sainsbury's stronger – that, if you like, it contributes to helping make the business greater. If this phase is now ready to move it will be the critical component in the acknowledged task of restoring greatness to the company, more so than anything that has so far happened under the present leadership.

Sainsbury's is a much happier company now than it was in the dark years. It is happier in its relationship with its customers, and those who have stayed with or returned to the company feel a greater sense of warmth about the shopping experience at Sainsbury's than, so far at least, its bigger rivals may have been able to attract. This renewed comfort, happiness in one's own skin, can be detected in looking at the company's attitudes to and treatment of its own personnel. From the beginning the King era focused strongly on building a degree of confidence and motivation among the employees, and this was assisted by a board decision to set some good levels of bonus or incentive payments that senior management was able to earn for target performance. King himself set about making much-needed corrections to what had become a thoroughly moribund and non-performing company culture, and he focused on the stores that had been a principal contributory cause of the problem. King's focus has had a positive effect and given the company a measure of self-belief, which it has needed to re-establish growth. The targets set in his early days were not particularly stretching, but in context they were demanding given what had not happened for so many years previously. We have a clear sense of a company team now operating at least as one entity and able to work towards a set of consensual but worthwhile targets. Progress has been made therefore, and it is to management's credit that it has happened. But, if we return to the overall requirement – 'to make Sainsbury's great again' – the need for a lot more work and for new and better resources to raise the company's game is only too clear. Sainsbury's does not have many really experienced people in its key roles, and essentially its core team still lacks both depth and continuity. While Sainsbury's has always been able to attract a sound plc board, it bears no comparison in focus or effectiveness with what Tesco has available, and the same applies to Justin King's operating team. Sainsbury's has a much higher turnover among management, and the company simply does not have the clout or the reward and remuneration tools to hang on to a high percentage of its key people, facing as it does both British and international companies that are world leaders in this regard.

Finally and perhaps most importantly, the store management effectiveness advantage that Sainsbury's was thought to possess has been lost to Asda and Tesco. The company will now need to raise its game as it seeks to move from steady recovery to solid growth and the desired position of future greatness. Asda and Tesco have devoted huge energies to improving store management effectiveness for many years, and this is the standard Sainsbury's will need to match. To achieve this, the depth and quality of management will need to be raised; retention of key staff will be required; and finally a much more ambitious set of goals alongside the processes and practices that can deliver them will be critical. Sainsbury's has come out of its nightmare years, and the team deserve credit for doing this. If the company is to get to the next level, the challenges will be far greater. Some of the present leadership team will need renewal if future goals are to be achieved. This is no doubt the major task facing the board in the period ahead, and it needs to make a realistic assessment to achieve its goals.

Financially the company is now sailing in slightly clearer water. While it is not yet an industry leader, its steady year-on-year improvement means that in five years net profits have doubled, reflecting a modest but consistent recovery. Can the business now move the figures forward substantially so that Sainsbury's gets closer to the returns of the high-performing competitors in the market? Through the current recession, Sainsbury's has weathered the economic conditions well, recording good figures towards the end of 2009. But it may be difficult to beat 2009 returns in 2010, and Sainsbury's is only partially in control of its own destiny on this score. The initial results for 2010 appear already to be under pressure. Sainsbury's has raised additional funds from the market to deliver the additional space it needs to grow, but in spite of this most analysts still look to the company to underperform or at best get close to market average results. It is very unlikely in the short term that new non-food areas will deliver much additional profit, and if this and the overall outlook are as forecast above (difficult) it is not hard to see why the CEO has listed structural simplification and therefore cost reduction as his highest immediate priorities. This is a responsible and realistic view to take in market conditions that are unpredictable, and the challenge will be in implementing this programme. There is indeed a view that, since Sainsbury's is starting late with some of the systems and process efficiency moves its competitors have undertaken, it can in fact move faster than others have done in the past. This will be an attractive outcome for the company if indeed it can be made to happen.

Detailed examination of achievement and prospects leaves us with many more questions than answers when one looks at the Sainsbury's business. Could there be more radical strategies available that could accelerate the company's challenging prospects and give it a better and quicker chance of finding its holy grail – making Sainsbury's great again? Even if the business has to trade some of its independence to get radical improvement, this would be worth doing. Already there have been predators lurking, and for some considerable time there have been signs that a Qatari-based group of investors want to buy the company; today they have a substantial shareholding, which, given the existing substantial family holding, means the Sainsbury's share structure is unusual for a big corporate plc, with two high single shareholders. Might there be worthwhile partnerships, alliances or even formal mergers available that could produce synergies and raise returns? In Peter Davis's time, an alliance with Boots was much in the board's mind. This has now disappeared, but there may be other prospects. What about a foreign purchaser keen to get a foothold in this major market? Wal-Mart would salivate at the prospect, but could not hope to get past the authorities with a bid. Carrefour, Metro or possibly in future an Asian business could join the Qataris as potential purchasers. Might Sainsbury's be able to use its growing managerial coherence to join with a European partner and achieve increasing scale and in due course profitability?

Unless the next five years produce accelerated progress and results, the chances of a successful bid from outside the UK look distinctly probable. Perhaps the best local option might be a closer relationship and perhaps a pooling of its food interests with Marks and Spencer. This could be a lot more than two erstwhile aristocrats huddling together for warmth in the cold new world. The business fit should make economic sense, and the two companies have cultural similarities as long-term, high-quality, Middle England brand owners, both of which have fallen on hard times. The Waitrose threat could then be handled with increased muscle and confidence by Sainsbury's, which would suddenly have a lot more strategic options. However, there are no signs that this is under consideration by either party – perhaps Marc Bolland's arrival at M&S may make the idea more active? If organic growth in the UK provides only limited prospects for the board, what about a return to overseas markets, where Tesco in particular has done so well from a standing start 10 years ago? Of course, there would be a funding need, but a worthwhile consideration making such a possibility more than academic might be that, by the standards of many international markets and certainly those of some of the European countries close at hand, Sainsbury's would bring relatively high retailer knowledge and good brand-building skills to help weaker international companies. Possible partnerships or even purchases may be available, in the French market for example. To summarize this discussion on the more radical alternatives, it is suggested that only perhaps by confronting some of these can the Sainsbury's business be given a real chance of growing more rapidly and being able at one and the same time to take on its mainstream mid-market competitors – which are now well entrenched – while simultaneously keeping the niche markets, where Waitrose is growing, as a source of some future strength.

The conclusion

First, the good news. The worst is over, the clouds are lifting and the company has stopped shooting itself in the foot. The Hampton–King combination put enough self-belief into the new board and operating team to bring this once great company back from the brink of virtual self-destruction. The standard measurements of volume growth and profitability have come off the floor, are moving in the right direction and have managed to do so now for five consecutive years. Warmth and harmony even extend to the customer base, and loyal Sainsbury's users are a lot happier about shopping in Sainsbury's stores than they were in the bad old days. The experience has improved, and markedly, and on this the team deserve recognition. But recovery has taken a lot of effort and a few more years than it should have done, and there are few signs yet that this company can move its strike rate to a level where Sainsbury's once again becomes a serious British mainstream competitor with a brand that sets some of its own standards. Now that Somerfield has gone, Sainsbury's, apart from the Co-operative movement, remains by some distance, the weakest of the big four competitors. If further consolidation happens over the years ahead, of the majors it is Sainsbury's that looks the most vulnerable. The absence of a strategy to change market factors in its favour remains a very worrying gap in future planning, and the company needs to be challenged to produce a strategy that can provide some better perception of competitive advantage. Above all from this company that provided the highest degree of brand differentiation the UK food market had ever seen – and for more than a century through many leaderships – Sainsbury's management must create some meaningful brand and business differentiation that can drive the company's activities forward with real purpose. Alongside such differentiation, it would be right to set discrete and stretching targets to give investors renewed confidence in Sainsbury's as a competitive company. Finally, the board and CEO need to think carefully whether there are not more radical strategies that they might consider, whether they were ready to trade degrees of independence and whether these strategies might not offer a more secure future for the business. If they reject this initiative out of hand, they may find themselves pursued at inconvenient times in the future. As we've seen, current management had the courage and prescience to set a hugely aspirational goal five years ago – to make Sainsbury's great again. They now need to ask themselves how and when this is going to happen and to put a differentiated strategy in place to achieve it. They also need to be honest enough to admit, once they know they've tried but run out of answers, that the time has come to pass the responsibility on to others who can be charged to provide some answers in their place.

Morrisons
Moving up fast

04

For many years, Morrisons looked a bit like Asda's younger brother: both were based in Yorkshire (Asda in Leeds, Morrisons in nearby Bradford); both concentrated on large stores, around 40,000 square feet; both aimed at working families, using a low-price, value-for-money offer.

Morrisons, a family firm, in fact has older roots: William Morrison opened a stall in Bradford market in 1899 (shades of Marks and Spencer, which started from a market stall in Leeds in 1884). The firm expanded slowly, and did not open its first town centre shop until 1958; the first supermarket opened three years later. Helped by funds from going public in 1967, growth continued, but at a steady pace; the 100th store was opened in the centenary year of 1999. Despite becoming a public company, Morrisons remained family dominated. Sir Ken Morrison ran the company for over 50 years (text box) and became a much-respected figure in the industry.

Morrisons for many years enjoyed faster percentage growth than any significant competitor, more than doubling business over a decade. Profits performance has also been compelling – over the same period, profits doubled and then proceeded to double again inside 10 years. Margins at around 6 per cent on sales are as good as any in the industry, surely a surprise for a company that is less than a quarter of the leader's size and that sells at low prices. At 20 per cent, return on capital beat that of most competitors, and Morrisons' gearing is negligible. Sales densities, while under pressure, are at the leading edge. The company had the fundamentals right and had the operating profile of competitors three and four times its size.

Morrisons has been able to match the best in the industry. Ken Morrison attributed this to an intelligent appreciation of what consumers require in terms of value for money. He viewed his approach as 'democratic' – shades of a once dominant and also northern-based

Co-operative movement – and believed, as the Coop did too, that political as well as economic choices matter. Financially prudent, Morrisons has avoided onerous leases and set out to own its trading land. It also owns its distribution systems and a significant percentage of its own packing of fruit and vegetables, cheese and bacon, believing this has given it better cost and quality control. Relationships with the brand manufacturers have been personally and consistently managed – suppliers rarely found it difficult to get in to see the Morrisons chairman. Finally, Morrisons is a people business, and it is no surprise to see the chain's wage rates, although the company is located in the not usually overpaid north of England, at a level higher than those of most national competitors.

A clear business strategy was reflected in the deceptively simple 'Low prices mean best value' proposition. The Morrisons formula eschewed corporate bureaucracy and avoided what it saw as trading gimmicks. Thus it stayed away both from trading stamps and then, bravely but coherently, from loyalty cards, preferring to compete strongly on known value item (KVI) pricing and using its distinctive yellow and black (now green) own brand to drive its price message home. Innovations, once proven, are persisted with, but Morrisons' philosophy of trading is not a new one, nor is it over-intellectualized. 'I'd rather you tripped up over a pile of cheap cream crackers than give you a loyalty card' is the way Ken himself put it. There was distinctive marketing in the lively and colourful 'market square' trading format. Increasing concentration behind service counters with some real people behind them, and heavy emphasis on the fresh foods offering compared with the best superstore offering. Finally Morrison himself seemed confident enough to bring the proven mixture south, and stores were opened in the environs of London, Banbury, Chingford and Erith, for example. There was every sign that these were succeeding.

Morrisons seemed set on its steady path: respected, growing, profitable, and mainly in the north of England. Dramatic change looked unlikely. But then came a defining moment: the opportunity to buy Safeway, the fourth largest chain (see the first or second edition of *The Grocers* for detailed background). Safeway had had a somewhat chequered history, but by 2000 was under the leadership of a very experienced international retailer, Carlos Criado-Perez. His strategy of focusing on product and price, being best in fresh food, best in availability and best in customer service, was coherent, and like-for-like increases were good. Safeway had serious underlying problems, however. Its estate of 9.5 million square feet was spread over convenience stores, supermarkets and superstores, but many were of poor quality. It had a reputation as high-priced, and struggled to attract customers to do their main weekly shop there. As a result, its sales densities were significantly lower than competitors', and margins were therefore also low. It had discussed a merger with Asda, but the talks had broken down. It remained an obvious takeover target.

Given the restricted market in Britain, Safeway had to be a tempting target, and it was certain that many or all of the big chains would bid: the Competition Commission would certainly rule out Tesco, and Sainsbury's was preoccupied with its own problems, but Asda, with Wal-Mart's might behind it, looked a good prospect; foreign bidders, a possibility at one time, looked unlikely. No one thought of Morrisons, then one of the second tier, so it was a surprise when it announced a bid. For Morrisons, however, it was a good fit: 479 stores, mainly in the south of England and Scotland, to complement its north of England bias.

Commentators were surprised, because Morrisons was less than half the size of Safeway (assets of £1.718 billion compared with £4.9 billion, and turnover of £3.918 billion to £8.72 billion in 2002). On the other hand, it might just be the only merger that the competition authorities would allow in this much-investigated market. Once the proposed merger was announced, Wal-Mart (Asda), Sainsbury's and Tesco also joined the bidding, as Safeway chairman David Webster had predicted. The bids were referred to the Office of Fair Trading (OFT), as was inevitable. The OFT in 2003 produced one of its exhaustive reports, recommending reference to the Competition Commission (CC), which reported in August 2003. To no one's surprise, the CC recommended that Asda, Sainsbury's and Tesco should be forbidden to bid; Morrisons would be allowed to proceed, but would have to divest itself of a number of Safeway stores where local competition might be harmed. The takeover went ahead.

Most commentators, in the City and the industry, were still worried. They doubted that Morrisons' management could cope with such a large and complicated integration, a challenging task even when the winning team is much the larger. The Morrisons management team, while much admired, was small and used to focusing on a single trading model in one part of the country. Safeway stores catered to a different market, more southern, more middle-class, perhaps more sophisticated in its tastes.

The Morrisons approach was uncompromising: the Morrisons range and pricing were imposed immediately across all stores. Although turnover leapt up after the merger, margins were hit hard: the old Morrisons had made over 6 per cent, but now margins fell, to 3.27 per cent in 2004–05 and a disastrous less than 1 per cent in 2005–06. Anecdotally, southern consumers complained that the revised offer was 'too northern; it's all pies'. The old management team were struggling; they simply could not adapt fast enough to this new world, and most of the Safeway senior management had left; Sir Ken had made it clear that he didn't think he needed them, but Morrisons lost some experienced and valuable managers, several of whom went on to senior positions elsewhere.

It may be that this traumatic period provided the shock that management needed. Sir Ken, once the most respected figure in the industry, was beginning to be seen by some, perhaps unfairly, as a drag on progress; superb at managing the well-tried model in the north of England, he did not have the skills to cope with integrating a large, complex takeover target. Since he dominated the board, which, contrary to best practice, contained no independent directors, there was no one to take a lead in this unprecedented situation. Like many strong, patriarchal leaders, he was slow to recognize the time to let go. City opinion, never marked by patience, was growing more insistent that change must come, especially after five profit warnings; eventually, the company agreed to replace the long-serving finance director, and later the managing director, Bob Stott. Sir Ken eventually agreed to take a back seat.

The first crucial appointment was Richard Pennycook as group finance director in July 2005. Although he came most recently from the relatively calm conditions at RAC (a service organization), he had previous experience of turnaround situations at Laura Ashley, the once iconic fashion business, the motorway service company Welcome Break, and the cider-maker HP Bulmer. He was very glad that Morrisons was not his first turnaround: 'it's not for the faint-hearted: you need the confidence to do the important things'. The first priority, in his experience, was to stabilize the situation before moving on to the second stage, optimization. Pennycook had developed what he called his Eight Cs, a checklist of essential steps:

- *Cash*: in a crisis, it is vital to get a grip of where the cash is and where it is going. Liquidity is fundamental.

- *Customers*: do you know what your customers want and whether their needs or their views of the company have changed?

- *Control*: it is urgent to have a system that you can believe in and trust; if the numbers you are getting are unreliable, you will be led astray.

- *Confidence*: confidence must be restored to a team that is probably dispirited and nervy; the turnaround team must exude confidence and spread it through the company.

- *Costs*: almost inevitably, you have to get costs out of the business, and quickly.

- *Concept*: is the basic business model still appropriate? In a rapidly changing world, the business's idea of itself must reflect reality, not what used to be.

- *Culture*: especially where there has been a strong company culture in the past, when the firm was successful, there may be a need to adapt that to changed circumstances.

- *Crises*: in the circumstances in which a weakened company finds itself, crises are inevitable. It is vital to make sure that there is headroom – in management capacity, in loan facilities and so on – to allow you to cope with the fires that break out. 'Without it, you are stuffed, basically', in Pennycook's words.

(Adapted from *Accountancy Age*, 5 June 2008)

The first stage, stabilization, was under way before the next, central appointment, a new CEO to replace Bob Stott, the long-serving second-in-command to Sir Ken. The replacement appointed came as yet another shock: Marc Bolland, a Dutchman in his mid-40s, from Heineken, a brewer. He had no direct retailing experience, but the appointment turned out to be very shrewd: what he did have was considerable experience of making a difficult integration work – just what Morrisons needed to recover from the mess. With Bolland and other new members appointed, a team began to emerge that combined experience with new thinking.

What Bolland also brought was a marketing perspective. The old Morrisons didn't need marketing: it knew its customers and was in constant touch with them (Sir Ken was in the habit of wandering round stores in his shirtsleeves, talking to customers). There comes a time, however, in the growth of a firm when it does need some marketing discipline (and sophisticated IT, for example). A telling example has Bolland walking round a store early in his tenure; he picked up a sandwich and pronounced it delicious. Of course, he was told, it was made fresh in the store that morning. 'But,' he pointed out, 'it doesn't say that on the packaging.' What Bolland improved, then, was the communication, so badly needed.

Box 4.1 Bolland: from beer to briefs

To say that the appointment of a Dutch brewer as the new head of Morrisons was a surprise is an understatement. Morrisons had the most singular personality of British supermarkets, a characteristically Yorkshire personality perhaps, moulded single-mindedly as it had been by its charismatic chairman Sir Ken Morrison. Now it was to be run by a man with no direct experience of retailing or groceries and, what's more, a foreigner. While many areas of British business were by now very familiar with employees and bosses from overseas, food retailing had remained almost entirely run by home-grown talent. Safeway's previous head, Carlos Criado-Perez, was a rare exception.

In fact, Dutch and Yorkshire folk are similar in many ways – down-to-earth and known for speaking their mind. Bolland had worked in the Congo and Slovakia, so had experience of adapting to different cultures. As he pointed out, he had watched many of the same TV programmes as Britons, and both nations shared a love of football, so the transition was not difficult. As to the charge of knowing little about retailing, he stressed that he was essentially an fmcg man, used to thinking of customers and communicating with them.

'He's single, quite dashing, and drives an Aston Martin DBS' was how one British newspaper introduced the new man to its readers (*Mail Online*, November 22 2009). The comparison with James Bond was irresistible. In practice, Bolland showed a hands-on approach, often wandering round stores, picking up litter and listening to staff (just like Sir Ken). He bought a house in Leeds and went to watch Leeds United play ('No greater love hath a man…').

The dramatic turnaround at Morrisons, started by Sir Ken and Richard Pennycook before Bolland joined, was brought to fruition under Bolland's leadership, and his reputation in the City was golden. When it was announced that he would be joining Marks and Spencer as its new CEO in 2010, Morrisons' shares lost 5 per cent of their value. What tempted him? Once again, he was venturing into new territory: M&S is famous for its clothing. He was awarded a handsome 'golden hello' amounting to some £15 million, but money can hardly have been the prime motivation. The job of CEO of Marks and Spencer has been likened to that of England football manager (which, for most incumbents, means you are on a hiding to nothing, your every move scrutinized and probably criticized by the British press). He must like a challenge.

A key question was how the new man would work with Sir Ken, who was still very much there. Bolland claims that it was no problem at all. He had worked under Freddy Heineken, a similar personality. He found it easy to establish a good personal relationship with his new chairman: 'I found him extremely interesting as a person and very good as a businessman. He is a remarkable man, very erudite, very passionate about a lot of things' (*Telegraph.co.uk*, 27 July 2009). He found that it was not necessary to change a great deal about the business, merely perhaps to hurry on what was beginning to happen; it was vital not to throw out the baby with the bathwater, but to keep and build on what was good:

'When I arrived, there were strong signals from analysts, the City and journalists that we should sell off the real estate as soon as possible, sell off our factories in the supply chain and move immediately into online sales and convenience stores or the company would not be successful.'

Instead, after setting up 14 internal project teams he concluded that Morrisons' status as the only major UK retailer to slaughter its own meat, run its own bakeries and produce its own cheese, bacon and sausages was a major advantage. He also opted to keep the freehold estate and to continue shunning convenience stores, which do not produce in-store food.

The 'More Reasons to Shop at Morrisons' was changed to 'Fresh For You Everyday' to reinforce the message.

'When I look back at some of the questions people were asking at the time, they were very logical questions because the company had made five profit warnings and was nearly loss-making. But the question was where to cut costs and where to invest. I found this supply chain a real point of difference with other retailers who are more focused on non-food. We prepare 1,700 lines of fresh food in the stores.

'I don't want to be seen as the rebel who doesn't want to do what the City does. But when we looked in depth at the Morrisons business model, some things that looked quite obvious from the outside were not that obvious.'

SOURCE: Interview with Marc Bolland, *Telegraph.co.uk*, 27 October 2009

Arguably much of the hard work was already under way, but Bolland completed it and added something. The marketing message to consumers was confusing, a long list of 'reasons to shop at Morrisons'. Many of the stores looked tired and needed investment. Bolland persuaded the board, supported by market research, to invest, and refurbishment started, with a clean new look of yellow (for the sun) and green (for fresh produce). The message was simplified, to focus on fresh food, both a compelling draw in itself and also shorthand for quality. Morrisons still prided itself on its greater control of quality, and felt that this would be a motivating point of difference. The advertising message used celebrities, but carefully, not only northern personalities.

Bolland continued the process of opening up new stores in the south of England, previously almost foreign territory. He liked and built on the can-do attitude he found: the process of development was fast and unfussy. The company bought 35 stores from the Co-op, remodelling them into the standard Morrisons model. Customers liked what they now saw: clean, bright stores with the distinctive 'Market Street' display of fresh produce. The message of Morrisons' control of fresh food through its vertical integration grew clearer, and prices were very attractive. The company began to outperform its competitors in like-for-like sales growth, scoring 14.5 per cent in 2006–07 and 8 per cent in 2007–08. While early gains contained an element of catch-up, the continuing performance is impressive.

While stressing fresh quality, Morrisons did not want to lose the important value credentials that it had built up so rigorously: it positioned itself just behind Asda, the price leader, but ahead of Tesco and Sainsbury's. It also scored highly on quality, moving up from fourth to second in one survey, behind Sainsbury's (Tesco was fourth). On fresh produce, meat and fish it was rated highest. The value message was driven home by great deals, supported by advertising. A schools programme, 'Let's Grow', provided simple gardening equipment, neatly supporting fashionable interests in real, local produce and growing your own. These efforts were led by Angus McIver, the marketing director, who had experience in Procter & Gamble and PepsiCo ('the best in the business' in the words of one analyst). He agreed that what Morrisons was doing was applying basic, classic marketing discipline.

The pricing strategy has remained firmly high–low: EDLP would not work for Morrisons. Bolland demanded industry-leading offers that would surprise and delight customers, such as the 'family meal for four for £4' (this was, of course, fresh produce, not a prepared meal). Like Asda, Morrisons is aiming at a family audience, and its customer profile is now similar, if a little older. Encouragingly, it is finding that growth in custom is faster in the young family groups than empty-nesters, and that ABs are increasing at 15 per cent compared with 3 per cent for DEs. Though that is partly a reflection of its new southern base, it has been helped by, for example, revamping the wine range. Morrisons wine had been seen as cheap, so it recruited a Master of Wine, improved the range, and tried to help customers match wine type to food. A brochure for wine shows bottles at mainly over £9 and some at over £10 (though of course with substantial offers on each). This is sending a pretty clear message: we know about wine, we know you want to drink better quality and we will help you to do it at a fair price.

The company is also working hard to learn more about the behaviour of its customers. As it is still firmly set against loyalty cards, it has to analyse credit card details by matching the numbers (anonymized) to track buying over time. It has divided stores into three types, and can flex the ranges to suit local preferences. It has also devoted funds to the rather neglected IT systems, devoting £300 million to the task of updating.

In 2010, Morrisons looked to be in a strong position. The optimization plan was signed off early in the year, having delivered £500 million of profit improvement and margins moving back towards previous levels. Its long-standing conservative strategy has left it with 92 per cent of its properties freehold (Tesco, by comparison, owns about 75 per cent, and Sainsbury's about 60 per cent). It also owns up to £1 billion of non-trading properties (malls, offices and so on). Like most food retailers, it has strong cash flow, allowing it to invest in acquisition opportunities as they arise. Its margins are climbing back towards their previous levels, and customer opinion is clearly favourable.

This rosy picture was spoilt by the announcement in late 2009 that Marc Bolland, who had gained a stellar reputation, would leave in early 2010 to join Marks and Spencer; the Morrisons share price fell by 5 per cent, and that of M&S went up by 6 per cent. The search for a new chief executive, such a long and difficult task previously, had to begin again. Many felt that Richard Pennycook, the finance director, had been responsible for much of the recovery and was a strong candidate to take the top job, but he was to be disappointed.

The new appointment was, like Bolland's, a surprise. Dalton Philips is a 41-year-old Irishman; he became the youngest head of a FTSE 100 company. Although unknown in Britain, he has a wealth of retailing experience, including in Wal-Mart's German subsidiary; he was previously chief operating officer of Loblaws, the leading Canadian group. Loblaws' president and deputy chairman is Allan Leighton, the former Asda boss, who described Philips in these terms: 'a very good retailer, he has a nice touch and is excellent with people'. His challenge will be to take the company forward in an increasingly competitive market. Morrisons, though strong, is small compared with the leaders.

It has little non-food and no online offering. These can be developed, but this will take time. Philips has experience of both, which may be a reason for his appointment. Morrisons may continue to outperform for a while, but this will become more and more difficult; Tesco and Asda will not give away share easily. For the immediate future, Philips has a comfortable ride as the group continues to deliver above-average growth. He will need to start thinking about, and will soon have to make decisions concerning, some major strategic issues. How long can Morrisons continue growing with its current model? What does it do about convenience stores, non-food and online shopping? Should it be looking for an acquisition to make the next big step-up in scale? Should it be looking overseas? Its competitors, and analysts in the City, will be watching closely.

In his first public statement, in September 2010, Philips made clear that Morrisons would continue to stress its advantage in fresh food as its major point of difference. It will experiment with convenience stores, and with an online offer. On the latter, Philips stressed that it would have to be profitable in its own right; it could not expect to be subsidized by the stores. The strategy will be 'steady as she goes', with cautious exploration of alternative sectors.

Waitrose
Building its brand for middle England

05

For many years, Waitrose was regarded as an interloper in Britain's food retailing industry, and certainly as no more than a fringe player at best. The supermarkets were able to disregard it. There were many reasons for this. It was a food chain fully owned by the bigger and, many would say, iconic department store John Lewis. Second, it was not a public company, since with John Lewis ownership came the addendum 'Partnership'.

The partnership

Box 5.1 The Partnership

Waitrose, like John Lewis department stores, is part of the John Lewis Partnership and is entirely owned by a trust that manages the two businesses on behalf of the (approximately 70,000) employees. They, as partners all holding equivalent partnership status, literally 'own' their company, have a significant say in its direction and management, and earn, on an annual basis, a significant share in its profits. Characteristically over the past 10 years this has amounted to levels of salary between 15 and 20 per cent annually. Today's Partnership is the third largest privately owned enterprise in the UK, and in the 90 years since its inception it has performed steadily and grown both volume and profits. In the first decade of the new century both have doubled, and the partners have seen their business grow to sales of £7.4 billion and profit of £390 million in 2009. (Waitrose has been a major contributor.)

John Lewis began life in its Oxford Street store in 1864 under the leadership of the first John Lewis, who handled its clothing business on a small scale, but

Box 5.1 continued

successfully, for 40 years from this one site, which the company still retains, albeit on a much larger scale today. The second store, Peter Jones, started trading in 1905, but initially was a lot less successful. At about the same time, Lewis's elder son, 19-year-old John Spedan Lewis, joined his father, initially in both stores, but subsequently, of his own volition, to take sole control of Peter Jones in Sloane Street. Spedan Lewis was a radical reformer par excellence and he had some remarkable and at the time revolutionary ideas for the company. He began to test these ideas in the Peter Jones store, not in the early days with much cooperation from his father, who was still in overall charge of the business and who viewed his son's notions as madness. Spedan Lewis's unusual notion was to institute measures of co-ownership in the Peter Jones store, and in time and as the store began to respond with good results this developed into a thorough-going and ambitious vision of nothing less than full-scale employee ownership. A long period of convalescence after a riding accident had its fortunate side and enabled Spedan Lewis to focus full attention on his new vision; in 1920 he formally bequeathed the company, which was now his to run, to the employees – to be known from then on, as they are today, as the partners. The Partnership was born from rational awareness by Lewis that three family members had been earning as much between them as all the rest of the employees together. 'Why should three owners ask for themselves more than defined levels of reward?' he asked. One wonders if any of today's corporate leaders ever entertain so astonishing a thought. If they do, it soon disappears.

Spedan Lewis was a reforming democrat with high ethical intent. He was not frightened of big concepts, describing his idea as 'Fairer shares, a possible advance in civilization, and perhaps the only alternative to communism'. Fortunately, he also knew how to run a successful company. After Peter Jones had become profitable, he was also able to create a strong business culture in the John Lewis stores, which under his guidance became leaders in their field. However, his company also aimed to set the highest social standards, and quickly such elements as shorter working hours, a third week's paid holiday, and staff contributions to the working process were proposed and easily accepted. The famous claim 'Never knowingly undersold' was also formulated at about this time and remains honoured today on all except internet purchases in the department stores. (It does not apply to Waitrose.)

Employees are able and encouraged to contribute to the business through their branch forums, where everyone is represented. The Partnership Council, which has 82 members, considers all non-commercial elements of activity and can discuss any matter whatsoever. Eighty per cent of its members are elected by the partners. Finally, the Partnership Board has 10 members, five of whom are elected by partners and five by the chairman; it considers all aspects of business including

Box 5.1 continued

results. Once again, there are no 'no-go' areas. John Lewis Partnership appears to have found an ideal combination of high performance and advanced social provision for its employees, and the recipe looks alive and vibrant today under a new and relatively young leader, Charlie Mayfield. Top-level staff conditions, generous insurance, sickness and holiday entitlements and even a six-month paid leave entitlement after 25 years' service are all examples.

Spedan Lewis remained as chairman until the 1950s, after which he reverted to the appropriate title of founder. He was able in his retirement years to put his philosophy and life story on the record. One of the best communications was a series of recorded reminiscences he made for the BBC in 1957. In this recording ('Dear to my heart') his gentle, slow speaking tones recall his original aspirations and the later achievements, and it is difficult not to feel that a unique business culture had been created by one visionary individual with a single but immensely powerful idea – partnership. Good ideas can travel, and Spedan Lewis's vision has done – now featuring happily in a distinctly different business (grocery at Waitrose) that Spedan Lewis had not envisaged. His essential vision is as worthwhile and certainly as successful as it was when he conceived it 90 years ago.

There is no doubt that for many years partnership constrained Waitrose's capacity to do all the things it might have wanted, to take on competition more frontally, and to acquire sufficient capital to compete with its better-funded and aggressive rivals. But Waitrose itself was hesitant to express its points of difference. It rarely raised its voice. The company, like its staff and managers, was noticeably polite and restrained. Service was something it was very, very good at, but mixing it in a tough marketplace with the likes of Tesco and Asda was not for it. It allowed the market to believe, and to some extent it itself accepted, that it was grown-up John Lewis's younger sibling (bright and good at its homework) but that it normally waited for its big brother to take any big new initiatives in this orderly and well-mannered family. Of course, its consumers knew that Waitrose always operated at the quality end of the market, and felt happy they were able to shop there. They readily conceded that there were others that did the same – Sainsbury's, where as everyone knew 'good food cost less', was the most obvious example and was itself highly regarded by many better-off British shoppers. When Marks and Spencer's new, distinctive and from the beginning highly rated foods offer came to market, Waitrose did not consider it needed to change tack. For the time being, it simply kept its head down and went on doing what it always had – selling the whole range to its public, at high prices. What consumers certainly knew was that Waitrose prices were a whole lot higher than the competition – any competition. Waitrose did nothing to disabuse them of this – the prices were high and, given the shortages of cash for capital expansion, management knew they were destined to remain so. So, while it was by no means a moribund business and was a company whose behaviour patterns and ethics in particular were widely respected, Waitrose was happy to pursue a low-visibility strategy for many years, copying the best practices of the parent company, keeping in loose touch with but never leading market developments, and holding firmly to the Partnership's comparable beliefs and values, but, while making good financial returns, not pursuing mainstream growth strongly. Waitrose was a niche business, doing its job for its narrow but contented southern English customer base, happy on the whole so to remain.

Oddly enough for this company where quality and prices have been permanently at the high end of the market, it is only now, in the midst of a fierce and lasting British recession, that much of this has changed. Perhaps it had to, and if it had not Waitrose would slowly have drifted into decline. We do not think this is or was the relevant background. Today, and for some years back, Waitrose has become a very different business, where many novel and unusual things are now happening. It is certainly possible to describe its approach over recent years as both innovative and dynamic, and it is today one of the unmistakable successes in the British food retail market. It looks like someone who has been indoors reading quietly and has stepped outside into bright sunshine, enjoyed the experience hugely and found a host of rewarding ways to pass the time.

The structural difference, in being a non-quoted business and being owned by the partners, has emerged as something that modern Waitrose now recognizes as not just an advantage but something that enables the whole company to behave in ways that internally, with the staff, and externally, with customers, create the crucial point of priority on which the company can capitalize. It is certainly the first thing Waitrose leadership mention when painting a picture of the company. Unhesitatingly, when Mark Price, today's CEO, was asked about it, he knew immediately what his answer was. So he goes on to point to a clear and measurable difference in approach, which customers observe and like in the stores and which, in his opinion, they rarely get elsewhere in the supermarket industry. Waitrose customer service is simply in a different league from that in the high street alternatives, and the difference is now organic. It is better informed and more courteous and has a very distinct and recognizable sense of style. Customers feel in a Waitrose store that there will certainly be someone nearby who will understand what they might want and will provide relevant guidance. This is not a common experience elsewhere. Even where competition have tried to instil it and organized lengthy and detailed training programmes to deliver it, there will be degrees of success and failure, and the responses customers are looking for will rarely be uniformly satisfying.

Waitrose's other core difference relates to its food quality. Since the arrival of Marks and Spencer in the 1980s there has been a true and dedicated high-quality alternative for consumers prepared to pay higher prices, but M&S has been constrained by its defined sets of premises and its consequently very limited product range. Meanwhile Sainsbury's, determined to keep in close touch with and even where it could match the leader's prices, allowed its prices to drift gently nearer to those of Tesco. Inevitably, the quality gap between Sainsbury's and Waitrose was going to widen through time. Eventually it has become quite obvious to consumers who know both brands where important quality differences lie, and they are nearly always in favour of Waitrose. As a result, Waitrose found itself increasingly in a position where it could strike out and occupy the pole position, where unbeatable food quality and distinctiveness were concerned, and it is a position from which it has now begun to take real and lasting advantage.

Marketing

Nowhere has this advantage been more clearly demonstrated than in the period towards the end of 2009, when after a year of universally bad economic news the key Christmas trading period thrust the two quality food retailers into direct conflict, as each sought to take advantage of this important trading period when consumer spending budgets are traditionally less inhibited. M&S elected to compare several of its products with products in the Waitrose Essentials range (see below) for price and quality. Far from helping M&S sales, the campaign appeared to do exactly the opposite and drive big share increases for the Waitrose range. Whether this was for reasons of perceived quality difference, price comparisons or wider availability in Waitrose stores is uncertain – probably all three reasons. Richard Hodgson, then Waitrose's commercial director, commented: 'Maybe we should thank the M&S marketing department for highlighting the quality and value of our… Waitrose Essentials range.' Waitrose recorded a 17 per cent increase over the period, while M&S growth was negligible. Sir Stuart Rose, the M&S chairman, admitted to having been trounced by Waitrose, but the writing had been on the wall for some considerable time.

Waitrose had indeed been enjoying splendid annual growth for the past several years. In 2009, growth was over 5 per cent, and the company's sales reached £4 billion for the first time. Revenues have risen in each year since 2005, and show more than 25 per cent net growth over the period – not bad for this erstwhile low-key, 'invisible' company. Similar handsome increases in operating profits (50 per cent), sales per full-time employee (FTE) and sales per square foot have been recorded. At the same time, Waitrose has been able to make strong increases to its number of UK stores, an increase of 11 in 2009, to a total of 197 stores. Gradually the geographic reach is beginning to spread northwards out of the company's strong southern base. The combination of uniquely well-informed and helpful in-store service, already noted, and a product range that, including its own label, stands for the best quality in the market has delivered Waitrose excellent levels of growth for many years. A steadily increasing market share has at least held firm through the recessionary conditions prevailing over the past 18 months in the UK, and the Essentials range was both timely enough and well enough managed to make an important contribution to this in 2009. Surprising as it may seem, and uncertain as many seem to be about the rationale, Waitrose appears today able to be a fast-growth business in a British market that seems to like its offer more as each quarter passes. Perhaps what Waitrose has found, which others in their resolute desire to trade themselves out of recessionary times have ignored, is the chance to build a brand its customers have long respected and can even love – 'trusted quality for Middle England' was the succinct way in which Mark Price summarized it. Waitrose as a brand is now delivering results for the Partnership (the younger sibling is more than holding its own), and Mr Price has enough innovation in the pipeline to ensure that the growth continues.

Let us now examine the brand concept specifically. Trust is associated with the Partnership, which looks like a comfortable 'collegiate' concept in a world where the big retailers experience regular bouts of outright hostility from some of the vocal middle-classes (see Charlie Brooks, 'Supermarkets must be brought to heel', *Daily Telegraph*, 7 January 2010). It is then confirmed by excellent store service. Concentration on food (no £5 shirts or cheap CDs here) enhances the notion of the specialist food store, and there has been a deliberate attempt to broaden the food range in ways that look exciting, different and modern. In this regard Waitrose appears to be out on its own in the UK; Trader Joe's in California has similar notions and enjoys a comparable lead there. Another notion Waitrose leadership articulate is that 'they can do things best that the others can't do', and the nature and style of the range extensions and new items confirm this on the shelves. This is no doubt attributable principally to the incomes most of their customer base enjoy. The Waitrose range is distinctly different in many respects from that of the mainline operators, and this is part of the quality element of Waitrose's brand kicking in recognizably. Style, clarity, distinctiveness, good design, different sourcing, an emphasis on health and well-being, and environmental appropriateness are all possible and independent elements that contribute to the quality component of the brand. Finally comes the customer, called 'Middle England'. How can we appraise this? We know middle-class shoppers patronize Waitrose; if you are hard up this is not the place to go and, if everyone knows this, the business will do well to recognize this reality. 'Middle England' as a descriptor may reflect this realism. There is too an aspirational, confident feeling in consumers who describe themselves as middle-class – the middle is nearly always a comfortable place to be. And, because they have aspirations and are confident, these same shoppers are prepared to pay the higher prices that Waitrose charges. We return to the subject of pricing later, because it is changing, but there's no doubt that Waitrose is and will for ever be located at the more expensive end of the British food market, catering for a customer who is not over-anxious about price comparisons and in some cases may not even be aware of what most of them are.

Meanwhile there is simply lots of new activity in Waitrose stores, and the pace of innovation has certainly been accelerating in the last few years. Some of it, even in an industry that knows its importance all day every day, may even be thought of as ground-breaking and is not what you expect to emanate from a minority player. Perhaps growth and stronger results have been the stimulus for this (which is chicken and which egg?), and clearly the capital to allow the business to grow in lots of different ways has been found – more than £200 million each year,

£400 million kicking it forward in 2005. The company has not been averse to highly adventurous marketing expenditure, at the same time. In a new and very focused drive to make the public aware of Waitrose's outstanding food and cooking potential, the company took the centre break in *Coronation Street* on 25 March 2010 – top peak time – to allow celebrity cooks Heston Blumenthal and Delia Smith to spend several high-cost minutes to help put across the company's best food message. Apart from the cost of advertising time, the campaign was extensively previewed in major newspaper and TV support. This would be bravura-level spending for any company, and for Waitrose it approaches being a 'bet the company' initiative. It confirms with no doubts at all the commitment of Mark Price's team continually to find novel ways to build their distinctive brand.

One big contributor to the excellent 2009 result was the introduction of the new Waitrose Essentials range, a strategic and in retrospect even inspired response early in the year to the recession. It may look like a strange thing for the high-priced brand owner to do – surely it will highlight just how expensive our main brands are, won't it? But Mark Price and his team took an even braver decision, which happily seems to have paid off in spades. They cut the price but did not reduce brand quality one bit, ie they relied on extra take-up and volume growth – the fact that consumers would be enthusiastic about Essentials – to pay for a big margin loss. The outcome has been a success – significant overall share growth, perhaps 20 per cent of the business now in the Essentials range – and a broader consumer offer. More important still perhaps is an enhanced brand reputation and so more 'trust' (see above). Providing the company can continue to grow its share, the chances are that this will further narrow its perceived price disadvantage. Waitrose knows that, if it wants to grow, it has to go on doing this – the competition know this too and they do not like it much. Thus over several years Waitrose prices have moved much closer to those of Sainsbury's and even Tesco. Tesco said openly in a recent statement, and Sainsbury's, all the time, are only too aware of Waitrose's penchant to go on building its brand. Waitrose, however, can see that Tesco has been the big long-term share winner, but believes that, if Tesco continues to win, it is different enough from Tesco still to do well. It is possible that the willingness to patronize higher-priced brand ranges may decline once the true seriousness of the UK economic position dawns. Such explanations as 'Consumers have down-traded from restaurants to home entertainment' (Mark Price believes this) or the engaging comment from Stuart Rose

Early Tesco store fronts (1930s)

Jack Cohen: Tesco founder

Sir Terry Leahy made Tesco a leading worldwide brand and a British business with the highest reputation

Philip Clarke's track record beat off strong contenders for the challenging succession to Sir Terry

Tesco Fresh & Easy, California: An innovative approach to US retailing finds progress slowed by the recession

John James
b1844 d1928
founder of Sainsbury's 1869
company service 1869–1928
chairman and governing director 1922

Mary Ann
b1849 (née Staples) d1927
founder of Sainsbury's 1869
company service 1869–70s

John Benjamin
b1871 d1956
company service
1885–1956
partner 1915
director 1922
chairman 1928

George
b1872 d1964
company service
c1886–c1915
responsible for
accounts and
some provision
buying

Frank
b1877 d1955
company service
mid 1890s–98
(from 1902 a
major supplier of
pig meat, poultry
and eggs to
Sainsbury's)

Arthur
b1880 d1962
company service
late 1890s–1929
director 1922
responsible for
provision buying
and supervision
of factory

Alfred
b1884 d1965
company service
1906–41
director 1922
responsible for
grocery and
canned
goods buying

Paul
b1890 d1982
company service
1921–38
responsible for
building
development

Alan
b1902 d1998
company service
1921–98
director 1933
joint general manager
trading 1938
chairman 1956
president 1967
created Baron Sainsbury
of Drury Lane 1962

Robert
b1906
company service
1930–present
director 1934
joint general
manager personnel
and administration 1938
chairman 1967
president 1969
knighted 1967

James
b1909 d1984
company service
1926–74
director 1941
awarded CBE 1960
responsible for
establishment of 1936
factory, and for setting
up Haverhill Meat
Products 1958
(later known as
NewMarket Foods)

John D
b1927
company service
1950–present
director 1958
vice chairman 1967
chairman and
chief executive 1969
knighted 1980
created Baron
Sainsbury of Preston
Candover 1989
created Knight of
the Garter 1992

Simon
b1930
company service
1956–79
director, financial
policy and
personnel 1959
deputy chairman
1969

Timothy
b1932
company service 1956–83
and 1995–present
director, estates, architects and
engineers 1962
MP for Hove 1973–97
held various government posts
1983–94, including
Minister for Trade and
Minister for Industry
knighted 1995
non-executive director 1995

David
b1940
company service
1963–98
director 1966
director and financial
controller 1971
finance director 1973–90
deputy chairman 1988
chairman 1992
created Baron Sainsbury of
Turville 1997

Sainsbury's family tree

Sainsbury's family directors at Chelsea branch

Asda Living Entrance: The Asda Living brand has significantly broadened the company offer

Asda Bournemouth 2010: Asda's few but larger stores enabled it to take and hold the no 2 UK market position

Asda recycling centre: Environmental performance is an increasing determinant of business success

The 'Market Street' is a distinctive feature of Morrisons' stores

Sir Ken Morrison, driving force behind Morrisons for decades

Marc Bolland, first foreign CEO, completed turnaround and launched new growth

Dalton Philips: Morrisons' new CEO charged with developing strategy for the future

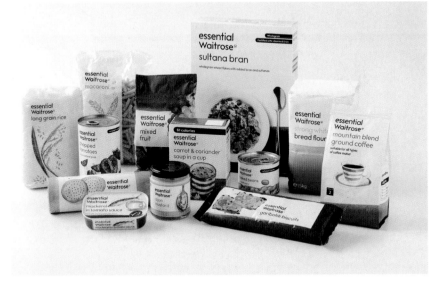

essential Waitrose range: Brilliant timing and execution helped Waitrose move ahead despite the UK recession

Waitrose Menu range: Waitrose widens its range of specialty foods and builds the UK's premier food brand

Waitrose Seriously range shows a company confidently communicating a distinctive consumer message

Marks & Spencer 1912

Marks & Spencer 1990s

Wal Mart: Santa Fe, New Mexico, USA

Wal Mart's founder: Sam Walton

that 'Consumers are fed up with being fed up' have been offered. For the time being at least Waitrose is not only unscathed but appears to have a (polite and modest) sense of triumph. So it should.

A big growth stimulant has been a new-found aggression in Waitrose to acquire new space in mainline stores and in new smaller convenience stores under the Waitrose name and to extend its Waitrose food brand into new locations. Today the company is still heavily biased to the south of England, with around 200 supermarket stores. Convenience stores, between 3,000 and 7,000 square feet, should double the store number, and the target is, one day not too far ahead, to get to a level of 1,000 sites where the Waitrose brand will be sold. Welcome Break motorway service stations are a further expansion area, where Waitrose has successfully followed the M&S lead, and Boots and Shell are two further locations where the Waitrose brand will now be available. Even the Middle East is becoming an opportunity for extending the brand – Waitrose has stores in Dubai. This is an adventurous new strategy for a primarily retail-driven brand, but indications are that brand Waitrose is now well enough perceived for these new extensions to add worthwhile levels of new business and further enhance brand reputation.

Supplier strategy is one further area where the company believes it has a different approach to the competition. This approach is well written up in the 2009/10 report in the section 'Provenance, traceability and [yes, once again] trust'. It stresses the value of long-term strategic relationships and points to its close involvement with the sourcing of food, to the higher percentage contribution from true local and British sourcing that Waitrose features, and to its farm ownership, enabling it the better to understand the supplying farmer's point of view. Probably Waitrose pays somewhat over the odds for the privilege of having these closer and more productive relationships, and the business would not deny it. This is not inconsistent with the core approach – to offer the best quality the market can offer and charge a level of premium for doing so. It is a strategy that only a few companies, in a competitive market like the UK, can afford to follow. There is a cost, certainly, but Waitrose feels it is making the strategy work for the company.

Online selling: the Ocado partnership

One final area where Waitrose has been able to extract consumer advantage from an early initiative has been its online approach to selling the brand. The Ocado relationship would appear to have worked to the benefit of the distributor, which after most of 10 years of exclusively selling the Waitrose brand has been readying its company for what was not a wholly successful flotation. The relationship appeared to benefit both parties and even today, as Waitrose extends its own home delivery in Waitrose vans, both brand owner and distributor appear to have gained. The John Lewis Pension Fund has been a major investor in Ocado. Waitrose has itself been able to extract benefit from early adoption of the online approach via Ocado, and from targeting a combination of high-quality food and professional service and delivery at a time-poor consumer segment well able to use what Ocado–Waitrose home delivery provided. Using Ocado now features as a conversation piece at middle-class dinner parties and invariably in approving terms. Ocado is not nearly as big as Tesco.com, and it is more expensive, but the quality of service does stand out. That Waitrose has now added its own online delivery service as a supplement to Ocado should not be viewed as anything other than a desire, manifested widely by the present leadership, to get the Waitrose brand in front of as much of the target market as it can. Meanwhile, if Ocado is for sale and is bought by a hostile competitor, Waitrose will not be left up the home delivery creek with no paddle.

We see Waitrose's growing operation as one of the most interesting developments of the last 10 years. After some years of securing what looked to all the world like a minority niche position, which might produce a decent margin catering for a stable but small group of affluent, southern English food shoppers, Waitrose has recently sprung to life and embarked on an active and innovative approach to growing its brand. This is obviously happening with the full, committed support of the Partnership. Waitrose has thrived on the arrival of new competition (Marks and Spencer at one stage appeared as a major quality threat, but no more) and is now making life difficult for Sainsbury's, which was a historical rival competing for its consumer segment. So far at least, shopper anxieties from living through a severe and long-term British recession, far from hurting Waitrose, has fuelled its level of growth – this would have been seen as surprising 18 months ago, but it has happened and it is persistent enough for us to treat it as an ongoing reality. Of all UK retailers, Waitrose has gone further in establishing its brand as a *sui generis* stand-alone food entry, and its acquisition of new high street stores, as well as the cultivation of some important new channel partnerships, will accelerate this process. We might hesitate to apply the adjective 'aggressive' to this partnership-based retailer, and the John Lewis or indeed Waitrose shopper would find the word particularly distasteful, so 'dynamic' will have to do. On the record, this seems entirely justified and, if it continues to do as well for the next 10 years as it has done for the last decade, it seems possible that Waitrose may be able to double its share of the British food market; this is what it regards as a good target to set for itself. The impressive point of difference is the inherent brand quality it has created – it will not be hard for it to attract new partners when it brings such a positive equity to the relationship. Meanwhile customers will happily patronize its stores for the identical reason – they like, respect and maybe even love the Waitrose brand.

The Second Tier

The top four companies, which we discussed in Chapters 1 to 4, account for 75 per cent of total retail business. What we may call the second tier of companies is not a homogeneous group, but is highly segmented. These are companies that vary in present importance. Some are lively and likely to grow in significance. Others are making little impact and may be dwindling in size or even disappearing from view (RIP Somerfield and Kwik Save). The discrete groups that make up the second tier of UK companies can be described as:

- *failing heritages*: independents and the Co-operative movement;
- *cheap but hardly cheerful*: hard discounters (Aldi, Lidl, Netto);
- *niche players*: Marks and Spencer and Iceland.

Failing heritages

The independent grocer

The decline of independent grocers has continued, seemingly inevitably. Their share of the total market dropped from 5 per cent in 2001 to 2.3 per cent in 2009 (Kantar Worldpanel). This is despite the fact that everyone seems to love the small corner shop, and many critics of the enormous, soulless supermarket sound as if they would prefer to do all their shopping in small independent shops run by people they know. As in other areas of life, it appears that people say one thing but do another. When it comes to the practicalities of shopping for food, the corner shop, with its limited stock and higher prices, does not cut it. Its old role of top-up shopping, a place that was local and open when you wanted something, has been taken over by the proliferation of stores at filling stations and the majors' shiny, inviting versions of the convenience store.

The numerical evidence of decline is confusing: the Competition Commission stated that, between 2003 and 2007, convenience store numbers actually grew, from 33,394 to 35,505, and the IGD reported that sales were growing faster than the total market (Competition Commission, 2008). The entry of Tesco and Sainsbury's to the sector accounted for some of this, but not all. The IGD reported that non-affiliated independents (not belonging to one of the symbol buying groups) had declined, but definitions are different. We may conclude that numbers are stabilizing, but at a very low level. There are always people wanting to run a small shop, so there is a constant supply of new entrants.

Those that survive still occupy their traditional and preciously guarded community role. On relative price, however, the whole world knows they are incapable of competing. There may indeed be bright new opportunity in the high streets, but the human, capital and marketing skills to succeed are rarely present among today's independents, and they are being replaced by a group of high street multiples, which are taking the best sites and have the systems and knowledge to make them work harder. Encouraged by some late-in-the-day hardening of national planning policies seeking to constrain the growth of out-of-town sites, and perhaps by a recognition that the use of cars for shopping needs to be restricted, the neighbourhood store could be due for post-millennium resurgence. Around the world, there seems to be a new awareness of the convenience and speciality store, catering to a growing group of aspirational but time-starved urban shoppers, some of whom clearly prefer this kind of shopping to the mainstream supermarket visit. However, it is unlikely that many of today's private shopkeepers will cater to them.

Successful multiple convenience store operators, such as Alldays and Dillons, have made good progress, and used the new learning of scale and expertise to fund expansion – showing a degree of purpose the independents could never generate for themselves.

It is not yet clear how far high street renewal may take us. In the long term it may depend on home shopping's advance and whether there remains a worthwhile role for local distribution. Short-term, there seems little doubt that high streets need vitality, breadth of activity and regular customer visits, providing the price premium is not too daunting. It will be the local convenience store's ability to offer excitement and relevant focus – through excellent meal solutions or a restoration of truly personal services – that will make recovery a reality. Sadly, it is hard to see many of today's independent food shops playing much part in the process.

The Co-operative movement

'Fifty years of unalloyed tragedy' was the outline summary of the performance of the Co-operative movement in the first edition of *The Grocers* 10 years ago. The tragedy was to continue for several more years thereafter. A picture of declining sales, dreadfully poor stores up and down the country, and a market share that had dropped at a staggering rate, from a market-leading 25 per cent in 1980 to between 4 and 5 per cent three years ago, continued to tell its own dire story. It seems that this fine historical movement, founded in Rochdale in 1843, was in free fall and that nothing could arrest the process. The Co-op had become the weakest of British food retailers and, despite having thousands of grocery stores distributed across the country and related businesses in sectors other than foods, it found itself unable to compete with the hard-nosed scale operators in the British supermarket industry or to find a way to make its distinctive business model – mutuality – sufficiently attractive to hold a stable customer base at any level in the market. But perhaps today things may have started to change, and the Co-op has its best chance for many years of becoming a decent place to shop once again.

What has happened to cause the change? Finally it seems that the Co-op has discovered sufficient resolve to tackle the issue that had always been its fundamental barrier to success, coherence or even, it seemed at one stage, survival – organization. Organization has prevented the movement from putting together a straightforward strategy or even following a simple business plan, and for too long it seemed there was nothing individual societies wanted to do about it. Then in 2000, after years of fighting each other rather than the competition, the Co-operative Retail Society (CRS), founded in 1934, merged with the Co-operative Wholesale Society (CWS), whose roots go back to 1863. However, the movement still lacked the capacity to produce a single cohesive business plan. The two parts of the organization had diametrically divergent views of the right way to proceed. Should the Co-op focus on its high number of stores and many high street locations by optimizing local presence and, in doing so, provide consumers with an offer from the

Co-op that was distinctive from that of the big supermarkets? The CWS component in management thought it should. Or was there no alternative but to challenge the big players on their own ground and work from an increased presence in big stores, as the CRS group felt? As usual, the question was discussed and left unresolved, and the Co-op decided to try to do both – which in the end meant it did neither in any meaningful way. Seemingly, nothing had changed. It was still the same old story from a group singularly unable, as it always had been, to get its collective act together.

Finally, however, change has happened. It has been driven by a group within the movement based initially in the Yorkshire Co-op, which is where the current CEO, Peter Marks, came from. Marks is a veteran of more than 40 years' standing in the Co-op, and he could see, as indeed many before him had appreciated but had done nothing about, that the movement needed to coalesce behind a single strategy, drive a common plan, and bring the majority of the movement's societies behind this common endeavour. As Marks summed it up, at a late stage in his own career in the Co-op he had 'absolutely nothing to lose'. It was a case of making the common plan work or facing disappearance. He was able to begin attracting important allies, starting with the United North West societies, and as time passed others began to follow. Today Marks can count on more than 80 per cent of societies being lined up behind his strategy. Now he could start to act.

The team chose a strategy of local presence, and has elected to use the very large number of Co-op stores (today, with acquisitions, more than 3,000 in food alone) as the spearhead for the new convenience store approach, where they feel they have the best chance of winning. Marks had some hard decisions to make. He saw clearly that there was no chance of consolidating the organization by joining up weak units, that is, huddling together for warmth. He had to take the few stronger components, set higher standards and then focus on amalgamating behind growing strength. The one Co-operative Group, which emerged in 2007, was put together as a basis with this in mind, and in the first year alone, not perhaps unexpectedly, the Group was able to realize substantial synergies of £70 million. Funding the changes required to make the group survive and then grow was a big issue, but it was able to raise the substantial sum of £2 billion, a considerable achievement for this straitened team, as the UK recession was looming. With this backing, the priority job became one of sorting out a collection of stores that had been allowed to deteriorate to an appalling degree. The catch-up process is now well on its way, and the Co-op is refitting, modernizing and rebranding at a rate of 700 stores each year.

Peter Marks's new team has not had the luxury of sitting on its laurels, however, and 2009 was to be what he describes as 'an historic year'. The Co-op bought the Somerfield company for £1.6 billion, which gave the movement its first market share increase for a very long time. Today the company is holding a share of between 7 and 8 per cent, so while it trails the big four by some distance it certainly has enough scale to continue to tackle cost synergies and savings with some energy. At the same time, 2009 was also the year in which the banking arm of the Co-operative Group acquired the Britannia Building Society, an ethically similar company to the Co-op but one that had a commercial attraction for the buyer through its branch network. The problems in other parts of the banking industry have provided a strong platform for the now bigger Co-operative banking arm to increase its share and its customer base in a sympathetic market that likes its distinctive approach to banking.

That a turnaround has happened in the Co-op's Manchester headquarters is no longer in doubt. Whether it will ultimately succeed is not yet certain, but it has at least got off to a promising start and indicates that the Group is operating with more coherence than at any time for many years. Results over the past five years have been moving steadily in the right direction. Borrowings have been necessary but are being accommodated within a manageable plan, and an industry-average return on capital is being attained, which might have seemed out of the question a few years ago. Profitability at a pre-tax level – if we can so describe a mutual's results – at £402 million, from revenue of £13.7 billion, is perfectly reasonable and has been achieved quickly. Underlying growth at 5.5 per cent in 2009 was above the market, and Marks points to 16 consecutive quarters when the business has grown. A fascinating question on the projected recovery is the extent to which the Group's origins and historical strength can play a part in its 21st-century 'restatement'. Perhaps they can. The movement will maintain the dividend, now in the modernized carrier of an electronic card, which can be simultaneously adopted as both a loyalty card and a credit card. The movement's ethical stance can add some appropriate weight to the perceived modernity of the Group's offer to customers, and a strong local presence may enable it to take advantage of a return to more local shopping – a phenomenon that appears possible or even likely. Finally, like all his mainstream competitors, Marks has ambitions to strengthen the movement's online presence. These aspirations no longer look in any way improbable.

A few positive years do not mean that this recently struggling Group has turned the corner once and for all. It is now numerically the most important force on the high street, with more stores than Tesco and a lot more than everyone else. The sadness is that it failed to capitalize on this potentially strong presence at a time when the high streets were unoccupied by competitors. Those days are past though. The issue is whether the Co-op can itself do a leading job in what is now a highly crowded local market, where volume shopping is still for the most part done in the out-of-town supermarkets that form the bulk of the big four's trading estate. Marks is not making any grandiose claims, and speaks now of 'sticking to the knitting' while seeking to hold a stable 8 per cent of the grocery market. This may take some doing. Convenience at £30 billion may account for nearly 20 per cent of the food retail market, and it will challenge this team to out-merchandise Tesco and Sainsbury's in an area where they are now both putting in real effort. Others have announced firm intentions to be there as well – Asda for one, Waitrose for another. There is no avoiding it – the Co-op's newly reorganized 'shock troops' are committed to a flat-out contest against the best UK opposition, now there in numbers, for a profitable share of the convenience food opportunity – can they deliver this demanding task? They believe they can, and in any case it is now the chosen strategy or exit, as these are the two options on the table. Peter Marks points warmly to the strength and commitment of his management team as a strong asset at his disposal in the contest ahead. If they do bring it off and deliver a long-term result, this will be a major turnaround story in British food retailing, certainly the most notable since the Tesco revival after 1978 – and look what happened to it.

Cheap if not yet cheerful: Aldi, Lidl, Netto, the hard discounters

Halfway down London's Old Kent Road, in one of the poorest parts of the urban south-east of England, is a large, singularly unattractive, windowless brick warehouse, with the blue sign that tells you that Aldi, one of Europe's largest and most drivingly successful retailers, is inside. Two miles east is a big and highly visible new site in a worthwhile, slowly reviving inner-city Deptford location with considerable presence – one of the bright new Lidl discount stores. Each is representative of a well-known German discounter company, with a recipe that has succeeded in many countries. A third hard discounter is also an import, Netto from Denmark.

Aldi offers incontrovertibly the lowest prices on a slim range – only 600-odd lines are stocked, usually of its own or tertiary (that is to say, branded but insignificant) lines. The process is an easy one to understand, and in Germany, where Theo and Karl Albrecht learnt their trade as one visible element in the post-war *Wirtschaftswunder* (economic miracle), the stores have become a saga in their own right, like a genuine German Coronation Street, a continuingly popular part of the national culture. BMW and Mercedes owners happily throng the stores, and widespread price awareness of the promoted lines ranks with the major news stories.

Manufacturers of brands justifiably trod warily where the discounter phenomenon was concerned, feeling there might be no long-term gains to be made, and seeing from Europe the effect on brand franchise as well as margins. In Germany, the strongest brands learnt from bitter experience to stay away from the seductive appeal of Aldi's prestigious volume-moving power – it is fine when you are friends, but when arguments break out the sudden change of heart can be both vicious and painful. Brand companies moved overnight from strong profit positions to barely covering their overheads, so great were the volumes that Aldi could generate. So you will not find brand leaders in the Aldi assortment. Nor will you find them anywhere else in this class of trade, with a few exceptions tactically stocked by Netto, and these may be token sales under strictly controlled buying terms from manufacturers anxious not to be charged with unwillingness to supply to the new discounter operations.

For some years the discounters made little headway: it took Aldi 10 years to go from 2 per cent to 3 in 2009, while Lidl crept up to 2.4 per cent. Netto is still below 1 per cent. Consumers seemed to prefer the wider range and much more pleasant atmosphere of the major supermarkets, even when the discounters' prices were significantly lower. The discounters offered very low prices, but little else. Products from their limited range are shown in the cardboard outers with the front cut off, stacked on plain shelves. The lighting is utilitarian, there are no bags at the checkout, and usually there is only one checkout operator and few other staff visible. The experience is enlivened by a central fixture displaying this week's bargain – often electrical tools of mysterious purpose at unbelievably cheap prices.

The perception has begun to change in the last few years: articles have appeared in the upmarket papers, revealing to astonished readers that these strange places existed and that they offered astounding bargains. Middle-class consumers talked, even boasted, at their dinner parties of the good deals they had found in Aldi or Lidl. Often specific items were mentioned – olive oil or Parmesan cheese – that were of high quality, at giveaway prices (in a blind taste test, olive oils from both Aldi and Lidl beat products from M&S and Sainsbury's, among others, and were some £4 cheaper). It became respectable to shop there. With the arrival of the recession, the economic pressure on household budgets gave the discounters a further boost, and sales moved ahead. Aldi in particular seemed to benefit, led by Paul Foley, who, uniquely for an employee of the secretive firm, was prepared to talk about his success. In 2009, sales went up by a staggering 25 per cent when the majors were struggling along on low single-digit growth. The industry was shocked when, in the middle of this new-found growth, the apparently brilliant CEO was fired.

Foley, who had spent 20 years at the German discount giant, was leaving the business by 'mutual consent'. Aldi, a notoriously secretive business, declined to comment further on Foley's departure. Its statement said that its former UK boss was 'widely credited as challenging and changing traditional market perceptions to establish Aldi as a leading brand offering high-quality and best-value products'.

Aldi was certainly very canny with its PR. The mainstream UK media were quick to coin the term 'Aldi effect' to describe the trend for shoppers at last to embrace discount chains that had been in the country for over a decade. Neil Saunders, consulting director at Verdict Research, believes Foley's time leading Aldi in the UK and Ireland should be judged a success: 'It is for the last few years that he will be remembered best: it was during this period that Aldi was reshaped to be more aligned to consumer preferences and appeared to open up in terms of communicating with stakeholders' (*source:* Just-Food.com).

Armin Burger, who had played a starring role in Aldi's continental operations, was brought in on a temporary basis; in October 2009, Matthew Barnes from the Australian business was appointed UK managing director. So tight-lipped is the company that it could not be confirmed that Burger had left, as had been reported. No one really knows, either, why Foley was sacked: did he simply talk too much, thus offending against the Aldi culture of silence? It may or may not be coincidental that sales growth is now back at its previous level.

Sceptical commentators believe that all Aldi's vaunted spurt was down to new space opened, and that shoppers have not permanently deserted their supermarkets. One analyst, David McCarthy, delights in stating firmly that the hard discounters' share is lower now than 10 years ago, when Kwik Save alone had a share of 5.8 per cent (Kantar Worldpanel). The majors, led by Tesco, had responded to the threat by tackling the price challenge head on: Tesco rechristened itself as 'Britain's biggest discounter' (a claim successfully challenged by Aldi before the Advertising Standards Authority). All the majors – and even upmarket Waitrose – launched a cheap range to fight the interlopers. For the moment, the threat has been contained, and it looks as if the hard discounters will make only gradual progress.

Lidl has many similarities to Aldi: both are German, privately owned, intensely private, and very successful in their home country, and have spread into many more (see also Chapter 7). Lidl's operation is similar, too: a small store with a limited range, sold at very low prices. Its share in Britain is lower than Aldi's but has been increasing faster: Lidl went from 1.4 per cent in 2001 to 2.4 per cent in 2009, while Aldi went from 2 to 3 per cent, and it is still opening new space as fast as it can find sites. Like Aldi, Lidl gained from the increasing acceptance, even trendiness, of the discounters.

A recent visit in one town found both in clean, modern buildings, Lidl on an industrial estate on the edge of town, Aldi nearer the centre. Both focus, as one would expect, on basic goods piled high on pallets, but Lidl's frozen cabinet included cooked velvet crabs and whole cooked lobsters. Both stocked fresh herbs as well as a range of fresh produce. It is then less surprising that a *Which?* report on supermarket quality rated Aldi and Lidl joint third: Waitrose was way out in front with an overall score of 79 per cent, followed by M&S at 64, and Aldi and Lidl at 61 per cent. The discounters scored five out of five for price, but also did well on product quality. This should give the big four a sharp poke in the ribs.

What Lidl in particular has suffered is frequent attacks in the media about its treatment of staff. The most serious allegations concern its German operation (see Chapter 7), but criticisms have surfaced in Britain too. The main complaints centre round very long working hours and challenging working targets (the number of items to be passed through the checkout or handled in the warehouse, for example). Lidl's notorious secrecy has not helped, but neither of the German companies has appeared inclined to change. The impact of the Lidl scandal has worked through to Britain, even though the CEO in Britain, Frank-Michael Mros, had previously been in charge in Germany and had been on extended leave as a result of the allegations about treatment of employees. CCTV cameras are no longer in the staff canteen (where they were placed because that was where suspected shoplifters were taken, according to management), and personal documents such as application forms have to be kept under lock and key. The public has noticed none of this and, as Lidl keeps on opening new space, sales continue to rise, albeit from a low level.

Netto has a presence in the market, but that is about all one can say. It has made little progress, its quality rating is abysmal, and one gets the impression that the Danish owners have forgotten about their British outpost.

Aldi and its imitators have spotted a market gap in the UK that is latent and growing. British retail margins have been among the highest in the world, and offer measurable incentive to provide other ways of getting everyday staple requirements into the hands of needy consumers. The surprising thing was that it took so long for these European powerhouses to enter the UK market. In delaying as long as they did, two things happened that make their opportunity now a smaller one. First, it became even more difficult, after 1993, without acquisition, to get good sites in tight urban environments. Second, British companies had most of two decades to establish the big-range out-of-town superstore as the universal standard and to claim that there is no better form of food shopping. The superstore is now rooted and more difficult to change, especially when it involves an obvious retreat from the good presentation and appearance of the out-of-town stores. This suggests that, if they do want to become a force in the UK, the existing discounters will have to change their approach, which after many years has brought them such limited success. Perhaps it also suggests that it may take a company with the global confidence and truly innovative record of US Wal-Mart to make genuine food discounting work for the first time in Britain.

Strong niche players

Marks and Spencer

Marks and Spencer had been for many years the stately liner of British retailing, sailing serenely on, basking in the glow of customers' loyalty and admiration. In the 1990s, it hit very troubled waters indeed. By 2001, it had a new executive chairman, Luc Vandevelde, and a new head of food, Justin King, recently recruited from Asda. We concluded then that, with capable leadership, the company could become more attuned to customer needs, remain reliable and once more offer the best value, and that its future depended on it achieving this. What has happened since then?

The seas have hardly been calm. Vandevelde remained as chairman until 2004, though with the addition of a chief executive, Roger Holmes, in 2002. Between them, they started the recovery, clothing in particular getting an injection of innovation and creativity. In 2004, Vandevelde was replaced by Paul Myners, a City grandee, but the real excitement lay elsewhere. Philip Green, a self-made billionaire with extensive interests on the high street (including iconic brands such as Topshop, Burton and Dorothy Perkins), started to show a renewed appetite for M&S. The company's profits were falling again, at a time when the rest of the economy was booming, and Green thought his proven retailing skills could turn it round. His declaration of interest sent the previously languishing shares leaping up. The board did not welcome the prospect, and invited Stuart Rose to become CEO. Rose, who had started his retail career as a management trainee with M&S, had gone on to make a name for himself, particularly at the Arcadia group. He was so successful that Green bought the group, and Rose left – though in an atmosphere of mutual admiration between the two men. Green had in fact pencilled in Rose's name as CEO in his bid, and he was not best pleased by M&S's pre-emptive appointment. At the M&S AGM in July 2004, the private shareholders, some of whose families had held the shares for decades, showed overwhelming support for the board: they did not like 'their' company being threatened by the barbarians at the gates. In the face of this entrenched opposition, Green withdrew. He had offered 400p a share, a price that the shares achieved again only in January 2010 (apart from a spike in 2007 to over 750 due to the irrational exuberance affecting the stock market as a whole, and Rose's effective PR in the City).

Rose had to prove himself, and he gradually did so, though he didn't publicly declare that the company was in recovery until January 2007. Like Sainsbury's, M&S had an enduring and powerful culture, a great strength in the past but a hindrance when radical change was needed. Its essential problem was that competitors had caught up, both in clothing and in food. In clothing, there were new competitors apparently more attuned to customers' changing demands, while in food its old reputation for quality, value and innovation was now shared, not only with Waitrose, but with the premium ranges of the majors. It is for this reason that we no longer see M&S food as the benchmark to which all others aspire.

Justin King, the new head of food, oversaw the opening of stand-alone Simply Food stores, and outlets at railway stations and airports (in partnership with Compass). The company had some good years, mainly on the back of this new space and an improving economy. When King was picked to run Sainsbury's in 2004, he was followed by a succession of appointees who made little impact. It is not true to say that innovation had entirely stopped: M&S introduced the Gastropub range in 2004 and the Cook! range (prepared meals, ready to cook at home) in 2005. Sales climbed slowly, from £2.9 billion in 2000–01 to £3.5 billion by 2005, with market share bobbing around between 3 and 4 per cent. Fundamental issues remained: there was not a pipeline of innovations designed to provide solutions to customer problems and to introduce excitement and differentiation; and the logistics systems were not upgraded ('20 years out of date', according to one commentator, a description accepted by current head John Dixon). Attempts to improve margins led to pricing drifting out of line, and the company was no longer seen as giving value, always a crucial element in the consumer offer.

The appointment of Steven Esom, former managing director of Waitrose, looked like a marriage made in heaven, but somehow it just did not work out. He lasted only 14 months. In 2008, a Marks and Spencer veteran, John Dixon, was brought in. He found the operation unprepared to face the recession, without a sound foundation. He immediately started to analyse the situation from scratch, starting with an 'enormous amount' of work with the Customer Insight Unit. The findings, not perhaps unexpected, were that customers expected M&S to:

- provide the best-quality food;
- be the most trusted;

- surprise and delight; and
- improve value.

Dixon took a number of actions, including replacing 75 per cent of the senior staff. Three segments of customers were defined – top, core and occasional – with ranges and promotions targeted at each. To attack the poor-value image, there were initiatives such as Dine In for £10 (a restaurant-quality meal plus wine for two), Wise Buys (staples at the same price as that of competitors) and multi-buys and money-offs. The innovation pipeline has been refilled, and new ranges such as Simply Fuller for Longer introduced to meet customers' health concerns. This range, worked up with scientific input from Aberdeen University, has been 'hugely successful', according to Dixon, without cannibalizing the Count on Us traditional slimming product. A start has also been made on identifying what systems are needed to improve availability.

A central concern remains: how to persuade more people to do their weekly shop at M&S. One answer was to make the products more available through increasing space. Another, and one seen as revolutionary by many, was to offer national brands. Although in the very distant past M&S did sell some brands, for decades it has been quintessentially an own-brand retailer. To entice more shoppers to spend more of their weekly budget in M&S, offering a few of the essential brands seems logical. Around 400 national brands such as Marmite and Heinz tomato ketchup have been trialled in 130 stores, and are being rolled out to all stores after promising results.

What all this activity has achieved is to stop the rot; whereas sales were falling, there has now been positive like-for-like growth for five quarters. M&S has not broken out, however. Its share of the total market was still only 3.9 per cent in 2009, and the most recent results were disappointing. It can go on opening space wherever possible – only 50 per cent of the population is within 10 minutes' drive of a store. That will help, but all the actions so far are catching up: they have not restored M&S to its former position as the leader in quality, innovation and value. Waitrose is now a much more formidable competitor, and in many eyes has taken M&S's place. Food is now fully half of total UK retail sales, a hugely important part of the business, and radical action is needed. John Dixon has, in many ways, done all the right things (and he was elevated to the main board in September 2009). But, frustratingly, it is not enough. The appointment of Marc Bolland, previously CEO of

Morrisons, may be a sign that M&S recognizes that something new is called for.

Iceland

Iceland is a modest-sized high street supplier of frozen foods, formed in 1970. Set up by some Woolworth's employees with an investment of £30 each, it has survived and grown, despite some turbulent times. Malcolm Walker, the ebullient leader (and one of the founders), has taken the company down interesting paths, left, and returned to rescue Iceland. It has ventured into organics, non-GM foods, a free online shopping service, and appliances, abandoning these at various times. The biggest adventure led to a merger with Booker, during which Stuart Rose became CEO briefly before leaving to make his fortune at Arcadia (for his later tenure at M&S, see above). The new CEO was Bill Grimsey; Walker was forced to resign under a cloud, having sold millions of pounds' worth of the company's shares just before the announcement of poorer results (he was later cleared). Iceland was renamed the Big Food Group, but results were disappointing; in 2005, the Icelandic group Baugur moved in and demerged Iceland. Baugur was at that time and subsequently engaged in taking shares in large swathes of the British high street, including household names such as Hamleys, House of Fraser, Debenhams, Whittard of Chelsea and a clutch of fashion retailers. When Baugur entered administration in 2009, Walker was quick to point out that it had never held more than 13.5 per cent of Iceland.

In 2005, after Baugur entered the picture, Walker returned to what he saw as his company. His views on the Grimsey period are pungently expressed on the company website, and they are not flattering. He refocused on the core business, and brought it back to profitability, partly by reducing the workforce. The appliance business was closed in 2009, so that Iceland is now back to its roots. Its positioning has been variously expressed, but has always been as the mums' friend, with low prices. Promotions have been curtailed, and a simplified pricing structure adopted – Clear Cut Prices. All prices are rounded to 25p, so £1.35 becomes £1.25, for example. The home delivery remains, and is a major selling point.

Sales have increased, and the share has been climbing back towards the 2.4 per cent achieved in 2000; so far, it has reached only 1.8 per cent. Iceland seems destined to remain an interesting, different, but small player.

The Market in Europe

07

European markets: retailers looking outwards

In 2001, we looked back at a period in which the retailing scene in continental Europe had been dynamic and sometimes turbulent. In particular, many firms had looked beyond their national boundaries, either because of the small size of their home market or because of government-imposed restrictions. It was striking that firms such as Carrefour and Auchan from France, and Metro, Aldi and Lidl from Germany were the most internationally adventurous food retailers (and cash-and-carry wholesaler in the case of Metro), much more than US firms and at that time much more than British firms. What we meant by Europe then was in fact mainly western Europe, and the biggest development since then has been the emergence of countries from central and eastern Europe as modern, free market economies. Estonia, Latvia, Lithuania, Poland, the Czech Republic, Slovakia, Slovenia and Hungary joined the EU in 2004, and Bulgaria and Romania followed in 2007. The other development has been the growth of Tesco as an international player, and the failure of Wal-Mart in Germany (though successful elsewhere – see Chapter 8).

Box 7.1 Wal-Mart in Germany

Wal-Mart's German adventure was a spectacular episode for Europe-watchers. Wal-Mart was – and is – the hugely dominant competitor that everyone fears. Europeans tended to assume that, once Wal-Mart entered a market, it would crush the opposition there, as it has in the United States. The German entry was a lesson for all of us.

Experienced commentators now tend to regard it as a prime example of how not to do it. It seemed that Wal-Mart was determined to do everything wrong that could be done wrong in entering a new market. It was not humble, and it did not understand that Germany is not the United States, and that the people, their habits and culture, the shopping environment and the competition are all very different from what Wal-Mart was used to. Wal-Mart assumed that what it did at home – with spectacular and unique success – would work here.

Many of the mistakes stemmed from the attempt to impose its own culture. Thus it offered greeters at the door, an idea that Germans did not like. Employees bagged customers' shopping, which was firmly rejected by the locals. Employees found the imposition of Wal-Mart culture in the workplace intrusive. The company clashed repeatedly with unions, not a surprise to anyone except Wal-Mart itself, which was used to imposing its strongly anti-union stance wherever it went and was quite unprepared for the powerful German versions.

Even more surprisingly, if possible, Wal-Mart underestimated the competition. Accustomed to being the lowest-priced, it found Aldi and Lidl undercutting it – and with far more stores. The invader had simply bought too small and perhaps too weak a target, and spent far too long improving the stores it had rather than building scale. It appears that the company was completely unprepared for the German market. It may have looked superficially attractive – the biggest, strongest economy in Europe – but few markets could be more different from the US market while seeming similar. The German *Mitbestimmung* (co-determination) system, in which workers are involved with management at works council and supervisory board level, must have shocked the US company. Regulations on shop opening hours and on what price cutting and promotions are allowed are a surprise even to British managers. A succession of managers, including later on some Europeans, could make little impression on the debacle – too little, too late.

Eventually, in July 2006, Wal-Mart admitted defeat and pulled out, with a loss running into millions of dollars. Even worse was the loss of face: the mighty, all-conquering, unbeatable Wal-Mart, humbled by one of the countries of 'old Europe'. While providing an enormous dose of that quintessentially German emotion *Schadenfreude* to Europeans, it must have sent the US company back with a great deal to think about. The experience may have put it off Europe for good. It has made no further attempts to buy there, and may think the whole area difficult and over-regulated, and offering only slow growth. To its credit, it does appear to have learnt from the experience: its subsequent entries into countries in Asia have shown much more respect for local culture, so perhaps it is a better company for it.

Most of Europe was beginning to look like the common market that its early supporters had evangelized for, although this is a superficial view. Some countries are more open than others, and some governments more eager to intervene than their co-members. Both France and Germany see a bigger role for the state, and are readier to intervene in markets than Britain is, for instance. Cultures still vary, as any journey through Europe will demonstrate. One of the first lessons that internationally expanding companies have to learn – and remember – is that people in new countries are likely to be different in their shopping, cooking and eating habits. How well food retailers have been able to reconcile their centralized business models with the need to adapt to local needs has been, and will remain, a central question.

National frameworks in Europe

The three primary national market growth engines have been located in France, in a very different retailing climate in Germany and, in a market different again, in the UK. The German champions have been Metro, mainly with its cash-and-carry wholesalers, and the hard discounters Aldi and Lidl, while several French retailers have built international chains. Before Tesco's emergence, Britain's retailers had seemed content to remain behind what they saw as impenetrable barriers against foreign entrants (though German discounters Aldi and Lidl are now significant elements on the UK landscape, perhaps the first ominous exceptions to the invulnerability rule). The Netherlands is an adventurous retail market, and Ahold has played a modest European role, as have important Belgian corporations, but it has been growth driven from either side of the Rhine that has been the formative influence. Ahold, whose international development had been among the most rapid, had concentrated almost exclusively on generating major equity finance to grow in the United States, before imploding after a financial scandal there; it has now climbed painfully back to sound health and profitability.

Today the European market is an entity that will integrate more rapidly in the years ahead, and it is so viewed by the key players. For more than 40 years, the normal pattern of development had been through the hypermarket, driven principally from a developing French model, which Carrefour is credited with initiating, but which has been imitated widely elsewhere over time. There are similarities in Germany, but there the major players have been much more individual in behaviour.

There has been a much greater tendency to rely on and communicate low-price strategies, a relic from the painful post-war years. The strength of the discounting format in Germany was one obvious direct consequence that is now rooted in the very core of German grocery trading. Aldi was a distinctive and genuine pioneer from the day the two Albrecht brothers started to create their powerful empire as early as 1948. Metro, Europe's largest single retailing entity, has competed in a bewilderingly complex array of market sectors, formats and fascias. The less well-known but significant Rewe is another large and diverse trading group and, at an integrated level, has been Europe's second largest player. It is a set of interlocking cooperative retail and wholesale developments but once again with no single or dominant pattern. The building of strategies that are becoming recognizable over the long term and the need for flexibility, particularly with regard to the importance of the discounting appeal, can now be observed as key factors. A further important development may now be the growing importance of the neighbourhood convenience stores.

The European companies

Germany's Metro is the biggest overall, but it has achieved its position without any obvious definition of retail strategy. After Metro, and in the top 10, there is a range of players, many one-time family businesses with considerable stakes in their home markets and traditional heritages built over many years, which are not very different from each other in size and power. All the way down to Leclerc, they have sales well in excess of €50 billion. Competition is now very tight, reflected in the slim net trading margins and an increasingly hell-for-leather drive for the new markets that are opening. With a few exceptions, the better European companies have not been able to achieve much more than around half the net margin that the best UK supermarket operator produced over the same period. Whether as a cause or a consequence, there is a simplicity and stripped-down operating and service climate in the European hypermarket or discounter that is very different from the well-engineered calm, cohesion and elegance of the British equivalents.

Format development in Europe

The European hypermarket format is now experiencing severe problems, a phase that has lasted 10 years and shows no sign of fading. Particularly in France and Spain, where the format has been most dominant, the major financial indicators are now all pointing downwards. Both discounters and supermarkets have greater current consumer appeal, and the 'convenience handicap' of the hypermarket – long driving times and even *too much* choice when you get there – has apparently not been overcome. Legislation, based on a thesis of consumer protection, limiting the rates of expansion and preventing goods being sold at a loss, has contributed substantially to the lack of scale advantage that hypermarkets can continue to generate. The hypermarkets' reaction, to expand their non-food assortments, has probably not helped, and there are signs that their consumer appeal is now weakening in the key food markets. Strategies with more precision, focus and clear areas of advantage, including a distinctive and topical profile for development of fresh food and quality grocery shopping, are now their crucial requirement.

Franchising has played a large part in European store development and has been a contributor to keeping down both capital investment and running costs. The best European companies have raised their net margins in recent years, usually through major moves in scale, accompanied by an increase in non-foods assortment and turnover. However, the 1 to 1.5 per cent range has been by no means uncommon for large and highly successful companies, eg Tengelmann in Germany, and shows just how tough life now is for some of these formidable and well-established operators. The obsessive secrecy of many competitors means it is not always possible to determine what margins and profitability are really being taken – a far cry from the visibility of performance and detailed financial analysis attaching on a quarterly basis to the results of British or US operators. What is clear is that their returns are nearer those of the US model than the UK's and, following recent US consolidation, most of the big European companies do not begin to match in scale the biggest US groups. Innovation, technology and scale as they have moved across Europe have delivered big efficiencies, but it is doubtful whether there is now a great deal more to go for. Hence there is a drive for new geography and emergent self-service markets. The growth of the discounter and its appeal in some of Europe's poorer markets to the south and east, with the global retail market now arriving at pace, suggest that margins may be set to contract rather than rise. Europe's biggest, highly diversified competitor (Metro) seems to recognize this and has put enormous pressure on consolidation, behind four focused fascias and resultant efficiencies. There will be inevitable shakeout among the second-rank players and, well within range now, there lurks the imminent threat of Wal-Mart, the world's largest retailer, on the way to building a world as well as European food retailing presence.

The importance of the family

The increasingly ruthless nature of today's market is a novel and unpleasant experience for many of these companies, which have proud and stable histories, some going back as much as a century. A roster of famous ruling families has played a major role in this industry's development. Tengelmann, more than a century after its German beginnings, still responds to the leadership of the great-grandson of its founder. It has become skilled at dealing with major interference, and regrouped and re-established its core activities twice in the 20th century, following its disappearance through confiscation at the end of two world wars. This has not diminished its resolve to recapture lost ground, eg in eastern Germany, and it has established a unique vertically integrated German foods business, while getting worthwhile footholds in the United States (with the purchase of A&P) and later in Italy (with Superal).

In France, the Fournier, Mulliez and Leclerc triumvirate of families played the crucial central roles in building the big and omnipresent French brand names of Carrefour, Auchan and Leclerc. There are more than embryonic signs now that they are with the utmost reluctance beginning to relinquish a powerful family grip on the reins of power. Carrefour, a widely spread company with apparent world ambitions, recognized that it had to put in place a strategic structure to manage its future, and that family voting rights had to be rapidly reduced. We will see what has transpired subsequently.

In Germany, Otto Beisheim was until 1994, astonishingly for such an enormous concern, sole owner of Metro. This is a 180-company conglomerate, where it is truly impossible to fathom the labyrinthine controls and systems that obtain in what is Europe's biggest retailer. At Aldi the twins Theo and Karl Albrecht have played a well-choreographed, but also highly secretive, part in the successful growth of their Aldi company, now well represented in both Europe and the United States. There is a suggestion in Germany that the dual-leader approach (north and south separate and competing) has been a deliberate ploy to maintain the tightest control of staff costs and conditions – on the grounds that it is easier for two leaders to say no to wage increases than just one!

The importance of these European dynastic families cannot be overestimated. Their survival in power has been a force for process consistency and the pursuit and acceptance of long-term strategies. The century-long hegemony of the Sainsbury family in Britain was entirely comparable in style, at least until John Sainsbury began to take the company public. In Europe, however, it is now set to change. In this regard, the change in Britain has preceded Europe's current re-examination. Sainsbury's floated the company in 1973, non-family board members have been in the majority for years, and there is a professional chief executive and a non-family chairman. Tesco's last family chairman stood down, albeit with considerable unwillingness, in 1970. Elsewhere in the UK, professional managers rule the roost, as indeed they do in the Netherlands: the expansion of Ahold in the United States accelerated mightily under Cees van der Hoeven's determined personal leadership after 1993.

There is a feeling that it has been the ethos of the individual companies themselves, and influentially the families in the shadows behind them pulling the strings, that has determined the essential nature of the continental European markets. Transparency has not normally been a characteristic. While it worked admirably when each ruling family knew and essentially respected the areas of potential dominance to which their competitors aspired in growth markets, whether these same companies can now change their behaviour, accept more visibility and accountability, and take on world competition is quite another matter. On the record, however, big market shares have been built in important new markets – Spain, Brazil and eastern and central Europe are all examples. At the same time, there have been notable and expensive failures, such as an innovative and expansive Carrefour throwing in the North American towel. As the need for capital intensifies, and as shareholders begin to make more insistent demands and want proper and regular performance information, the rate of change will accelerate and many, more visible mistakes will be made. Such unsuccessful acquisitions as Casino and Cora in France and the poor post-acquisition performance of Euromarche for Carrefour (which forced out the CEO as a consequence) and of Catteau for Tesco (which knew it was hugely lucky to find a quick buyer) are cases of past errors. We can be sure there will be more, as hostile acquisitions play a significant part in the market's consolidation and growth.

Governments and legislation

A further important difference between the British and continental markets has been the attitude of national governments and the role of legislative constraint on the big retail companies. In France, through the *loi Royer*, there has been considerable restriction on development of hypermarkets, usually exercised through the imposition of absolute limitations on new site developments. The motivation has been to protect the centres of French towns and villages and thereby the livings of small shopkeepers. In this regard the policy can be said to have been achieved its objectives. Comparing a French and British high street today is illuminating, and shows the extent in Britain to which decades of laissez-faire government planning and inconsistent local policy have created a threadbare high street and communities deprived of many former local shops. The French high street and communities have in this respect fared better.

Elsewhere in Europe, restrictions have also been considerably more demanding than in the UK. In Germany, there are legislative constraints on outlets above 1,200 square metres in size, called the *Baunutzungsverordnungen* (building regulations), not dissimilar to France's *loi Royer*. Restraint in Germany has operated as much through the limitations of price and cost as overt government controls, but the resulting position is not very different from that of France, and a stronger local community has been preserved. While Britain, after 1993, was forced into a process of learning from previous mistakes, it has on the whole been Europe's good fortune to have been influenced by a series of more interventionist social policies and therefore to have been able to avoid most of the problems of the disintegration of local communities in the first place.

Building brands

There has been little genuine brand building in most European retail operations. Companies have been content on the whole to behave as holding companies behind a veil of secrecy and to create new store fascias or brand portfolios where they were needed operationally. There are large aggregations of market sectors and operations grouped under a single holding company name, with food usually predominating. Albert Heijn was originally a tiny family business, founded 100 years ago in Oostzaan by the side of a Dutch canal and its chain of stores is highly innovative, having experimented early with technologies such as scanning in-store and home sales. Heijn is the gold standard in the Netherlands, with a firm grip on the Dutch market and a share three times that of its nearest rival, but Ahold has shown a capability of building a strong consumer brand in Holland.

Just about as unlike Ahold as it is possible to be, Aldi is predictably positioned and confidently operated. Aldi is uncomplicated and down to earth and, where price is the paramount requirement, its determination speaks for itself, both in Germany and elsewhere – it took more than 10 years for it to make Denmark profitable, for example. Although Aldi branding lacks any element of emotional aspiration, the company has shown that it can use its skills and speed to reproduce German success in developed markets (eg the United States, where 10 per cent of its sales, from its Trader Joe's stores, are now generated, and it has over 1,000 Aldi stores). Strategic commitment shows in its willingness to wait patiently for success. Fifty years of terrific consistency and tradition in Germany cannot be ignored. 'The rich want to come here and the poor have to' has been the Albrecht brothers' persuasively simple claim. The formula obviously translates successfully, as Aldi is now in 18 countries, 16 of them in Europe. Given the obsessive secrecy about their plans, but their acknowledged ability to measure retail performance with exactness, the Albrecht brothers may now know a lot more about strategic market dynamics than they are given credit for. Their standardized brand is already travelling successfully into places far removed from the poverty of 1948 Germany, and many markets exist where Aldi's coherent brand, ability to focus and clear value appeal will be a strong proposition.

Germany

The clear leaders of the grocery market are Aldi and Lidl, with 15 per cent of fmcg value and 11 per cent respectively in 2009 (*source:* GfK). Their similar business models are now familiar, not least because they have stuck very firmly to their knitting: they are stripped-down hard discounters, whose shops offer few frills but very good, often unbeatable prices. The only excitement in the stores is the weekly bargains in the centre aisle, but customers know what to expect. Their secrecy makes it difficult to penetrate far into their operations, but it is clear that they are supreme at keeping costs down. So central is that goal that Lidl in particular has been accused of unsavoury practices in Germany, including spying on its employees, even to the extent of noting down their emotional involvements. The company claims to have cleaned up its act, and there have been no recent recurrences, but the scandal left an unpleasant taste. It has not stopped its commercial success, however, as Lidl has been creeping up on its bigger rival, increasing its market share in Germany, while Aldi has been growing only slowly. Both have exported their model, Lidl in Europe and Aldi further afield. If Lidl continues to show its current form and carry on producing leading growth figures, it may take over leadership in Europe. Certainly, Aldi looks vulnerable in Germany, where Lidl seems the livelier.

Where Aldi's strategy has been clear and integrated, the same cannot be said for the two leading German retailers – Metro and Rewe. Metro grew rapidly but haphazardly for 30 years from its establishment in 1964. Following Beisheim's retirement in 1994, Metro has embarked on a long-overdue process of consolidation and simplification of its retail empire, which embraces a huge range, sold through every conceivable retail format from hypermarket to cash and carry. It has expanded aggressively abroad, and now operates in 30 countries; international revenues account for almost 60 per cent of the total. The cash-and-carry business is by some way its most successful, although recently it has suffered from the recession. The eastern European countries have been particularly hard hit: cash-and-carry revenue was down 7.6 per cent in 2009, and overall income was flat. Although Eckhard Cordes, the CEO, boasted of Metro's success in overcoming the harsh recession, other companies fared better, so management of the unwieldy empire is still a problem. The cash-and-carry business has been split in two, with Frans Muller taking on Asia and new countries while Joel Saveuse, head of Real supermarkets, looks after the mature markets of Europe (Saveuse seems to be part of the exchange of executives between Metro and Carrefour: Daniel Bernard went from Metro to run Carrefour, while Saveuse moved between the two more than once). As cash and carry is an ideal way to move into new countries with undeveloped retail market structures, Metro has huge opportunities in future, but it is unclear how far it will be able to profit from them.

Metro is a third bigger than its next biggest German competitor, the equally complex Rewe group. This very large German business is domestically powerful and has grown rapidly. It is represented in the east and western German markets, and now is present in many of the central European markets. With 80 per cent of sales in food, it is, by sector at least, well focused, as is Metro. Apart from hypermarkets, Rewe has concentrated on developing its Penny Market discounter brand, and has begun to enter more foreign markets. While it failed with the joint operation with Budgens in the UK, it did a lot better in Austria with a subsidiary that was wholly owned. Apart from the moves to the east, it has now reached a partnership agreement with Esselunga, a significant northern Italian operator. Rewe is another conservative company that has grown quickly through pragmatic evolution but now faces a host of new changes – formats, geography and competition – so that it is difficult to forecast its prospects in the more global market. In 2010, it took over 65 branches from Tengelmann, suggesting that Germany is still a primary focus.

Finally in Germany there is Tengelmann, perhaps, over the longest term, the most impressive of German-based competitors, although it is smaller than Metro and Rewe and equivalent in size to the bigger French companies. Founded by the Schmitz family in 1867, it is distinctive for its pursuit of vertical integration policies, enabling it to concentrate on high-quality own-label production. Tengelmann has moved progressively from a luxury approach to create a more mainstream profile, and 75 per cent of its volume is now in foods. Rapid German growth through the post-war years rebuilt the business that Tengelmann twice created and lost through confiscation after the world wars. Acquisition in Germany of the Kaffee Geschäft chain and of significant Co-op stores fuelled growth, as did the development of their PLUS (Prima Leben und Sparen) discounter operation. With what could be called a sense of adventure, Tengelmann bought the failing but once great American A&P chain, with 1,100 stores and a big but notoriously low-margin revenue stream. Tengelmann too has an Italian business (Superal) and is increasingly becoming better represented in the main western European markets, including France, Spain and the Netherlands. It has developed retailing skills, good technologies, a sound innovation record, and enough confidence to enter the biggest world markets. How these competences and its ability to survive on tight margins support them in the years ahead against bigger but hitherto less focused German competition will be a key issue for

Tengelmann. It can also expect eastern European competition from many sources, an inevitable clash with French and German companies in Italy, and challenges in Europe and the United States from Wal-Mart. Tengelmann's stretched profile suggests the need for rapid success or focus and rationalization in the immediate future.

France

French retailers behave by inclination as committed European exporters, driven by restrictive legislation at home and economic stagnation in post-Mitterrand France. Carrefour is, after the takeover of Promodès and its international expansion, now the biggest French retailer, though Leclerc continues to be the leader in France itself. Founded in 1959 by Badin Defforey and the Fournier family, Carrefour is credited with inventing the hypermarket format, and it now has more than 100 in France itself. The largest French retail multiple (as opposed to buying group), it has used non-food to build new growth and margins simultaneously, and has been alert to the opportunity for new discounter formats alongside its main Carrefour brand. Very much more willing than its competitors to experiment, Carrefour is not at all afraid of entering joint ventures, including one with Metro AG. New markets – savings, banking, insurance, telephone services – have all been tackled, and the Carrefour strategy is by no means risk averse. While the hypermarket has been the main engine of Carrefour growth in the past, it has built new growth from discount operations, admittedly unlikely by itself to hold or raise margins.

Carrefour was the pioneer of growth overseas, investing round the world before its rivals had woken up to the opportunities. Under the leadership of Daniel Bernard, it planted its flag in 30 countries. Unfortunately, this crusading mission seemed to take most of its focus, and it took its eye off the home base, where the market was changing. Price was becoming more important, leaving Leclerc well placed, and leaving room for discounters to move in. Bernard left, to be replaced by Jose-Luis Duran, previously CFO. Duran pulled out of countries where Carrefour was not in the top two, to concentrate on markets that are more profitable. Results at home were still poor, and the atmosphere had become tense with the arrival of two active investors, Bernard Arnault, one of France's richest men, and Colony Capital, a US private equity firm. The two had bought shares at €50 in 2007, and were unhappy that they stood at €30 in 2010. Duran too was fired, to be replaced by Lars Olofsson, a Swede previously number two at Nestlé. Olofsson reportedly briefs the two active shareholders once a fortnight, a practice that Duran was unwilling to adopt. He has reorganized the portfolio, tried to modernize the IT systems, and tackled the pricing problem. He has stated firmly that the company will not abandon its growth markets, particularly Brazil and China; much of the future growth is expected to come from international markets, as France is still difficult. Sales, however, continue to languish. Carrefour is suffering from the disaffection with hypermarkets that is pervasive: between 2003 and 2009, sales per square metre in its main hypermarkets in France, Italy, Belgium and Spain fell by 15 per cent (Citigroup estimates). The company has closed its operations in Russia and southern Italy, is negotiating in Portugal, and has tried to shut stores in Belgium (causing strikes in the process). At home, apart from the hypermarket difficulties, it seems not to be able to get a grip of the discounter segment, despite having two fascias (Ed and Dia).

Olofsson is credited with creating a new aura of confidence, introducing eye-catching advertising, and bringing in new talent from Tesco and P&G. A share buy-back raised the share price to €38, but did not find favour with analysts, as it was seen to reduce the company's flexibility. Sales in the first quarter of 2010 came in above expectations, so some progress is being made.

Quite what the dissident shareholders expect is not clear, though no doubt they have their own ideas. The French market is highly competitive, and not very rewarding at present; quick results are unlikely and, if the two active shareholders pressure Olofsson too to leave, who would take the job? Carrefour's future remains open to doubt.

Carrefour's French rival Auchan is difficult to assess, if only because of the secrecy that permeates its policies and operations. Until recently the Mulliez family owned 80 per cent of Auchan, which opened its first hypermarket in 1967. Auchan has from its earliest days banked on size – the Asda of France – and some of its aptly named Mammouth stores are well over 40,000 square feet. It invested abroad early, from 1981 onwards, and is now in 13 countries, eight of which are in Europe. At home, it has developed the 'Simply Market' (in English) as a discounter, and has tried to *réenchanter l'hyper* (bring enchantment back to hypermarkets). Sales are still sluggish, reflecting the recession, price deflation and currency swings. Auchan's strong reputation in France is a valuable but perhaps declining asset, but the company is in a good financial position and should be able to emerge from present difficulties to continue its expansion.

Spain

The current economic difficulties in Spain, among the worst in western Europe, disguise the buoyancy and innovation that were previously characteristic. Carrefour has built a leading position, especially since rebranding all its hypermarkets as Carrefour; indeed, it is relatively more powerful in Spain than in France. But the biggest in the straight grocery market is Mercadona. Based in Valencia, the company is led by Juan Roig, a strong personality not afraid of making bold decisions. Early success was based on an innovative format: 50 per cent own label and 50 per cent popular brands, a hybrid straddling discounters, hypermarkets and traditional supermarkets. In many ways, it looks closer to a discounter: it has a narrow product range (around 9,000 stock-keeping units), stocks only one brand and its own label in each category, and was ranked the cheapest supermarket in Spain by the Ministry of Industry, Tourism and Trade. In early 2009, in response to the worsening economy, Roig decided drastically to reduce the number of products stocked, especially brands. This was a controversial move: competitors Carrefour and Lidl reacted by stocking more of the brands dropped, and a price war started. Sales and profit results for Mercadona for 2009 were poor, with profit down by 16 per cent, and all the rest are suffering too. How this fascinating battle turns out will have to await an improvement in the economy.

The Netherlands and Belgium

Two of the smaller countries in Europe are home to some of the most successful food retailers. The Dutch company Ahold has recovered from its near-death experience and is now a well-established company, not only at home but almost uniquely in the United States. Although total sales of €28 billion in 2009 do not put it in the front rank, it has proved its strategic and operating competence, which is demonstrated by its 5 per cent operating margin and substantial return on capital employed of 13 per cent (*source:* AlphaValue). It operates in eight countries outside its home base. In its home market, the Albert Heijn brand, founded in 1887 and a pioneer of the supermarket format in the Netherlands, is highly regarded for innovation and quality. The US businesses, Stop and Shop and Giant, produce almost 60 per cent of group sales and over half of the profits. The group has maintained growth even during the general downturn, and may in future join the elite club of major European players.

Belgium is notable for Delhaize, which also has stores in the United States and five other countries including Indonesia. At home, its main fascia is Delhaize Le Lion, focusing on own-label products sold through neighbourhood stores. It is showing little sales momentum, and seems likely to remain a competent but minor competitor.

Another Belgian group, Colruyt, stands out from the crowd with best-in-class pricing, management and results. It operates hard-discount supermarkets, competing directly with Aldi and Lidl, but at *lower* prices; it is therefore also lower-priced than its other main competitors, Delhaize and Carrefour. Over the last 10 years, it achieved a staggering 9 per cent annual growth in sales. Its operating margin is 6.7 per cent, one of the highest in its class.

Summary: European strengths and weaknesses

Our main conclusions on the European market, and the strengths and weaknesses that exist, have not changed in any major way since 2001. First, we consider the strengths. There is a group of powerful competitors, with substantial operating experience, not only in home markets but in cross-border situations. Many are genuinely international in outlook as well as in business performance, and those that are not will either learn internationalism quickly or subside into less effective national units, ultimately falling victim to purchase by one of the international groups. Successful expansion worldwide by Carrefour, Metro, Aldi, Lidl, Auchan and others has created the prospect of a few major international trading groups. Size and international expansion can be supplemented by a widening array of formats, flexibility and efficiency. Most competitors have had to respond to national legislation controlling their growth prospects and even their prices, and to the usual stop–start European level of economic performance. They have lived through, at best, sluggish and difficult home markets, managing to create a range of retail formats, including strong discount operations, and to survive in a highly competitive world with, for most companies, most of the time, the thinnest of net margins. Continental European retailers could reasonably claim to have had an open and world-directed view of the market for many years. Other contenders for the world market – US, UK and Asian companies – have only discovered this more recently, if indeed they are yet persuaded the market will be global. The rewards for vision and for identifying and taking the risk to expand have been perceived, and there are now companies with strong track records.

There have been, and there certainly remain, significant weaknesses. First and foremost must rank the obsessive secrecy surrounding the strategies and results of many competitors, Ahold and Carrefour being exceptions, and the unfortunate climate persists. The family structures that have sheltered behind the facades of these major companies have controlled strategies in ways that are now surprising in the free democratic cultures where they trade. The question 'Who needs shareholders anyway, and what can they tell me about running my business?' has never been very far away in the continental European retail markets. The atmosphere of secrecy and behind-the-scenes family control raises the question of how well placed the main players and the industry are to face the best of professional free market competition. The cultural and leadership change required and the speed with which strategic and management adjustment must be made to face global competition are daunting. On the other hand, several companies can claim they are properly positioned to compete. Metro, providing it can overcome its present difficulties, should be a confident performer, with its cash-and-carry format. Carrefour has been the most assured international operator, though it is currently bogged down and under attack from dissident shareholders. Aldi, building on its secure home base, has shown the ability to export its model, not only in Europe but, most impressively, in the harshly competitive US market. Its compatriot Lidl has also expanded quickly, but so far only in Europe. Auchan, though perhaps underrated, is another strong contender.

A comparison of continental Europe with the UK

The comparison of the European market and the domestic market in the UK remains fascinating. As so often when comparing UK and European processes, it is unfathomable how these markets have developed in such different ways. The causes determining divergence, and the wide gulf now separating retail practice, make suggestions of future implications delicate. There may be three primary sources of difference that account for divergent developments over the past half-century. They are:

1 the nature of the industry and the companies that make it up;
2 factors concerned with government, and the communities where the developments have been located; and
3 consumers themselves, their experiences and their attitude to the role of food in their lives and specifically to food buying.

Nature of food retailing

First are the industries and the companies themselves. The importance of family-controlled concerns in Europe needs to be acknowledged, whereas in Britain only Sainsbury's experienced comparable dynastic influence and this is now exhausted. Enormous secrecy about European plans and performance is countered in Britain by constantly debated strategies, and records of performance catering to an investor community where little or no news is very bad news. Greater visibility for the innovations and the results of retailing development, and the impact of competition in the UK has not occurred elsewhere in Europe, where news is spasmodic and controlled, and financial performance rather than retailing strategies and competences are the focus of interest. Radically different investment policies have obtained in the two markets. Continental European retailers, from as early as the 1970s, began rapid expansion out of their home markets. In the UK only Sainsbury's atypical and isolated Connecticut venture was significant. US influence on the market in Britain – Sainsbury's and Safeway are both key examples – was greater than in mainland Europe, where indigenous models, particularly hypermarkets, grew up and extended from France and Germany south and east across the continent. In summary, two fundamentally divergent models now coexist, each successful in its own right but so far owing only a little to the other.

The impact of governments

Societal and governmental impact on development and performance in grocery retailing is next. No UK companies will concede they have had an easy reception from national or local planners, and since 1993 the UK's own version of environmental restrictions has begun to bite more seriously. But restraints have been imposed late in the day and at a stage where retailers have stakes irrevocably rooted in out-of-town locations. Locking the British stable door long after the horses have left is the classic European view of British public policies. Restrictive legislation and a concept of hostility to the big national self-service food company – and especially to its most gargantuan demonstration, the hypermarket – have been ongoing features of retailing's existence in mainland Europe, as they were, interestingly, for many years, under the aegis of the Robinson–Patman Act, in the United States. This has taken the form of tight limitation to the physical expansion of selling space, and constraints such as preventing predatory pricing in visible market sectors. Fighting the restrictions neither diverted the intent nor limited the efficacy of the planning processes put in hand.

The UK, described – ironically, many years ago, by a famous Frenchman – as a 'nation of shopkeepers', adopted the free market model, notably through the crucial decade of the 1980s when literally hundreds of out-of-town superstores began to dot the landscape and a new-style 100 per cent car-based shopping behaviour became dominant. The European model, at its zenith in France, but copied elsewhere, was a profoundly philosophical attempt to retain the essence of town and village high streets, and existing shopping configurations with their plethora of small specialist food suppliers. This offers immeasurably greater protection to a whole gamut of small shopkeepers.

Whether as a cause or a consequence, the UK legitimized car-based shopping earlier and to a greater degree than mainland Europe did, and apparently this was a difference deliberately created. A further important difference is that UK supermarket leaders have traditionally exercised more public policy-making influence than they have been able to do in Europe. The several successive Lords Sainsbury, Lord MacLaurin, Sir Alistair Grant and so on – their titles speak for themselves – are prestigious establishment figures with high levels of public awareness, whose public statements and opinions carry real weight. Grocery retailing has come of age and is formative in British life in a way that must now surprise French and German retailers. This has enabled a visible and soundly managed industry to play a part in setting for itself the free market conditions where it operated, to ensure acceptance of codes of behaviour and, equally important in some instances, the preservation of the status quo. In most of Europe, this was less possible.

Public interest was normally defined differently and by a different consultation process.

Consumer influences

Finally come the influence and predilections of consumers. Post-war reconstruction was a gentler, more evolutionary process in Britain, which had after all not been invaded. The country where the Albrechts started trading was a tougher environment than post-war Britain, and the same was initially true of France. If the market is viewed as a continuum with high quality and high cost at one extreme and low prices and standard quality at the other, it is now clear that the markets elected to behave differently. In Germany and France, low prices and the role of the discounter in supplying them in a simple, uncomplicated store environment have been more prominent features than they have ever become in the UK. The giant European hypermarkets were a natural extension of the discounter phenomenon. Their consumer appeal was derived from superior economics, that is to say a much bigger range and much lower prices were an indisputably winning formula. Consequently, affected by the headlong expansion of UK superstores in the 1980s and the capital investment requirements for new stores, trading margins in the UK have been markedly higher than in Europe – currently, they are on average three times higher than in France, for example. But UK consumers have been prepared to pay for the difference, and the quality of the shopping experience in the best UK superstores compares very favourably with that of the equivalent European hypermarket and is certainly superior to that of any discount store. This perhaps explains the failure of the hard discounters in the UK to date.

The final issue is the role of food, the importance of quality in food purchasing and its acceptance by consumers in their respective societies. That there has been an element of late renaissance in aspirations to and provision of British food quality nobody would contest, but at the same time few would claim that the UK consumer achieves a higher standard of food awareness or provision than in France certainly, Italy probably or even perhaps Germany. What has happened is that British retail multiples play a larger role in providing the market's response than their French or European equivalents. Retaining main street town and village shops with the high-quality small specialist food shops that still exist in French and many European towns and even small villages means that consumers can find and rely on quality and variety at a price, when and where they want it. In Britain, high streets are now usually the home of building societies, estate agents and restaurants, though the re-entry of Tesco and Sainsbury's may change the picture dramatically. It is now uniquely and specifically more often the supermarket's responsibility to provide the right balance of quality and variety, and at the right price, and usually the location will be out of town. So two very different social outcomes have been reached, and in each case, superficially at least, the two societies seem content that it should be so. It will be interesting to see what elements of convergence may in due course start to happen. In Britain particularly, where high street decline went to an extreme, the return of serious investment to the high street and a resurgence in the range and quality of local and speciality stores may be the start of a new trend. It is now the superstore operators, to some degree for defensive reasons, that are keen and ready to provide new choices themselves, thereby keeping their hands firmly on the food quality, range and price combinations that consumers are offered.

The outlook

The prospects for cross-border mergers or acquisitions seem dim, not only because of the temporary shortage of capital, but because each market is so competitive or constrained by legislation. The days when we could think that Ahold or Carrefour might be buyers of a British chain seem remote. Ahold has recovered from its near-collapse, but like Carrefour is certainly in no shape to contemplate such a venture. Wal-Mart remains a colossus that has the means to buy any of the European companies, but its German experience may have scarred it and scared it off. China looks a more tempting and worthwhile market for Wal-Mart. If it did fancy a purchase in Europe, Carrefour might be a tempting target, though the French government is notoriously protective of its companies. The picture is similar for all the European companies: why would they want to buy in western Europe? Eastern Europe and Asia present much more alluring prospects. The reaction of governments in Europe is unpredictable, but seems unlikely to be to welcome a foreign company unless they feel it would transform their home market. The near future, it seems, will be one of domestic consolidation and intercontinental expansion.

Contrasting Fortunes in the United States

08

T he market in the United States has been one of bewildering contrasts over the years since the Second World War. As you might expect of the land of the free, there have been periods of enormous innovation and high attendant success in which the United States has led the world in retailing practice. However, alongside these phases of free market development and business innovation, there have been periods of apparent quiescence when local and federal government policy and legislation have constrained free development, followed by periods of pronounced and deliberate deregulation, which have not always been to the benefit of the leading players in the industry.

One historical feature of the US market has remained influential: that of local and regional companies, many of them privately owned, adopting profiles that were the best for their discrete local area populations. This uniquely US pattern still obtains widely today and, as we will see, there are companies with strong local franchises, some with high national market share rankings, that are more significant than niche competitors and that have been trading profitably and successfully over many years in their local market. The most extreme example might be Stew Leonard's Norwalk dairy.

Box 8.1 The amazing Stew

Forty miles north of New York City lies Fairfield County, an affluent part of Connecticut where commuters live and board the Newhaven railroad to New York City from towns like Norwalk. Norwalk is much like any smartish Connecticut small town – except that it has since 1969 rejoiced in having Stew Leonard's very first store, 'the world's largest dairy'. Leonard's dairy is unusual in lots of ways. For a start, its astonishing curving pathway-like shopping aisles are invariably packed full of shoppers, usually with hordes of excited children in tow. Stew Leonard's has been recorded as having the greatest sales per unit area of any food store in the length and breadth of the United States, not a bad achievement for a little New England chain with just half a dozen stores. Jobs on the staff in Stew Leonard's stores are highly prized – not surprisingly, since Fortune rates him as having one of the best 100 workplaces in the United States. So far, so very normal. But Stew Leonard has some outlandish notions.

When he bought the land in Norwalk 40 years ago, the farmer who sold him the land insisted as a term of the contract that her existing farm animals were to survive for the length of their natural lives, and be protected, no matter what kind of enterprise took place on the site. Nothing daunted, Leonard, himself the son of a milkman who knew the trade, decided he was going to make his new store work perfectly well first and foremost as a dairy and then as a grocery supermarket. Thus was born the world's largest dairy, where animatronics rules – mechanized cows burst into song and colourful roosters sing uproariously. The original live animals have given way over the years to the more mechanized variety – which Leonard believes perform just as well. The wooden store is built like a barnyard, round which a wide and colourful set of rustic paths wind. Entertainment is the name of the game. It is difficult to characterize the sense of humour on display – 'breathtakingly infantile' was one such attempt. A *New York Times* reporter visiting concluded that 'Mr. Leonard's dairy has shattered forever the tedium of grocery shopping.' Seriously enquiring retail commentators noted the much reduced level of emotional stress that Leonard's unique environment engendered among the eagerly thronging Connecticut shoppers. Indeed it would be difficult for the tensest of suburban bargain hunters to remain serious while milk cartons dance, celery stalks sway and sing, hidden banjos sound forth from fruit displays, and round the corner is a small zoo where children enjoy the geese and goats. Staff play their fantasizing parts, willingly attiring themselves in farm animal 'uniforms', while robot dogs bark at their heels, and the proprietor sports an imposing cow suit and bellows out 'Good moooorning' in stentorian tones. Harmless fun perhaps, but this proprietor knows his onions as well as his dairy. Prominently displayed as you enter the store is a big, brief and highly visible two-line notice. Line one states: 'The Customer is always Right'. Line 2 goes on: 'If in doubt read rule 1'. Each week almost a quarter of a million customers push their oversized trolleys round Leonard's high-capacity aisles, running up unimaginably large grocery bills.

Box 8.1 continued

The fame of Connecticut's very own big butter and egg man soon spread far and wide, and a handful of similar stores followed Norwalk, opening in New York as well as the home state. Business guru Tom Peters unequivocally approved the dairy's level of shopping excellence. Senior Wal-Mart management were reported to have been seen snooping surreptitiously round the store – 'unlikely to scale easily', they might have decided. The US president handed Stew Leonard his very own personal award. But nemesis was soon to strike. It transpired that Leonard had for years been systematically using his own very special private computer program to skim inordinately large amounts of cash from the till rolls, and shipping the proceeds to his Caribbean bolthole. The cows no doubt mooed in displeasure. More importantly, the state of Connecticut took the proprietor to court, mounting its biggest ever criminal tax evasion case against Leonard, and the judge handed him down a 52-month jail sentence. Leonard engaged in a round of rapid and energetic plea bargaining, stood down from the dairy, and handed the stores over to his sons, Stew Junior and Tom, admitting 'I have made a big mistake... I'm very sorry and I'll take the consequences.' (One of the boys was to follow him into the same court some years later on similar charges.) So was this the end for the iconic New England dairy? 'No Sirree', they responded. 'We're packed out – our customers are very supportive!' Down at the diary it was business as usual, and it has remained so ever since. Yes, the customer *is* always right – if in doubt read rule 2!

On the other hand, it is a remarkable fact that there are several European invaders now present and in many cases trading successfully across the United States, whereas US companies, with the single and notable exception now of Wal-Mart, have penetrated foreign markets very rarely. It is only in the Canadian and recently Mexican markets that proximity and similar trading conditions have encouraged US retailers to open there. The traffic in the reverse direction on the other hand has been diverse and frequent. A dozen international, principally European companies have invested in the United States over the past 20 years. There have been some big winners: Aldi, Trader Joe's, Delhaize in part, Southland/7-Eleven, and Ahold for some years at least; the last named was awarded the title of US retailer of the year in 2000. Equally there have been some well-publicized failures: Sainsbury's, which was an early entrant in New England, Carrefour, which is a significant missing player, Auchan and, given A&P's continuing woes, Tengelmann. On the most recent major entrant in the western states, Tesco, it is too early to make an assessment. The fact remains that business success in the US food retailing scene has been more than an ongoing possibility for more than two decades, whereas, so far, few US companies look at all likely to venture outside their national boundaries – apart of course from Wal-Mart, numerically well capable on its own of compensating for a host of hitherto absent US competitors.

At home, domestic retailers' strategies have become more coherent, the drive for competitive advantage has created focus, and a wider range of retail formats has emerged. The supermarket remains individually the single largest outlet where people in the United States choose to shop, but there are now many more choices. Internet shopping has so far produced only limited impact in food shopping. The major failure of Webvan, the virtual disappearance of Peapod – acquired by Ahold – and the lack of major credible new entrants have meant that initial judgements on the penetration of the internet and home shopping in the United States have not always proved accurate. Gary Hamel, writing in the 1990s, felt that the internet's presence would now be ubiquitous; it is anything but. Wal-Mart is recognizing the vehicle as a powerful future driver of growth and has a big enough range of products, attractive enough pricing, and a universal enough presence to make it succeed if anyone can. But to date it is the lion that on the whole has failed to roar.

The arrival of the supercentre is quite another thing, however, and at one stage it looked as if it might be the single phenomenon that would dwarf and ultimately choke off all other trading formats – which has not happened. However, Wal-Mart alone now owns over 2,700 supercentres in the United States, with an average floor space area of 200,000 square feet in each. The largest, in Albany, New York is 260,000 square feet, and on a single 20-mile stretch of Arizona highway there are six Wal-Mart supercentres trading successfully. While there are statements suggesting some slowing of the Wal-Mart supercentre drive, there are no signs of it stopping yet, and the United States' ever-present desire to effect a one-stop shop is well catered for in this format.

Does this mean that the era of the small store is over? Not necessarily. Some of the more exciting developments are taking place in small stores. Trader Joe's in California is one stunningly well-managed example, which is considered below. Perhaps its presence there was one reason the new Tesco small store development (Fresh & Easy) chose to start close at hand. Certainly, we can assume the subsequent arrival of several Wal-Mart-owned Marketside small stores in Arizona was yet another attempt to confront the best world-class competition available.

Meanwhile close by is the unique, organic and fast-growing Whole Foods Market, another amazing growth story detailed below. Consumers of southern California and Arizona can rejoice in their good fortune. This is a battle of the titans where they have the ringside seats.

At the other end of the scale there are the warehouse clubs – principally three in number: Costco, Sam's (Wal-Mart) and the smaller BJ's. Costco appears to be the overall winner and has had some notable wins in its 27-year lifetime. It was the first company to grow from zero to over US$3 billion in six years, and today it ranks as the third biggest US retailer and the ninth worldwide. Sam's remains below Costco at number two in the market, and has recently been forced to close the business in Canada, where Costco's model was better implemented and strongly preferred. There were rumours in 2007 that Wal-Mart might be contemplating the sale or at least spin-off of Sam's, but this was denied by the company. Sam's is overall less profitable than Costco, and has recently responded by making significant cost reductions, in 2010 reducing the workforce by 10 per cent (11,200 employees) through outsourcing its on-site product sampling activities. The success of Costco in warehouse clubs is a significant marker. Although still sparsely present outside the North American continent, its worldwide retail ranking (nine) entitles it to recognition in a market where perhaps only the European Metro cash-and-carry model could claim greater international success.

Kroger

Second among major US companies, Kroger, founded in 1883, has hung on to the position of US food leader and is now operating as a successful player in the major US regions, with a performing supermarket model and a growing hypermarket presence. Following the takeover of Dillons in the 1980s, Kroger has been led by four separate Dillon family CEOs. Kroger's manufacturing is well established through 42 manufacturing plants, its brand range has the traditional tripartite subdivision (value, banner, private selection), and its overall claim 'More value for the way you live' has taken over from 'Right store, right price' as more appropriately geared to recessionary times. Meanwhile innovation (Kroger Personal Finance) has moved the company outside food, a partnership with the Disney company has sought to introduce a dose of magic into the store portfolio, and Kroger has been a buyer of

Dunnhumby's proprietary consumer loyalty measurements. If any large business has the capacity to take on Wal-Mart it must surely be Kroger.

Safeway

Safeway, which was Kroger's equivalent in earlier times, is now barely over half Kroger's size, and holds fourth position. Safeway's turnover is around $40 billion and, since returning to public ownership in 1990, it has begun to acquire companies once again – Randalls in Texas, Dominick's in Illinois, and a reacquisition of Vons in California. Safeway and its subsidiaries are marketing-driven companies and have a huge range of sub-brands in their store brand range. They have tried hard, under a range of overall slogans, to rebrand the business using a lifestyle format, and search for novel ways of branding the shopping experience. Safeway has tried a range of new formats, but most of these have failed. Unlike Wal-Mart, which unequivocally is driving to an EDLP philosophy, Safeway relies heavily on the effects of brand promotion. There are some modest recent signs of share improvement, but organically Safeway appears a much more diffuse company than any of its three larger competitors, while it faces several of the most competent growth retailers on its own doorstep.

Privately owned retail businesses

So much for Wal-Mart's big three competitors. There are several companies that are appreciably smaller but intrinsically better placed, and they have gained ground steadily but significantly over several decades. It is to their stimulating record we next turn, starting in the south with Florida's Publix. Publix is a highly effective, well-managed private company, now present in five south-eastern states. It is Florida's largest and the United States' tenth biggest private company, and overall is ranked seventh among US food retailers. Today, having recently purchased 49 Florida stores from Albertsons, thus eliminating this one big competitor from its core market, Publix is one of only five US companies owning more than 1,000 stores, a remarkable achievement for this employee-owned enterprise. Publix has genuinely attractive stores in the US sunbelt, 'where shopping' they claim 'is a pleasure'. Dating from its foundation in 1930 by entrepreneur George Jenkins, affectionately known as 'Mr George', Publix has been able to take on all comers. It keeps up with technology, has an advanced system of hand-held POS terminals in its stores and is understandably highly rated in its communities and by its workforce. Its ACSI consumer satisfaction rating is at the highest level; it is rated by Fortune for being one of the 100 best US places to work, and has been continuously for 10 years. This is a company with substantial sales revenues, growth and good profit levels, which has pursued consistent policies for many years. It looks certain to succeed for years to come.

Still in the south, HE Butt is also a high-performing US retailer. It has been successful for years, and its progress has been well maintained. Based in Texas, it is slightly smaller than Publix, but it shares some common attributes that account for its long-standing success. HE Butt is the largest private company in Texas (another privately held winner), 11th overall among US private companies, and was ranked 13th among US food retailers in 2006. However, its ranking is set to rise, with sales of $15.5 billion in 2008. HE Butt has been a powerful Texas competitor for more than a hundred years and has high, even dominant, market shares in many of the major population centres (eg San Antonio and Austin) despite the existence of highly qualified competitors including both Kroger and Wal-Mart. Family owned, and with a member of the Butt family in the leadership role from its inception until today, HE Butt is a highly rated local company. House-based store product development has been given a high priority, and the company has many owned manufacturing locations in its home state of Texas. Its new Central Market brand represents a move into the more affluent gourmet foods segment, while HE Butt Plus takes the company into non-foods, and Mi Tienda will cater for the sizeable Hispanic market. Meanwhile the company is opening stores south of the border in Mexico itself.

This is a company with a high level of environmental awareness, and one that enjoys its high level of community approval in part also because of its level of local charitable support. It is interesting to observe how such private companies as HE Butt, which cannot depend on the market for capital, can still cover and finance the wide range of activity required of today's modern food retailer, seeking to retain a market leadership position. Consistent policies designed to preserve and enhance long-term brand and business reputations have to be one explanation. These are founding families who are to be congratulated on their far-seeing approaches, exercised over many generations.

We track north-east now to Rochester, New York, the home of Wegmans, our third privately owned retail business. Originally known as the Rochester Fruit and Vegetable Company, it was founded in 1916 and is now led by the third and fourth generations of Wegman retailers. Though smaller than Publix or HE Butt, this is a significant performer in five north-eastern states, fringing New York itself, where it has 75 stores and a turnover of some $5 billion. It ranks number 29 among US food retailers. This company is highly policy-driven and consistently innovative. It has embraced the superstore concept effectively, and it is the local leader in a part of the country where much of the retail scene can look tired and run-down. The Wegmans store brand is a focus of attention and is highly rated. Wegmans seeks to offer 'food you feel good about', and it carries a first-class wine range. Tobacco on the other hand has since 2008 been eschewed as company policy. By any standards Wegmans is a customer service champion – it has a shelf-ful of awards recording this. Fortune has consistently recorded Wegmans among the top 100 US companies in which to work, and over the past eight consecutive years Wegmans has been placed in the top 10: in 2009 it ranked third overall. This is a clear case of a fine, long-established business getting better with time. Food Network described Wegmans as the best US grocery store in 2007, and US Consumer Reports called it 'the best large grocery store in the US'. Once again it seems likely that well-established processes and innovative attitudes should sustain continued growth; family members retain operating direction and management of the company, a sign of their ongoing commitment.

Aldi's low-price, limited-range offer, based on its German positioning, was already a success in the United States when Theo Albrecht, one of the two brothers who share the Aldi franchise, invested in a wholly different kind of store, named Trader Joe's, whose only obvious similarity with Aldi is its shared intention to keep prices low. Once again we are dealing with another privately owned company. Trader Joe's, founded by imaginative entrepreneur Joe Coulombe before Theo Albrecht's family trust took it over, has grown quickly and made a big impact. Over a 10-year period from 1990, it multiplied its store count by five and its profits by 10, while gaining huge plaudits for the quality of its service: Consumer Reports rate Trader Joe's second only to Wegmans overall. It has elected to operate in small, friendly but relatively plain neighbourhood stores, concentrating on a product range of gourmet foods, organic produce and offerings sourced with an eye to ethnicity from unusual places (black beluga lentils, Thai black pepper sauce, teriyaki tofu, feta-stuffed Norwegian salmon, etc) From its inception, Charles Shaw-branded wine featured strongly and at ruthlessly low prices. Environmental policies are pursued with commitment, and such negatives as artificial preservatives, colours, flavours and trans-fats are publicly avoided. Trader Joe's pays staff above-average wages and a bonus, and in addition offers health benefits. This is in every sense a modern, carefully profiled and go-ahead company, and its well-patronized stores are quite unlike others even in go-ahead southern California, and are a joy to browse through. Trader Joe's now has more than 300 stores, revenues of $7 billion, and at number 2 in the US retailer list is already making major inroads in the US market, primarily in southern California. The brand looks well placed to make further progress across the country, and Trader Joe's is already present at modest levels in 24 states.

A third company from the southern states, Whole Foods Market, was founded in Austin, Texas by college dropout John Mackey in 1980, and 30 years later he remains at the helm of this organic and natural foods company. Throughout this period Whole Foods Market has pursued a simple policy of acquiring often small natural or health foods companies across the United States and turning them into a spirited, distinctive and highly visible national business. Today Whole Foods Market has some 280 stores, principally in the United States, and it ranks 23rd in the US grocery list, with a turnover of $8 billion. Whole Foods Market has a unique profile, with a range that spans organic and conventionally grown products and brands, in which its owned brand list is both unusual and prominent and in some sectors entirely dominates the shelves. There is a big aspirational and social responsibility component in this company's make-up, stemming no doubt from the personal attitudes and ambitions of its brave and highly articulate founder. Mackey has been on record as claiming two key and personal goals: 1) to change the way the world eats; and 2) to create a workplace based on love and respect. Fortune rates Whole Foods Market as number five on its list of great companies to work for, while the Environmental Protection Agency places it third on the national Green Power Partners list. Despite its considerable chutzpah, however, the company's progress has certainly not been uniformly smooth. Extending its operations to the UK through its takeover of Fresh and Wild and its occupancy of the Barkers Kensington site in London (just before the UK plunged into recession) caused major losses, and the company swiftly cut back its UK presence as a result. Mackey's own uniquely challenging communication style has at times caused havoc and has even landed him in the US courts, where his revelations were alleged to infringe SEC rules, but he got off. He admitted engagingly to selling 'junk food'. Subsequently his ferocious and improbable opposition to the Democratic health plan caused a widespread consumer store boycott. Mackey does not travel quietly, and he gives shareholders and sometimes customers alike a rocky ride, but his resolution seems undimmed by reverses. His brand generates innate appeal from its Austin headquarters, through the west and into Manhattan, where Whole Foods Market's Bowery store is the largest on the island.

The liveliest period in Whole Foods Market's life has been its last five years, including its proposal early in 2007 to acquire Wild Oats, a parallel and sizeable organic and natural foods competitor. After terms had been agreed between the two companies, the deal was reviewed by the Federal Trade Commission and a decision made to block the merger. The Commission claimed that the parallel activities of the two companies in 'premium natural and organic supermarkets' would give rise to an ability of the new company to raise prices and simultaneously to reduce quality and service standards. Both companies challenged the decision and on review won their case, the rationale being that competition was not confined to companies like theirs but included, for example, major supermarket chains present in their markets. In the following year calmer waters were reached when John Mackey was cleared of the SEC indictment for illegal disclosures on his personal website; he has recently stood down from the chairman's position, although he remains on the board on a salary of $1 per annum. Whole Foods Market has legions of admirers, but vocal critics exist who suggest that latterly it has 'copped out' and become a commercially driven big-box retailer 'just like all the others'. In spite of an uneven profits record, Whole Foods Market's unique natural positioning is highly topical and, as recessionary factors become less important, the company's many positive features may have a great consumer influence and deliver rapid growth in the future.

There are two final points to be made from studying these different retailers – Publix, HE Butt, Wegmans, Trader Joe's and Whole Foods Market. First, they show once and for all from their collective and deep-rooted success that innovation remains alive and well across the length and breadth of the United States today. It takes many distinctive forms but is evidently very capable of producing enduringly strong brands with powerful and valued reputations. Second, one does not have to be big to grow and to win; it is remarkable how successful retailers that were the brainchild of entrepreneurs in the United States' past are still driven forward in 2010 with purpose and success by their descendants half a century or more later.

Wal-Mart

And so to Wal-Mart, retailer extraordinaire, about which company many words have been written. Can anything new be said? Maybe not, but the steady and relentless onward march to potential dominance of Wal-Mart, as a US and now increasingly worldwide phenomenon, continues. For its first 30 years its founder, Sam Walton, led the charge – and what a charge it was.

Under its third CEO since Sam Walton, his colossus marches on relentlessly. Would Sam have approved had he been here to see it? Of course he would. His successors have stuck to his mission, driving an identical strategy now across the developed world. But it is in the United States that Sam's business has made the most progress, and it was in the United States that Sam made his immense and lasting contribution. He wanted his company to be the country's number one 'grocer', and this, among many other achievements, it now is. In so doing, Sam Walton amassed a private fortune for himself and his heirs of astonishing proportions. At one time six of the United States' 10 richest people were Walton family members.

Yet Sam hated to display visible signs of his wealth. He was in so many ways a conundrum, possessing restless probing curiosity and a driving ego, but at the same time he was capable of utter humility. The stories of his unusual behaviour during his 30 years at Wal-Mart's helm are legendary. Sam started work early – very early – 5 or even 4 am was normal. He used to drive to business in a rattletrap old truck, often smelling of wet dog, a reminder of hunting expeditions. Neighbours complained about the noise his truck made while they slept. When he got to work, frugality remained the order of the day. He insisted his executives, whatever their seniority, share rooms when away from home on overnight trips, and made sure that his offices were careful not to throw anything away, even used pencil ends. Don't spend a penny that you don't have to was his approach. Sam never lost the common touch.

He thrived on the market and was frequently found sneaking unobserved into competing stores to get information on their practices.

But whatever his methods discount retailing quickly became Sam's forte. After learning his trade at JCPenney, Sam went into business in Arkansas's small rural towns, and his message was blindingly simple – 'We sell for less'. Later this developed into 'Low price always', and this has never changed over half a century since. Initially Sam couldn't persuade the big brand owners to supply him, but when he eventually succeeded the results were eye-popping – in the early days he sold Crest toothpaste at a knockdown price of 27 cents and it was said customers drove 100 miles to buy from him. Sam knew lowest price meant high volume, and he never looked back. As he opened more stores, he got better and better at winning customers. At one new store opening the crowds were so big that the local fire department made him open the doors for five minutes, and then they locked the crowds in until they were allowed to leave.

Sam liked to think of his staff as 'his family', and he formally termed them 'associates'. Cost was again a primary consideration. He paid as little as he could get away with, and for many years never hired college graduates as they were far too expensive. There was an employee stock ownership plan from the early days, but not too many took advantage of it. The company meetings and the ritual chant that began the day became a feature, and Sam was happy to encourage a culture where his staff had lots of freedom, as long as they delivered the results he wanted. Even when he was at the head of a big business he encouraged an informal, 'down home' ethos, and this involved not taking the boss too seriously. Once when he lost a bet on Wal-Mart's 1984 result he was found dancing down New York's Fifth Avenue with a hula hoop, wearing a grass skirt. 'Nobody's too important to lead a cheer or be the butt of a joke,' he said in *Sam Walton: Made in America, My Story*.

The Wal-Mart that Sam created became and has remained America's biggest company, and the results have left other retailers miles behind. With a return on capital that reached 30 per cent, and a level of compound growth over 20 years of 35 per cent, the figures speak for themselves. Wal-Mart's aggressive approach to growth does not appeal to everyone, but it has been the company's record as an innovator that has taken it so far ahead. Sam's three successors, David Glass, Lee Scott and Mike Duke, have stuck to their guns and maintained his impetus. Sam had ended his business career as the recipient of most of the honours the world's biggest free market can give its outstanding business heroes. On awarding him the Presidential Medal of Freedom, Ronald Reagan said that 'Sam embodies the entrepreneurial spirit and epitomizes the American dream.' US retailing is unlikely to see his like again.

By the time of his retirement Sam had lived long enough to see that he had built a potential colossus. By today's standards the 1988 figures look pathetically small – sales of $16 billion, which today's team have multiplied no less than 25 times, 1,200 stores in a single country (the United States) and 200,000 employees. This is not bad, you might say, for one man's business lifetime. Perhaps more significant was the arrival of the supercentre format for the first time in Washington, Missouri in 1988. Today Wal-Mart has 2,737 supercentres alone, and in total it owns 3,800 stores. Wal-Mart is certainly not averse to alternative formats and lists five separate types – discount stores, Neighborhood, Hispanic, Marketside and supercentres. There are indications that the level of emphasis may be shifting somewhat as the company seeks to gain increased levels of penetration in the big cities where, aside from other considerations, there will simply not be space available. But the growth of the supercentre in the United States is certainly not over yet by any means. Today Wal-Mart is credited with a share of grocery and consumables of somewhere over 20 per cent, and that level of market share leaves a great deal of opportunity still available. Meanwhile, it is in the supercentre that the Wal-Mart level of competitive advantage is the greatest, since it is here that leveraging scale leadership through major volume sales and the biggest cost efficiencies can translate into the lowest prices, which still today is known to be Wal-Mart's fundamental calling card, the area where it scores best.

Wal-Mart has decided in recent years to move away from the simple 'Low price always' slogan that had been adopted formally 17 years previously, which, in essence, had been the universally recognized claim for the business from the earliest days in Arkansas when Sam Walton first started out. Today's claim is to 'Save people money so they can lead better lives', and this indicates some developments in the company's strategic thinking. For all its almost 50 years of life Wal-Mart has been quite brilliant at trading down. Its combination of a ruthless determination to offer its customers the lowest prices – always – was matched by equal resolution in using its uniquely powerful sourcing processes to deliver costs that nobody else could match. It was a simple but enduringly powerful strategy and, in a world where price remains a critical customer requirement, Wal-Mart knew this and knew that it could deliver it better, more widely and for longer than any of its competitors. So, if it is working, why the change now? The simple answer is because the company wants to grow faster and to grow more, and to do this it needs to be able to widen its consumer appeal. This means trading up and perhaps trading out, as well as trading down. Lowest prices always are not about to disappear, but they are destined to have some alternative and additional 'fellow travellers' on the forward journey. The present Wal-Mart customer base of around 200 million is skewed to lower-income-earning groups, and also to conservative and therefore predominantly Republican-voting Americans. One-fifth do not have a bank account. The new Wal-Mart target reflects a different and much more specific six-segment grouping, as follows:

- African-Americans;
- affluent shoppers;
- empty-nesters;
- Hispanics;
- suburbanites;
- rural dwellers.

This is a significant and highly ambitious change of gear, and it will be interesting to see how successfully Wal-Mart can implement it. For the first time in 50 years Sam Walton's simple and unadorned strategy looks as if it has been at least modified.

Perhaps, after so many years of resounding and continuous success, now is the right time to start changing, on the principle 'Quit while you're ahead.' For ahead it most surely is, whatever criteria you adopt. Revenues in 2009 for the first time exceeded $400 billion, and they have more than doubled in the past decade. Eight years ago, for the first time the company became the world's largest in any category, and for every year since, apart from 2006, it has remained so, with the gap between pursuers and the leader steadily widening through time. Looking at the absolute figures among retailers, that is direct competitors, and especially predominantly food retailers, there is simply no meaningful competition. Wal-Mart is five times the size of its US nearest follower, Kroger, and is growing faster. In worldwide terms the company is four times larger than the second company (Carrefour) and again is showing much faster growth. Wal-Mart is in fact about twice the size of the four biggest worldwide retailers – Carrefour, Metro, Tesco and Kroger. By any measures this is dominance on an unarguable basis, and it is a lot more pronounced than it was 10 years ago. Identical relationships and a similar picture obtain when one looks at operating profits, albeit some of the ratios may be a little lower – but essentially profitability reflects Wal-Mart's immense scale advantage. Perhaps this is even a level of international advantage that should begin to trouble legislators on a worldwide basis. While Wal-Mart's share of the market is appreciably lower than say, Microsoft's, its relative lead over its direct competition is bigger and is widening.

Wal-Mart's future could indeed be brighter even than its illustrious past. It seems to expect to be the low-price marker with a big share in the biggest world markets, notably the United States. US consumers increased their visits to Wal-Mart as times became hard, and the company saw discretionary spending in 2009 rise as a result and was able to raise its market share. Thus among its traditional customer base, with incomes of around $30,000 per annum, there were increased volumes; from more affluent groups, increased penetration of Wal-Mart's discount stores also produced a net volume increase. You win on the swings and you win on the roundabouts. Despite 'consumer confidence being low', according to management, Wal-Mart's price cuts rammed the best price message home: bargains such as Sharp TVs, reduced to $698 from $1,158 did the trick. In 2009, Wal-Mart revenues rose by an impressive 7.2 per cent.

But there is more, much more, to go for, and again the company's confident message tells the story. Outlining the moves to develop the new 'high-efficiency supercentre', Castro Wright, head of the US stores division, observed that 'the amount of potential which Wal-Mart has in its 15 leading US region markets is greater than the value of the entire retail markets of Russia and India put together'. He is right. Just taking four big northern and eastern metro cities – New York, Chicago, Boston and Philadelphia – Wal-Mart has virtually virgin territory in which to gain a presence. Can it do so? It seems that the company's political as well as its consumer acceptability is now greater than it has been and that its message as the low-cost, low-price vendor is now a lot more acceptable even in middle-class urban areas than it was in the past. The answer is probably yes. In any case, even if reactions were less than encouraging, the company has become adept over the years in persuading less-than-enthusiastic communities to take on its store offer. To add to the opportunity, there is online selling, a field where Wal-Mart is now investing heavily and where it has some unique high-volume tools available, specifically ways of persuading suppliers to help develop the Wal-Mart online offer on a basis where both can win. Certainly Wal-Mart knows what it will need to do to succeed online, and its strategies are becoming clear. Recently in a little foray into bookselling, Wal-Mart was able to make the mighty Amazon blink first where price comparisons were the issue. Even without banking, which it appears will not be tackled, Wal-Mart has major US growth capability ahead for at least a decade.

International performance needs to be considered as part of future opportunity, and already a quarter of the company's revenues derive from outside the United States. While the past record was distinctly patchy, with failure in Germany, South Korea and perhaps Japan, there are now more successes than there were. The UK is covered in Chapter 2, and Mexico, Canada and Brazil are major market winners for Wal-Mart. Meanwhile the company is pressing ahead hard in China, having made labour relations concessions, and has opened a potentially rewarding partnership with Bharti in India, taking its presence there as far as restrictive Indian regulations permit. More important still are the impressions one gets about the new more mature approach to foreign expansion. Some things have not changed. Wal-Mart focuses exclusively on big markets, now adding exploration of Russia and an acquisition in Chile to the list above. It is willing to spend heavily and to buy big – when it can. In one fiscal year, 2009–10, $5.3 billion was earmarked for foreign expansion. But a change can be seen in the overall approach to market entry. Alternative local brand names can be adopted. Local shopping and eating habits are now studied and acted upon (in China and Brazil for instance). An article by Michael Bustillo in the *Wall Street Journal* in August 2009 confirmed this: 'After early errors, Wal-Mart thinks locally to act globally'. There's little doubt Wal-Mart's learning process has made an important U-turn. Here is Anthony Hucker outlining current policy in Brazil: 'What we've learned in recent years is that one size does not fit all.' This is worlds away from the hot dogs and golf balls 'ugly American' entry into Germany 10 years back. The new approach may to a degree inhibit the extreme elements of worldwide cost and scale advantage that the company can exploit, but it does have a lot of room for manoeuvre. In any case, as Anil K Gupta, business professor from the University of Maryland, points out, 'Any company's ability to leverage being a $400 billion company has its limits.'

Indeed this may be the case, and Wal-Mart's adjustment of some of its international policies reflects a clear and entirely rational intention deliberately to vary the nature of its approach to satisfy particular market needs. China, Brazil and no doubt India will all be prime examples of this new element of flexibility, and the company is increasingly sure it will pay off. Meanwhile, however, there remain the areas of substantial cost-effectiveness advantage that Wal-Mart enjoys against all comers, purely as a result of having built such enormous scale advantage first in the domestic United States but over the past decade internationally as well. Sourcing naturally is one such area where Wal-Mart, as we have seen, is taking steps to ensure it builds on today's experience and drives its advantage home further. Logistics has become a known and expected area of expertise, which again it can claim to enjoy against all comers. Finally, Wal-Mart has built experience of running effective supplier and sourcing information systems around the world, often using its presence in China as the base for advantage. We have noted the big wins with the consumer that Tesco was able to extract once it learnt how to interrogate Dunnhumby as a vehicle. Wal-Mart's approach may be simpler and more aggregated, but it is outward-looking and embraces supplier activity. As its major suppliers know, it is now well able to marshal its worldwide experience across markets. Only a handful of its suppliers have the requisite expertise in their own information processes to do anything other than respond to the strategies and ideas that Wal-Mart can then bring to joint forward plans with supplier organizations.

Sustainability and corporate social responsibility

Endless academic argument has tried to assess whether the economic impact of Wal-Mart is positive or not, and it is difficult to say which side of the debate has emerged more persuasively. What is clear is that Wal-Mart has put specific effort into ensuring it is a 'good citizen', not just in the United States but in its markets round the world, of which the UK is a fine example. The company, under its fourth CEO since Sam Walton, has recognized that consumer, community and government perceptions of its approach will make a substantial difference to its ease of operating, and considerable efforts to improve its sometimes uncompromising and brutal reputation have paid off handsomely. Wal-Mart was a major logistics provider in the aftermath of Hurricane Katrina and gained considerable kudos from its intervention. Its stance on global warming and on the need for significant green initiatives has been positively received, and appears to be one that is now being sustained into the longer term. In 2009, Wal-Mart announced it was putting in place the Worldwide Sustainable Product Index as a regime to assess and control its global sourcing activities. The questions raised about Wal-Mart's ultimately beneficial or damaging consequences for communities as a whole will continue, with legitimacy, to be asked. So they should, with an enterprise as widely spread, far-reaching and successful as this company is. The company now appears to understand that it needs, alongside its evident desire to bring low-cost, low-price goods to market, to provide the rationale for the ways in which it pursues business growth, and to satisfy an adequate proportion of its audience that its activities are both reasonable and ethical. This brings us therefore to one final critical area of policy and performance, worker remuneration, where once again much has been written about the company's unique policies in relation to its 1.6 million workers, and the burden of the debate has not usually been on Wal-Mart's side.

One of the more balanced critics has been Nelson Lichtenstein, who argued that Wal-Mart created its own corporate subculture in the (white, rural and poor) Ozarks region, where it has its Bentonville headquarters. Sam Walton felt he had a 'family' in his workforce. Lichtenstein says he 'created a self-contained culture, an ideology of family, faith and folk communalism that exists in strange harmony with a Dickensian world of low wages, job insecurity and pervasive corporate surveillance', a culture where the female workforce was 'cheap and grateful'. Apart from chronically low pay (31 per cent lower than that of comparable large retailers), the workforce suffers chaotic day and night shift schedules, and is indeed regularly encouraged by management to claim relief from 'public safety net' programmes. Low pay and poor conditions in turn produce massive staff turnover, the cost benefit from which drops straight through to profit, creating surprising but recognizable competitive cost advantage. This explains the dedicated and hitherto entirely successful resistance of the company to union recognition.

Lichtenstein is a historian and sees a contextual change ahead. He believes that the Reagan, Clinton and Bush years, with unions in retreat, lax enforcement of labour laws and stagnating wages, leading most Americans to seek cheap consumer goods, have been Wal-Mart's glory years, but he suggests that era is now ending and that Wal-Mart's day of reckoning is here and now. Democrats led by Obama will raise minimum wages, encourage unions and enforce rules on hours and wages more rigorously, none of which Wal-Mart will welcome. Whether

Lichtenstein's forecast proves accurate we will see, but a year into the new world the initial portents, on health reform for instance, portray a much less violent degree of change and less radical reform. So Wal-Mart may continue to sleep easy – and, as it points out, it has no difficulty in recruiting new occupants for the jobs, at all levels in the company, as they become available.

On the other hand, Jay Nordlinger, writing on 'The new colossus' in *National Review* (19 April 2004), dismisses the criticism of Wal-Mart's personnel practices as largely nonsense, describing it as little more than envy of 'a great American business success story'.

As the United States confronts the worst recession in its history, we can offer a conclusion on the health and strength of the US retail market. The verdict must be a balanced one. Perhaps it is right to deal with the 'glass half-empty' appraisal first. European companies have hitherto been better worldwide performers than their US counterparts, which for the most part have just stayed at home. Even Wal-Mart, which can be counted as a likely future global winner, has had a patchy worldwide record vis-à-vis the best world-class competition – probably now Tesco. Foreign businesses have done a lot better entering the US retail preserves than vice versa, and there are perhaps a dozen worthwhile examples that have set up shop and are doing nicely. European retailers have done better in developing, promoting and gaining good market shares for their stores' own brands than have US retailers. The core US format, the mainstream conventional supermarket, has had weak strategic leadership, has been indifferently managed and delivers an undistinguished all-round shopping experience, certainly where distinctive and high-quality food provision is concerned. But there are some great positive features of the US scene, and the world will do well to consider them carefully as new countries develop their own retail models in years ahead.

First, the United States has, after some early uncertainties, maintained a free market model. Planning is largely left in the hands of the customer rather than the bureaucrat. Second, in Wal-Mart the United States has developed in less than 50 years a genuine industrial colossus, which four generations of leader have driven to extraordinary domestic and now global strength – and the game is not yet over. Can it be caught? Probably not in our lifetimes or those of most of our readers. Third, the US industry has shown ingenuity and persistence in the development of new and appropriate formats, and in this regard the astonishing, omnipresent and consumer-endorsed supercentre must be accorded pride of place.

Yes, the United States has available space, but someone had to work out in the first place what to put there and to ensure it survived. Fourth, there are now signs that the Wal-Mart-led global sourcing model carries enough economic advantage for it to survive and grow for years ahead, not just creating advantage for its owner, but raising cost-effectiveness standards for the entire US and probably global industry (and it generates many new jobs in poor countries). Fifth, the United States has put together a highly successful club store offer, which has not only worked very well in that country but is able to make an impact outside – the Costco company is a high-performance operation, as its ranking versus Sam's Club confirms. Finally, innovation is alive and well, and its home in the consumer goods and food retail markets remains firmly located on the western side of the Atlantic. The United States is still home to many great consumer brands and companies, and as we have demonstrated earlier there are several US-grown retail models, several of them private, that are run with imagination and successful long-term commitment.

The Internet and Other New Ways of Shopping

09

It is a brave person who would venture firm forecasts of how the applications and uses of technology will develop over the coming decades. We have lived through the dotcom boom and bust and, indeed, through some bold predictions. Gary Hamel, one of the leading business strategy gurus of the time, was one of those predicting a 'convulsive development' in retailing in the 1990s. He argued that easy cost comparisons – 'frictionless capitalism', as Bill Gates calls it – made possible by the internet would drive down retail prices. 'Money comes from knowing people won't comparison shop,' said Hamel. 'People make enormous amounts of money out of friction' (*Financial Times*, 11 September 1998). He foresaw the existing supermarkets ending as dark hulks around our cities, and he predicted that the firms that took over would not be those currently dominating the market, as had happened before. He was wrong on all counts – at least so far.

We now live in an internet age, when the majority of households have access to the web, and online shopping is familiar and well established in most advanced countries; in the UK, 63 per cent of households had broadband access in 2009.

Why should new ways of shopping be needed?

We know that new technology – or rather the entrepreneurs involved in and surrounding it – looks for problems to solve. In the end, it is the market that decides, when consumers are convinced that the new product offers them real benefits, in a form they like and at a price they are ready to pay. What forces suggest that there is a need for new ways of food shopping?

We know that some social groups already have serious problems with food shopping, especially those in some deprived areas, the old, those without cars, and those living in the wrong place: it is a problem of access. Most of us, from experience and anecdote, would agree that there are other problems: time, traffic, parking, queuing, wobbly wheels on shopping trolleys, screaming children (other people's or our own) and so on. The retailers are tackling many of these, but there are residual issues around the fact that much supermarket shopping is repetitive and unrewarding. As people's lives become more crowded, alternatives that will save time or effort may be attractive.

What do we mean by 'new ways of shopping'?

Discussion of home shopping often focuses on the internet to the exclusion of other modes. In fact, there are many ways in which the traditional shopping model – customers go to shops to buy what they want – could be adapted. Some of these are long-standing, such as mail order and catalogue retailing. Internet shopping is, in some ways, just a technologically advanced method of mail order.

The basic variables of the shopping process are six:

- product and service range;
- pricing;
- fulfilment;
- service provider;
- interface between customer and service provider;
- point of order.

From these flow almost 40 possible solutions.

Some of these are simple and are available now. A shopping list, produced from loyalty card data, can be produced by swiping the card when the shopper enters the store; store staff could pick the routine, packaged items while the customer spends time on the more enjoyable tasks of choosing fresh produce and wine, or has a snack, or indeed goes somewhere else (if there is anywhere else to go within reach). Other experiments use telephone, fax or internet ordering, while some offer home delivery.

In fact, we should separate the two main aspects – order capture and physical delivery – as they are quite distinct and can be tackled separately.

What do consumers want?

'The issue is not remote shopping but how to service customers,' said one retail executive. We cannot generalize about customers as if they were all the same. We know that they are very different, with different needs, preferences and resources.

We know that there is a segment that welcomes internet shopping. Originally, they were mostly young, 'time-poor, cash-rich', computer-literate, with fast access to the web at work or at home, and willing to pay for a service that gave them value. The ability to order from their desk appealed to them, as it saved time and avoided the unpleasant aspects of shopping (crowds, queues, traffic). They are confident in their ability to choose the right products, and not particularly interested in browsing (around supermarket shelves, that is). Internet shopping has now spread well beyond this group to embrace more and more of the general population, although it is still age related. The peak age group seems to be 35–44, as younger people use the internet most, but not for shopping. Usage among older groups is increasing (the 'silver surfer' phenomenon), but the poorest sectors of the population are still least likely to be internet shoppers. Interestingly, between 2006 and 2008, the proportion of the population saying they did not want internet access at home rose, from 3 per cent to 24 per cent (Office of National Statistics).

It seems certain that many people currently do not want to shop for food online but there will be alternatives. It may be that mobile access through smartphones will become a significant way of shopping. Pervasive computing, digital TV, voice recognition and other technologies will make the whole process much more user-friendly. This may draw in a new segment of people who basically do not like shopping: providing the technology is available to them, in an accessible form, they may be interested.

What we cannot know is how big these 'non-shopping shopper' segments will be. We may speculate about what exactly retailers can offer them out of the total shopping experience and what they cannot. We know that offering shopping lists, reminders, linked purchases and tailored promotions is straightforward. Although the first trial by a new remote shopper may take quite a long time (perhaps even longer than a real shopping trip), after that the process should take no more than five or 10 minutes. How to simulate browsing, however, is more of a problem. Most shoppers go into the store without a shopping list, so impulse purchases make up a significant proportion of the final basket. The products we buy through browsing – fresh produce, unusual or luxury items, chocolates, prepared meals, wines – are not only the more enjoyable purchases for us, but they are likely to be among the higher-margin products for the retailer. So-called virtual reality cannot reproduce the shopping experience for such goods at present, although sophisticated data analysis can prompt purchases that fit in with customers' other choices. Estimates of the size of the segments that will take up remote food shopping vary widely, from 5 per cent to 20 or even 40 per cent. Even at 5 per cent, of course, that is still a large amount of purchasing power, so every retailer will want to make sure that it is not losing sales to a rival. In 2010, almost 60 per cent of consumers use the internet for shopping, but online purchases account for only 7 per cent of total UK sales – most people shop infrequently and spend little. For the grocery market, 13 per cent shopped online in 2009, according to the Institute for Grocery Distribution (IGD) but, of those, 30 per cent shopped less than once a month, so the online segment amounts to only 2.5 per cent of the total. The IGD expects the market to double by 2014.

Beyond true remote shopping, the rest of the population will still have needs that existing systems do not meet. Some may respond to self-scanning, others to a personalized printed shopping list, others to a screen on the shopping trolley, some to the ability to collect an order previously phoned in, others to home delivery of goods personally selected in the store, and so on. Experience of other new technologies suggests that many of us do not know in advance exactly what we do want; when the reality is presented to us, we see how we like it. Most electronic cash experiments, for example (using smart cards that can be loaded with cash value and used for a variety of small purchases), have failed – but no one could have predicted that without trying it.

What are retailers offering?

Remote ordering and home delivery are, of course, well established: mail order has been around for decades, and newer forms of direct marketing such as TV shopping channels are also successful. Internet commerce, though the majority is now business-to-business, has also made inroads into consumer markets such as computer hardware and software, CDs and books. When we look specifically at grocery shopping, the field is much less developed.

We should perhaps separate out home delivery as such, since in its basic form it has always existed and still does in some parts of the market. In the United States, many smaller chains offer home delivery as part of their service, and it can be a useful competitive weapon (though the costs must help to keep margins very low). Generally, home delivery of groceries disappeared in the UK along with counter service, and is only now reappearing in combination with new ways of ordering.

First, we can distinguish between what the grocers themselves are doing and what new rivals offer.

The lead in Britain was taken by Tesco: in May 1984 Jane Snowball became the first online home shopper for groceries when she ordered from her local Tesco via a ground-breaking initiative from the local council that allowed residents to order shopping using their television remote control. This was a one-off, but Tesco started online shopping on a small scale in 1994, had developed a more robust service by 1996, and began offering a full online-ordering home-delivery service in 2000. The approach the company took was what we would characterize as typically Tesco: carefully planned, pragmatic, starting from a low base, expanding only when it was satisfied that the thing worked, and then driving growth aggressively. It chose to pick orders from existing stores rather than setting up dedicated warehouses, despite the opinion of some experts who thought this the wrong way to go. The early efforts were fairly low-tech and beset with teething problems, but Tesco persevered. Gradually, it developed its operations. It worked constantly to improve quality and lower costs. As an example, it introduced six trays per trolley to increase picking efficiency. The trays were originally numbered, but the company found that this led to errors, so now it uses coloured symbols. It also, of course, uses technology: the orders are sorted by algorithm to mimic the route round the store and to fit into a van for a specific delivery route; this information is displayed on a screen attached to the picking trolley. As Laura Wade-Gery, CEO of Tesco.com, says:

Simple principles drive our operating model and process design:

- Jobs must be interesting and simple to do.
- Technology must reinforce the process.
- We work with the flow of human nature.

As the service was extended (to cover some 99 per cent of households), sales rose, from under £500 million in 2001–02 to £1.9 billion in 2008–09. This represents 5.5 per cent of Tesco's total sales excluding petrol, more than double the figure for other national supermarket chains with online operations).

The service now offers non-food shopping as well as grocery shopping, and it added a printed catalogue in 2004 covering non-food items only. It is an ironic return to what some see as an old-fashioned model but, if a sizeable group of customers wants to shop that way, Tesco is happy to oblige. In 259 stores, there are Direct desks at which customers can both order and collect items from the non-food range. Grocery is still by far the biggest area, at £1.5 billion in 2008–09, but much of the future growth potential is clearly elsewhere. In addition to products, Tesco adds services such as an online diet programme, which it says achieves high levels of customer satisfaction and loyalty.

An obvious objection to adding an online service is that it will cannibalize store sales. What Tesco has found is that over two-thirds of online sales are incremental. Thirty per cent of online customers are new to Tesco, and existing customers initially spend less in store, but within a year their in-store spending is back up to its previous level.

Moreover, Tesco claims that the operation is profitable. Tesco.com pays all of the additional costs caused by its in-store picking, including the wages of its own employees and additional costs arising from increased volumes. Its capital expenditure has been relatively low, mainly IT, software development, some in-store adaptations and vans, so return on capital employed is fairly high – 28 per cent in 2008–09.

Capital expenditure will increase as the company runs out of store capacity and has to build warehouses. This had already happened in south London by 2007; there are two warehouses (or dotcom-only stores, in Tesco-speak), in Croydon and Aylesford; another will open in Greenford in 2011. The company expects to build one a year for the next few years, so that perhaps 15 per cent of turnover will pass through this format by 2014. The warehouses will increase capital expenditure and fixed costs, but reduce variable costs through more efficient picking.

Internationally, Tesco has introduced the service in South Korea (the country with the most widespread broadband coverage of homes) and Ireland. It will continue to expand to countries that it judges ready, that is, with enough broadband penetration and a positive attitude to buying food online.

Tesco is now the leading online grocery retailer in the world, a distinctly unusual position for a British company. It has problems with quality, scoring unimpressively in consumer surveys; the company says that it is working steadily on putting these right. Even so, given its lead, it will be difficult to catch. The numbers two and three in the UK market, Asda and Sainsbury's, have followed and, as they are playing catch-up, their headline sales increases are impressive, though total sales are still far behind those of the leader. Sainsbury's started selling wine online in 1995 and food in 1998. Asda started in 1998, initially by opening a warehouse in Croydon, south London, but this soon closed, and the company reverted to a store picking model. It revamped the service in 2004, and in 2007 embarked on a major expansion. Sainsbury's is currently selling £500 million online and Asda over £300 million, despite its geographic coverage now approaching that of Tesco. An estimate of current market shares, based on company accounts, is:

Tesco	51%
Sainsbury's	17%
Asda	14%
Ocado	18%
(including Waitrose)	

(**Source:** Ocado)

Ocado

Ocado is the potentially disruptive newcomer, an online-only grocery retailer allied to Waitrose. Founded in 2000 by bright young men from the City, Tim Steiner, Jonathan Faiman and Jason Gissing, this was the first online-only grocery business since the dotcom bust, which saw such spectacular disasters as Webvan.

Box 9.1 The Ocado boys

'I think we just wanted a proper business and some control' was Tim Steiner's explanation as to why three 30-ish Goldman Sachs brokers decided on what many thought a crazy idea – to set up an online-only grocery business in opposition to the big boss, Tesco, not to speak of Asda and Sainsbury's. The last people to try anything like this, at Webvan in the United States, had crashed in flames after losing billions of dollars. Steiner, Faiman and Gissing started Ocado in 2000, and have run it since with increasing sales but no profits.

The three had absolutely no experience of the supermarket business, but they were young and confident enough to think that didn't matter. They thought it would be easy and, though they know better now, they are still remarkably positive. As Steiner said, 'We just thought if we hired the best IT, integration and logistics firms we could quickly put this together.' All three come from well-off north London backgrounds: Steiner's great-grandfather set up Steiner Leisure, which has gone from a hairdressing chain to one of the biggest operators of cruise liners in the world; Faiman's father ran dress shops in north London, while his mother ran furniture shops; Gissing's parents ran an import–export business to and from the Far East. As Faiman admits, 'we were arrogant and naive', but they had that priceless attribute, confidence, though confidence alone would not have got them far without their City contacts and plausible presentation.

Talk of an imminent flotation (which has been imminent for at least two years) makes them only a little more cautious. Asked if they want the money to set up another warehouse in the north, an obvious next step, Gissing starts, 'Actually, the reason we appointed Goldmans was I got fed up with individuals and institutions phoning up and telling us what we should be doing…', and Steiner interrupts diplomatically, 'We found it difficult to manage the expectations of some very major supporters…' It's not like a conversation that you would have with a typical supermarket executive.

As the most unusual and, to some, most exciting development in the otherwise staid world of food retailing, Ocado is the subject of close scrutiny by many in the business, especially, claim the boys, Terry Leahy at Tesco. Tesco has made no obvious moves against the upstart, though Ocado has challenged it by matching prices on a range of products. Indeed, it seems it is the Ocado team who are more than slightly obsessed with Tesco.

The three have a clear vision of how they can expand their model to other product fields, and to other countries; their outward confidence, at least, is undented, and they can see a very bright future ahead.

(Adapted from Andrew Davidson, 'The MT interview: The Ocado boys', *managementtoday.com*, 1 June 2008)

Despite not having made a bottom-line profit, Ocado has attracted investors such as the John Lewis Partnership, Swiss bank UBS and Tetra Pak billionaire Jorn Rausing. Procter & Gamble paid £5 million for a 1 per cent stake in 2008. The firm has invested £300 million since the beginning, mainly in its high-tech warehouse and in developing its own software.

Ocado's approach from the beginning has been determinedly different. Although it started in a manual warehouse in Hemel Hempstead in 2002, it opened a semi-automated warehouse in Hatfield to run alongside it until the Hemel Hempstead building was closed in 2003. The Hatfield operation was converted to an automated system over the next two years. The Hatfield hub operates through seven spokes (cross-docking warehouses) opened successively around the country. Products are shipped from Hatfield to the spokes by HGV and then delivered by local vans, thus covering 66 per cent of households by 2010.

At first sight, this appears unlikely to compete with the highly developed logistics systems of the likes of Tesco. Ocado claims that its proprietary route management software is streets ahead of any competitors. It recruited super-bright mathematicians to produce algorithms that reduce drive times (and hence carbon emissions); they have also designed the company's management systems, giving complete visibility of items from order to delivery. Vans are equipped with technology giving satnav, order details, the ability to change orders at any moment up to customer sign-off, and communications allowing routes and orders to be changed.

The company claims that its model gives it a cost advantage over store-based competitors of 11–12 per cent through a shorter distribution chain, much lower wastage, more efficient picking and higher stockturn. It can stock a very wide product range of about 21,000 grocery stock-keeping units, with an average holding of only eight days' stock.

The tie-up with Waitrose has continued, being renewed in 2008 for five years and for ten in 2010. This provides products of a quality known and appreciated by consumers willing to pay the prices. Ocado has also introduced its own products, such as the Ocado Everyday lower-priced range, has matched Tesco on all identical branded products, and has introduced internet-only prices on Waitrose own-label goods. This suggests that it is conscious of the upmarket image of Waitrose, and wants to compete more directly with the supermarket leaders. There is no doubt that the Waitrose reputation for customer satisfaction has transferred to the online operator, and been enhanced by Ocado's picking and delivery prowess. Its website has won awards, and in consumer surveys such as those published by *Which?* (the magazine of the Consumers' Association) has consistently been rated best online service. It scored five out of five for the order-placing experience, accuracy of order delivered and driver's service.

Already profitable at the level of earnings before interest, tax, depreciation and amortization (EBITDA), the company has ambitious plans for the future. The Hatfield warehouse can cope with £1.3 billion of sales, and the company believes it has plenty of room to grow even within the existing market, through extending its geographic coverage. Further, it can introduce non-food ranges, exploit its technology and network, and expand in Europe (perhaps through joint ventures with a local retailer). More importantly, it is a firm believer in the rapid growth of online shopping. It clearly believes that a significant change in society is under way, equivalent to previous dramatic transformations. In such a remade society, a penetration by online grocery shopping of 20 or even 40 per cent is perfectly believable. If the company is right, the business has a very bright future indeed. Even if this is too high, Ocado has a good business model and would do well at a level of 5 to 10 per cent. After persistent rumours, the company finally announced its flotation and the IPO launched in July 2010. In a market where several firms had pulled flotations, this was a success, but at a price: Ocado had set an unexpected range of 200–275p per share, but was forced to drop to 180. The shares have since moved between 130 and 155, reflecting widespread doubts about profitability. The owners remain upbeat and optimistic.

What could go wrong? The relationship with Waitrose is crucial, and Waitrose has started to develop its own online operation. The John Lewis holding has been put into its pension fund: does this imply that it is starting to distance itself? Will the contract be renewed in 2020? Ocado says that it is perfectly happy with Waitrose, and they can all fish profitably in the same large pool. Will Tesco set its sights on Ocado and attack it with low prices? Ocado has obviously thought about this, and thinks that such a move would damage Tesco's own business most. The situation will arise only if Tesco believes that the upstart is a genuine threat to its business. The stage is set for a fascinating struggle.

What is likely to determine the outcome is the open question of the rate of growth of online shopping. This will depend on customer acceptance, and firms' ability to deliver a satisfactory service. If it does grow rapidly, can the established retailers compete profitably, and will they want to? If online shopping is taking a greater share of the market, the property holdings of the incumbents will become less valuable, and some stores could become unprofitable. Many observers believe that the companies cannot compete profitably online, and even Tesco's claimed profit is illusory. On this view, online shopping is an extra service to customers that they have to offer (but probably would prefer not to). When online shopping is an add-on serviced from stores, they can cope without spending large sums. If it becomes a big market in its own right, the companies will have to start investing in new real estate, buildings, machinery, vehicles and staff (as Tesco has found). That would be a drag on their already thin margins.

The future

It is not possible to predict with any accuracy, but what can we say about the future? The outcomes for food shopping depend on the interaction of many variables, but we will concentrate on three major influences: technology, economics and competition.

Rapid, or even steady, development of new ways of shopping will depend on the wide availability of technologies that offer bandwidth and ease of use. These include interactive TV, voice recognition, smart telephones, and kiosks (and, of course, things we have not yet dreamt of). Interactive TV is already with us, although it has had limited success except among specialized TV shopping channels.

The challenge is to produce a new model, and that is where new competition may come. Gary Hamel argues that, every time there has been a big change in retailing, such as the growth of out-of-town shopping or the arrival of huge 'category killers', new arrivals have attacked the current occupants. 'With each of those shifts, never did the leaders in one paradigm become the leaders in the next. I think it is just as unlikely that the winners in out-of-town shopping centres will be winners online' (*Financial Times*, 11 September 1998).

This is the scenario preferred by Ocado aficionados. They argue that people will continue to become busier, have more ways to spend their limited leisure time, and will prefer to spend it on more rewarding pastimes than shopping. They will welcome the chance to shop online, using their laptops or smart phones on the way to work. The service delivered by online retailers will outperform that of any other channel in efficiency, accuracy and quality. A problem with this view is that it is mainly held by people in the top target segment for such services: young(-ish), educated, well off, technophile and time-poor. There is little evidence that other parts of society – the great majority – think in such ways. Some people actually enjoy shopping, for a variety of reasons: to get out of the house, to meet friends (notice the number of small groups chatting in a supermarket), to see the produce and judge it, to use the supermarket visit as part of a round of chores or pleasures, and so on.

However, we are confident that there will be a demand for new ways of shopping – not just remote ordering or home delivery, but a variety of modes and combinations – and that the existing retailers will have to meet those demands if they are not to lose control of a significant share of their market. It seems likely that each competitor will reach a different solution, depending on the specific situation and strategy. Ocado may succeed and grow, and in so doing will stimulate others to follow. The danger for the majors is that the specialists could cherry-pick the most valuable customers (those most willing to buy high-margin items, for example, and concentrated in inner-city areas that are easy to serve economically). That could have a more-than-proportional effect on the retailers' profits. It will be a fascinating battle to watch.

Supermarkets, Society and Sustainability

10

The effects on consumers, food quality and safety, and the death of the town centre

In every revolution, there are bound to be winners and losers. Some of the winners from the retail revolution are obvious: the shareholders, managers and employees of the successful supermarket chains. On the other side, the owners, managers and employees of the firms put out of business by the revolution – not only small independent grocers, but butchers, greengrocers, fishmongers, dairies, wholesalers and, increasingly, other trades – have lost. This, you could argue, is just the normal operation of economic forces, the 'creative destruction', as Schumpeter called it, unleashed by innovation.

But business operates within society. What of the other interested parties that are affected? Consumers and suppliers are the most closely involved stakeholders, but there are also questions of the wider environment, and of people as citizens. Have the all-powerful superstore groups helped to kill off the traditional town centre?

Critics have levelled many charges at the supermarket groups, as they have at any big and successful organizations. The issues are complex and interrelated, but they are important, and we need to look at them squarely. As the Competition Commission found, critics will raise a whole range of issues that they believe supermarkets are involved in:

> The broader public policy issues concerning grocery retailing raised with us during this investigation include the social cohesion of urban and rural communities, the character of UK high streets, the social and health consequences of alcohol sales by grocery retailers, the impact of grocery retailing on the nation's health, the environmental impact of the groceries supply chain, working conditions among agricultural workers both in the UK and abroad, and the security of UK food supplies and the sustainability of the supply base.
>
> (Competition Commission, 2008: 22)

Now we will look at some of the specific criticisms that have been made, starting with consumers: how well are they being served?

Consumers

Shoppers have gained many concrete advantages: a huge range of products, sourced from all over the world; a one-stop shop, where this range is gathered in one place, increasingly with other services such as pharmacies, dry cleaning, access to cash, a post office and petrol; the sheer convenience of being able to park easily – and free – while they shop; and a choice of competing stores offering this range. Shoppers have voted with their feet – or rather their cars – patronizing the supermarkets and superstores at the expense of other outlets. The vast, gleaming superstores –open seven days a week, some 24 hours a day – are the clearest possible evidence that consumers are getting what they want. When asked, the great majority of shoppers are pleased with the advantages of superstores (Peston and Ennew, 1998; Competition Commission, 2000, 2008).

The quality of the supermarkets' offer has meant that, until very recently, they seemed immune to criticism. There have always been some critics, to be sure, but they were in a minority, and their voices were not widely heard. Broad public support for supermarkets brought political support. In 1998, however, something changed. Articles in serious newspapers and weighty television programmes began to appear, charging the grocery firms with all manner of things; these criticisms, albeit from a vocal minority, have continued.

Diet, health and the price of food

In both Britain and the United States, inequality of wealth has been increasing. In Britain, there has been growing evidence of increasing inequality of health: for the poorest group in society, all the health indicators are significantly worse than for the wealthiest. They have lower life expectancy, higher incidence of many diseases, lower birth weight, and generally a lower quality of life.

There has been evidence that some of these differences are due to a poor diet, and many commentators waxed eloquent on the topic. Hard evidence was more difficult to find. In 2010, however, the Food Standards Agency reported on the results of its Low Income Diet and Nutrition Survey. Key results were:

- *Food consumption:*
  - For many foods, the types and quantities eaten by people on low income appeared similar to those of the general population. Where differences did exist, they were often consistent across different age groups.
  - Generally, those on low income were less likely to eat wholemeal bread and vegetables. They tended to drink more soft drinks (not diet drinks) and eat more processed meats, whole milk and sugar.
  - For men and women, consumption of pasta, pizza, burgers and kebabs, chips, fried and roast potatoes, crisps and savoury snacks and carbonated soft drinks (not diet) decreased with increasing age. Consumption of wholegrain and high-fibre breakfast cereals tended to increase with increasing age.
  - The majority of fat spreads used by the low-income population were not polyunsaturated.
  - Children were more likely than adults to eat sausages, coated chicken and turkey and burgers and kebabs.
- *Fruit and vegetables:*

  The average number of fruit and vegetable portions eaten daily by people on low income was: men 2.4, women 2.5, boys 1.6, girls

2.0. Like the fruit and vegetable intake of the general population, this is well below the government's recommendation to eat at least five portions a day.

- Weight:

  The numbers of underweight people were low (2 per cent). However, large percentages (62 per cent of men and 63 per cent of women) of people on low income were overweight or obese, in about the same proportion as in the population at large.

Such facts are shocking and disturbing, but supermarket executives might be forgiven for saying that they reflect deep-rooted social and political problems, and questioning what this has to do with supermarkets. Part of the answer lies in the availability of cheap food for those who need it most. Many researchers had been documenting the problems the poor and the old have in finding, let alone affording, a balanced diet. They claimed, in both the UK and the United States, that 'food deserts' existed in poorer parts of cities. Eventually, the issue hit the front pages.

Perhaps surprisingly, the Competition Commission dismissed this whole argument about food deserts. Its research found no evidence that multiple retailers were avoiding low-income, urban areas. 'In fact, the proliferation of supermarkets was higher in the poorest areas than elsewhere... Some multiple retailers have also been actively involved in opening up areas that have historically offered less access to the range of products available to consumers elsewhere' (Competition Commission, 2000, Vol 1: 55). It also found that, in low-income areas, prices were not inflated, but that supermarkets were likely to increase the number of economy products available. Again, as with pricing, careful, objective research has found in the supermarkets' favour, and has rejected populist and sensational criticisms.

Food quality and safety

The safety of food has become a topic of concern to the public since the scare of BSE, and outbreaks of serious food poisoning from listeria and E coli bacteria.

Here, the supermarkets have a good story to tell. Their own standards are generally high, and they have often been in advance of government advice and regulation. They have been quick, for example, to remove products from shelves at the slightest suspicion of contamination.

More proactively, they have taken a lead in trying to remove genetically modified (GM) ingredients since the issue blew up in 1998 and 1999. Iceland, a modest (under £2 billion sales) frozen food retailer, announced in early 1998 that it was banning GM ingredients from its own-label products. Although this caused controversy at the time, the firm is convinced that it helped it to achieve a 13 per cent like-for-like sales increase (its home delivery service contributed too). The major companies took similar action in 1999, when the issue hit the headlines and the general public became seriously (if unscientifically) worried. Consumers seem to have lost faith in the government's ability, or willingness, to enforce strict standards of food safety against the interests of agri-business, but the setting up of the Food Standards Agency may have helped (though public opinion is more likely to be shaped by the media than by government agencies).

The supermarkets know that they rely absolutely on their customers' confidence in the safety of the food they buy. They work hard to deserve that confidence, and their record shows that they do. Beyond that, they have also promoted healthy eating (led in this by Tesco), though it has to be said that they also sell a great deal of processed food, since that is what many of their customers want.

On food quality, and the welfare of the animals that supply much of our diet, there has been more criticism of supermarkets. Campaigns led by celebrity chefs gained great publicity: Hugh Fearnley-Whittingstall on factory chickens, and Jamie Oliver on pigs. The chicken campaign in particular had an immediate effect, and sales of 'welfare' chickens and those raised in barns with access to the open air increased, along with the more expensive free-range variety. More generally, there is a significant segment of shoppers who are interested in the quality of the meat and vegetables they buy, in terms not only of flavour but of how the animal was treated and how the plants were grown. Those on more restricted budgets continue to buy the much cheaper battery hens and cheaper, processed meat and frozen vegetables.

Supermarkets and the town centre

The health and vibrancy of a town centre may be affected by many things, such as changes in the local agricultural and industrial scene, population shifts, and wider regional changes. Food shopping in the centre cannot alone be responsible for its success or failure. Yet food shopping is the most common and frequent type of shopping, and a trip to a food store is often linked to other shopping. If the food store is removed, then that may contribute to a more general decline in shopping and in the viability of the centre. Even a marginal loss of trade, say of 10 to 20 per cent, may make the difference between trading profitably and failure.

Unquestionably, new superstores do have effects on town centres. Food retailers in the centre suffer, though to varying degrees. Other retailers, and the centre as a whole, may or may not decline as a result. Larger centres should be better balanced and better able to withstand the loss of food retailing, though as we saw there may be very serious consequences for some inner-city areas. It is striking that in many other countries, for example France, Germany and Italy, government has been far more proactive in defending small stores and town centres. Laws limiting large superstore development appeared far earlier than in the UK, and laws prohibiting the use of loss-leaders are common. The British free market approach has contributed to, even connived at, the effects of unrestrained superstore development.

A striking and contrasting development in the last two decades has been the re-emergence of several supermarket fascias on high streets and in local shopping areas: Tesco Express and Metro, and Sainsbury's Local. Tesco's expansion was considerably aided by the Competition Commission's bizarre decision that supermarkets and convenience stores formed separate markets, so Tesco was allowed to take over the 850 shops of T&S in 2002. The market leader claims that, in practice, its return to a town centre is positively beneficial: that other retailers are attracted back and the centre regains its vitality. Even critics would agree that the supermarket groups' shops are cleaner, brighter and better stocked than the usual convenience store – but they still bemoan the overwhelming sameness of a dominant brand. Critics would also allege that the multiples are not being high-minded, but simply reacting to the shortage of viable large sites. For its part, Tesco argues that it does take the plight of the town centre seriously, and it points to developments in centres such as Orpington, Kent, where it led a general development that included a Tesco store, but also other buildings (other retailers, residential buildings and leisure facilities) that would benefit the community as a whole. Tesco is launching more of these developments.

The supermarket groups are running businesses. The success of the superstores shows that they are meeting the needs of shoppers (at least, the majority of them). The retailers, having discovered the right business model, recognized the opportunity; government policy supported them. People want to use their cars, and will do so whenever possible, especially to shop for bulky, heavy goods such as a weekly food order. The supermarket chains are merely reflecting changes in society, not leading them. Their return to the town centre is also a reflection of changing shopping patterns and preferences, they argue.

If we as a society want to change travel patterns, reduce pollution from cars, and lessen the cost and frustration of traffic jams, then we have to find ways of achieving that, probably through government action. In any case, the revision of PPG6 locked the stable doors after the horses had bolted. Most viable sites had already been bought, and some areas were beginning to look over-shopped. The multiples continue to look for new sites, and are being more imaginative about the sort of site they can use and how they develop them. The Office of Fair Trading and the planning system will act as constraints, and the pace of expansion will be inevitably slow.

Climate change and sustainability

Climate change is the biggest of the big stories of our time. It may move on and off the front pages, but it doesn't go away. Regardless of the political wrangling and shortcomings of the scientific data, the overall case is broadly accepted: human activity has contributed to potentially disastrous climate change, and humans have to do something about it. While governments around the world take up various attitudes and set more or less challenging targets, businesses have been setting their own agenda and getting to work.

Grocery retailers, being closest to the majority of citizens, have been made more aware of their responsibilities, and have received a great deal of criticism: for the amount of waste they create through packaging, for excessive energy use in refrigeration, for adding to food miles through importing products and delivery miles, and even for encouraging consumers to buy more than they need through offers and multi-buys, thus contributing to food waste. One estimate suggests that 5.9 million tonnes of packaging and 8.3 million tonnes of food waste are sent to landfill annually in the UK; 50 per cent of this comes from the top five supermarkets (WRAP, 2010). They have responded, and may now even be said to be leading from the front. Most people probably noticed this when the supermarkets' practice of giving out free plastic bags in huge numbers began to be challenged. In Britain, the chains responded in different ways, from encouraging less use to giving away reusable bags, to charging for bags. Some French supermarkets, by contrast, simply stopped providing them at all, and Aldi have never done so. There is, of course, far more to a sustainable business than plastic bags.

In the UK, Marks and Spencer and Tesco have made the most public commitments as part – an increasing part – of their corporate social responsibility strategy: let us see how well they have done in practice. In January 2007, Marks and Spencer publicly announced its Plan A, 'because there is no Plan B' – perhaps the best slogan coined in the whole welter of words surrounding the subject. This set out 100 commitments on what, according to Sir Stuart Rose (2009), were 'the most important social, environmental and ethical challenges facing our business'. On climate change, M&S says it has achieved 10 of the 29 goals for 2012, including reducing its carbon emissions by 18 per cent, improving the energy efficiency of stores by 10 per cent, and reducing the fuel use of delivery fleets by 20 per cent. As its stated goal is to make its operations in the UK and the Republic of Ireland carbon neutral, it is testing hybrid vehicles, small-scale wind turbines and anaerobic digestion facilities. It recognizes that it has some way to go, and it tries to involve business partners and customers in energy-saving initiatives.

On waste and recycling, all food retailers have come under attack for the amount of packaging they use that is sent to landfill. M&S claims to have reduced the number of single-use plastic bags given out by 83 per cent (by charging 5p), and to have reduced non-glass food packaging by 12 per cent. Other efforts include a clothes exchange initiative with Oxfam, reducing paper waste through a Christmas card recycling scheme, and support for the Love Food Hate Waste campaign by the Waste and Resources Action Programme (WRAP).

Overall, M&S is making a serious effort across the business: it has set specific goals, and it measures them as accurately as it can. It has also appointed Jonathon Porritt, one of the best-known campaigners in the UK, to monitor its efforts and report on them. As Porritt says, the whole thing could be 'just another CSR pitch'. On the contrary, he concludes that Plan A is different: 'it covers the whole gamut of corporate sustainability issues. It's outcomes-based, it's got serious traction through the whole company, and it rests on the measurement and management of non-financial data... at a level of detail that few companies can match' (Marks and Spencer, 2009: 43). M&S further claims that the process is now cost-neutral, and has positive benefits in that customers appreciate it and see it as marking the company out as different. There is clearly a long way to go, but the company is serious about its responsibilities.

Tesco, too, has been a leader. Like M&S, it has recognized for some time that its responsibilities cover not just shareholders, but also its employees, customers and the wider community within which it operates. In 2006, it added 'Community and Environment' as a fifth segment to the Steering Wheel that guides its actions. Even during the recession, it claims that the environment has remained a priority. The CEO, Sir Terry Leahy, has written that 'Climate change remains the major strategic challenge of our age. I fundamentally believe that business has a crucial role to play in tackling change, setting an example, guiding consumers towards more sustainable forms of consumption, making them affordable and providing the information on which to make informed choices' (Tesco Corporate Responsibility Report, 2009). Leahy's rationale is on record:

> The starting position... is it's a choice between growing or going green and a concern that you give up a bit of potency and focus in the business if you go in pursuit of these things... my strong belief is that's not the case... that actually going green will be a good way to grow and add value... my reason for saying this is that modern western economies will have to operate on about a fifth of the carbon they operate on today and that will require a complete rebuilding of mass consumption systems. Change is opportunity in marketing and I can tell you that's where growth comes from. A business that starts to read that well and gets ahead of those changes will be a faster growing business.

With this degree of clarity of purpose, an operating response becomes a whole lot easier to generate.

So Tesco has led UK CEOs in their sponsorship of the green agenda and the need to act, through its leadership role of the Sustainable Consumption Institute at Manchester University. Important and visible moves were made prior to the Copenhagen conference to ensure business was ready and committed to take relevant actions. Energy saving delivering a low carbon footprint is a real target for the company. New stores have shown an impressive rate of carbon reduction, and the arrival of the Cheetham Hill store in Manchester produced savings of 70 per cent from the 2006/07 base levels and prompted the Climate Change Institute to wish that other businesses would follow the Tesco example.

A refreshing aspect of Tesco's approach is that, in reporting on its achievements, it also sets out the challenges still remaining. So, in the 2009 report, it lists as achievements:

- being the first major retailer to carbon-label 100 own-brand products;
- opening the first new-format environmental store in Cheetham Hill, Manchester;
- halving energy use per square foot in UK stores against a baseline of 2000.

The remaining challenges are:

- the doubts about the long-term impacts of bio-fuels, which Tesco had introduced into their filling stations (it has asked the Sustainable Consumption Institute – SCI – to examine the problem in more detail);
- its inability to report on water use (and, again, it has asked the SCI to help with the issue);
- how to reduce packaging: it had been working on weight reduction targets, but feels that this may not be the best way of measuring environmental benefit, and is working with suppliers on a better approach.

As a growing business with global ambitions, Tesco has to keep on driving down environmental costs. It points out that, in 2008–09, its net sales area grew by 16.4 per cent, but its carbon footprint by only 3.7 per cent. It achieved this, not just by target setting and advocacy from above, but by appointing energy champions: there are around 4,000 in UK stores, for example, whose task is to engage staff. The 2009 report sets out in detail the company's targets and actions over the many fields in which it is working. While this will set the company up for its critics, it is an open and honest statement of how committed it is.

The SCI is an interesting example of business–academic cooperation. Tesco committed £25 million to the Institute, which will focus on four areas: sustainable consumer behaviour and lifestyle, sustainable production and distribution, climate change and carbon levels, and making development more sustainable (*source:* SCI website). As an academic institution, the SCI will publish much of its work, so, while some investigations may be for Tesco's own private use, much will also benefit other users round the world. This is a far-sighted and generous action.

Other major retailers have of course been active too. Asda works within its parent company, Wal-Mart's, campaign. Wal-Mart first set sustainability targets in 2005: the three core goals were: 'to be supplied 100 per cent by renewable energy; to create zero waste; and to sell products that sustain our resources and the environment' (Mike Duke, CEO). Critics at first objected that this was merely part of its attempt to burnish its poor reputation, and it certainly faces an enormous challenge. In 2008, the company estimated that its stores globally emitted 21 million tonnes of carbon dioxide equivalent, and that this will increase by 10 per cent a year as it opens new stores (Asda's share of this is not revealed). Typically, perhaps, for the company, it does not see its efforts as part of its corporate social responsibility, but as a way of being a better business. Instead of setting up a corporate social responsibility division, it set up 12 sustainable value networks to drive and promote the effort. These are still US based, and the very detailed 2009 Global Sustainability Report covers mainly US activities, as might be expected.

Asda's contribution does appear, in items such as: the opening in 2008 of the second low-carbon store, which will be 40 per cent more energy efficient and produce 50 per cent fewer carbon emissions; cooperation with suppliers to reduce embedded carbon in products; improving fleet efficiency by increasing front-haul and back-haul journeys (not running trucks empty), to reduce carbon emissions by 40 per cent; reducing plastic bag use and packaging waste; and reducing waste sent to landfill by 65 per cent.

Sainsbury's, too, sets out its achievements in its 2009 report. Interestingly, it puts water as a major focus. Sixty per cent of water globally is used in agriculture, and clearly much of that reflects supermarket sales. It also mentions pesticide use as a concern, showing perhaps a wider appreciation of global problems than the others. Beyond that, we find the familiar achievements: the opening of a green store in Dartmouth, Devon in 2008; 15 per cent savings in energy efficiency in 200 stores; targets for carbon emissions of a 25 per cent reduction by 2012, and of packaging weight of 33 per cent by 2015; a zero waste programme for all stores; and the reduction of truck miles by 7.7 million kilometres, and of plastic bag use by an impressive 58 per cent in two years to April 2009. A conspicuous initiative is that it has four trucks running on bio-methane, which is gas produced from rotting waste.

Morrisons, in its turn, claims to be a green and responsible company. One achievement was that in 2008 it was one of only 12 companies, and the only supermarket, to be awarded the Carbon Trust Standard for managing and cutting carbon emissions (the other three have followed since). It reports that it has achieved its emissions reduction targets of carbon by 36 per cent and haulage by 8 per cent. It identifies future challenges as finding ways to further reduce carbon savings, preparing for the introduction of the Carbon Reduction Commitment in 2010, balancing packaging reduction with the prevention of food waste, and finding long-term, sustainable solutions to reducing waste to landfill. Its unique vertical integration gives it better control of waste higher up the supply chain, and it is also different in setting up a Let's Grow campaign in schools so that pupils can learn about fresh produce, and piloting a Fresh Food Academy to train 100,000 colleagues to NVQ Level 2 by 2011. Morrisons reports the results of its efforts in admirable detail, for example breaking down packaging savings by product, and waste reduction by type. It prefers its energy saving to be economically sound, so it does not, for example, indulge in small and ineffective wind turbines.

To sum up, then, the major grocery retailers have reacted to growing public concern about climate change by adopting policies and setting up action programmes. Compared with only a few years ago, this is a dramatic change. All the major grocery retailers are measuring their carbon emissions and publishing the results in detail. They are all working in three main areas: their own activities, the operations of their suppliers, and the habits of consumers. Their reports set out, in varying detail, their targets, what they have achieved so far, and their plans for the future; some describe the challenges they still face, again in more or less detail. Some publish an outside appraisal of their work.

As they are so visible, they will always be subject to more criticism than less obvious candidates. Criticisms range widely, the most sweeping claiming that all the retailers' efforts are merely 'green-wash'. Critics point out that large supermarkets are some of the least energy-efficient buildings in the sector. In this and other fields, what critics are really saying is that the supermarket groups should have done more, and done it faster. It is true that most shopping trips to supermarkets are in cars. Given consumers' known preference for using the car, it is hard to see what the retailers can do about this, beyond what they have already done in opening smaller shops in town centres. They still move huge amounts of goods around the country by road; although some have gone back to rail, this is a tiny proportion of the total. Efforts to reduce waste could go much further. Consumers could be helped to reduce food waste, rather than encouraged to buy more than they need through offers and multi-buys. All the labelling (added to nutrition data) could just confuse people. A report by *Which?* found that, although most groups have reduced the use of plastic bags in stores, they still use them in quantity in their delivery of online orders. In all this, grudging and occasional praise is overwhelmed by criticism, but really all the critics are saying is 'Could do better'.

As the climate change debate grows more and more strident, as it will, supermarkets will be expected to play their part, along with government and consumers. Within the limits of their business model, they will; they have already made some progress. Very significant change, such as meeting the government's target of 80 per cent reduction in carbon emissions, may need much more radical action.

Conclusions on consumers and society

The supermarket groups have done extremely well, then, certainly for themselves. For shoppers, they provide a broad range of products in a pleasant, safe environment. Their food is safe and hygienic, and generally thought by shoppers to give value for money. In some categories, they have led a drive against excessive manufacturer margins. They respond to, and lead, changes in taste; they help to educate consumers (for example, in wine); they try to be responsible (in offering healthy eating options). They are so trusted by consumers that, of all deposit takers (banks and other financial institutions), they are growing fastest.

On the other hand, they have reached such a point of concentration that they wield enormous power. We cannot assume that they will always use it for the common weal, rather than for their own selfish interest. They have undoubtedly driven thousands of small shops out of business, possibly increasing overall efficiency, but reducing choice. They do not always serve the poor and the old well. They contribute to increased road traffic, with all the ills that brings.

Have they served their turn, as some critics argue? The argument is that they played a valuable role in breaking down previous oligopolies, particularly where manufacturers charged higher-than-necessary prices, but now they are too big, they are themselves an oligopoly, and they have outlived their usefulness. We may compare them with the clearing banks, which for many years enjoyed an unchallenged hold over retail financial services. Now, new competition has made people realize that they do not need banks as such: they can use telephone or internet services, other retailers and a whole raft of providers. The clearing banks were notoriously slow to catch on to the fact that they were there to serve their customers, rather than the other way round. The supermarkets, certainly now, are not making that mistake. But what will happen if the public come to believe that what they have lost may, in the end, be more than they have gained? The supermarket groups have enjoyed high levels of public and political support, because they have persuaded us that they are doing a good job. The stores will have to demonstrate – continuously – that they truly have consumer interests at heart and that they are not abusing their enormous power just to enrich themselves.

The effect on suppliers

If consumers are the biggest group affected by what supermarkets do, suppliers are also intimately involved. For some indeed the decision of a single buyer from one major retailer can make the difference between profit and loss – in extreme cases therefore between survival and closure of a business. When four buyers between them control the majority of the market, probably 75 per cent of most active categories, then the threat of delisting is a serious one and the negotiating power brought to bear is enormous. There is no doubt that decisions of this kind are operationally some of the most critical that sales leaders and even boards of manufacturing companies have to take, and there is a constant anxiety, especially in smaller and middle-ranking companies, and particularly those that depend upon a single brand for their existence, over the ever-present possibility that their supply contract can be lost with limited warning, and for reasons not directly concerned with the performance of the company's product – the arrival of a new product on the market, for example, in a sector where only one product is felt to be viable. This position – whether real or merely perceived – where a sword of Damocles is constantly hanging over a single critical brand stocking decision, has had a material effect on decision making among smaller and middle-sized suppliers. Rather than concentrating on innovation, development and creating strategic moves forward, it has in many cases caused immediate and continuous focus on operating relationships with the key distributors, which in turn results in a culture that becomes too short-term and in some cases overly political. This level of short-term criticality is probably not in the interests of consumer choice or effective brand development in the longer term.

We focus on two major groups of suppliers, which account for a major proportion of purchases and have been visibly affected by the growth of multiple retailers – manufacturers and farmers.

Manufacturers

By manufacturers, we mean makers of the packaged goods that form the bulk of supermarket products – fast-moving consumer goods (fmcg). Many of these are huge companies in their own right and are considerably more representative global players than the retailers they supply. Good examples are Procter & Gamble (P&G), predominantly accepted today as the 'thought' leader, Johnson & Johnson, Colgate, Gillette (now owned by P&G) and, from Europe, Unilever and Nestlé. Powerful as these companies remain, they are a lot less powerful than they used to be, viewed against their retail distributors. Wal-Mart's brand is now bigger than the company brand sales of any of them. Not only is Wal-Mart growing faster, but its worldwide potential, in terms of unoccupied markets, is much greater. The balance of power has shifted hugely over half a century. By the 1990s, retailers simply did not want or need to stock secondary brands, and they wanted a sensible margin on the brand leaders. Now the shift has moved significantly further.

Today, for market leaders in brand supply, it is no longer the brand that forms the basis of the negotiation between manufacturer and retailer. Today retailers will choose to review the category – say detergents, pet foods or coffee – and they will expect (or require) the suppliers to take an interest in (or responsibility for) the profits made by the retailers in the whole category. This process was born years ago as category management, and was described as a joint activity or a partnership. So, in theory, it remains today, but the controlling partner in all significant categories is now the retailer, which emphatically calls the shots. The nature of the negotiation remains a partnership, since it is only if adequate profits can be generated for both manufacturer and retailer that survival for both parties is possible. Over the years two things have happened, and on a continuous basis. In successful categories, the retailer's share of the available profits has risen, whereas the manufacturer's has declined. In successful categories it is possible, in categories where there is sufficient innovation or increased consumer appeal, for profits to rise, so there are growth possibilities for both parties. However, in the majority of categories where there is consumer search for best value and price advantage, the requirement is for costs to be reduced so that margins can still be maintained. This search for cost-effectiveness has been delivered, in the majority of cases, by the manufacturer, although the benefits from the reduced costs are shared by the two parties. Huge pressure is thus exerted on the manufacturer's systems and processes, and only the best have the levels of experience, scale and competitive advantage in their own areas to respond and survive. For the brand owners this has been a rude awakening. They now operate in a hard world where they are answerable for the levels of cost-effectiveness that they can produce – and woe betide them if they fall behind in delivering the category targets. In fact the best of them become first-class operating category partners, and become adept at managing to retain their brand's integrity in challenging conditions. The weak, however, live on borrowed time for a brief period before they simply disappear, to be replaced by alternative category leaders or quite possibly, in many categories, by the retailer's own brand(s) (see 'Own label' below). Retailers could reasonably respond that the same rough justice was meted out to many independent shopkeepers in the 1960s and 1970s by a range of powerful brand owners.

It is when one considers the case of the smaller manufacturer or brand owner that an uneven contest becomes a certain win for retail. Single-brand suppliers, family owners and start-up companies are ill equipped for the contest, and avoid taking on the might of the retail buyer. If their innovation is intrinsically compelling, they will stand a fair chance but will normally possess inadequate experience to get a fairly balanced set of selling terms, specifically price and margin. Where the proffered new brand is more run-of-the-mill, the suppliers have little or no chance – and perhaps in the world of the market, where consumer choice rules, this is right. However, it is not, directly, the consumer who is making the call; it is the tough, hard-nosed buyer on behalf of the retailer, interpreting probable future consumer choice. Is this so obviously correct? Possibly not. What we are describing is a distinct change in industrial structure, achieved gradually over half a century. Does it matter to society?

We saw earlier that concentrated buyer power is not bad in itself. If lower prices are passed on to consumers, their welfare is increased. There has been some evidence that British retailers do not always pass on as much as those in other countries (we discuss below what happens to lower farm prices); rising margins at certain periods suggest that countervailing power has not always operated and that retailers have been able to use their dual power to increase profits. The existence of stable or even slowly declining net margins over recent years should indicate that retailer power is decreasing. This argument is unconvincing; it seems much more likely that it is intra-retailer jockeying for share advantage that has trimmed margins and prevented some quite sizeable companies from getting close to the average (Sainsbury's). It would be a brave bet that margins will continue to fall much further. A more insidious danger according to manufacturers is that the stranglehold exercised by the big four will reduce the attractiveness of markets, and therefore reduce suppliers' commitment to them. In a report to the OFT, economists seem to agree, concluding that 'buyer power may be socially detrimental where it undermines the long term viability of suppliers and their willingness to commit to new product and process investments' (Dobson, Waterson and Chu, 1998). The Competition Commission, for its part, did not find any deleterious effects on manufacturers' profits, or on the rate of innovation.

Own label

Into this context arrives own label, a huge and growing worldwide phenomenon. The growth of retailers' own brands has delivered devastating damage to the fabric of even the strongest manufacturer brand citadels, nowhere more effectively than in the UK, where penetration at 40 per cent is considerably higher than elsewhere. Long gone are the days where own label was a cheap, under-formulated and usually imitative version of the national brand leader. In the UK, 83 per cent of shopping trips include some own-label purchase. More than half the British believe own label is 'at least as good' as a brand – coffee 57 per cent, razors 74 per cent (against the mighty Gillette). About a quarter 'would change store' if their brand was not available (Gillette more than Colgate). The arrival over the last decade of the premium private label (Finest from Tesco, Taste the Difference from Sainsbury's, and Asda's Extra Special) has 'rearmed' the own-label category, and it has not stopped there. Tesco adds premium sub-variants such as Organics, Free From, Healthy Living and Fair Trade, a virtually endless series of thoroughly relevant brand variants, and these are certainly *brands*. Paul Polman, head of worldwide Unilever, talking about Aldi, is both realistic and correct when he says, 'These people are using brands just as much as we use brands. They believe in brands. Don't be fooled.' He knows what he is talking about. In 2005, Aldi, not in the world's top six retailers, had worldwide sales just 20 per cent lower than Unilever's and were catching up fast. There is a new and rational respect for the calibre of the own-label assortment, and manufacturers – whether, like the majority, they produce own label or, like P&G and Unilever, they prefer not to – recognize the new game. It fits neatly into the negotiation context we described earlier. Category management *starts* with own label and goes on to consider the brand assortment. The emerging pattern is becoming clear. In markets where there is limited meaningful brand innovation (yoghurt in the UK, for example, although leading global food brand Danone is present), own-label brands will create the new brand structure and the nature of competition – flavours, health or hedonism, packaging, 'free from', price and so on – and brands will take a back seat. In markets where brands show commitment, where product advantage preferably of an enduring nature exists, and where the manufacturer can sustain a long-term performance difference, at least the brand leader and perhaps one other 'performance' contender will survive and aim to lead the consumer market. Even here, however, own label will expect, through partnerships or straight pressure, to gain a share of the performance market, and will certainly set out to dominate the 'value' or price-driven market, using the level of pricing that can deliver the required value share component. This is the new reality, accepted with varying degrees of composure by all concerned.

There are two further nuances to recognize in assessing the current own-label context. Where the brand has a capability of innovating and brings this development to market, a frequent element of the retailer response is politely to enquire when its own variant of this innovation can be available to be marketed under the own-label name. With many manufacturers, this is a simple case of scheduling the date, since they will produce both, and may seek to achieve differentiation in favour of the original brand both in formulation and in a time lead. But the retailer's version will invariably follow the original pretty quickly, and often with not much difference between the two. Since the retailer's version will be cheaper, it is obvious which way the market will swing – in favour of the retailer brand. From this came the erosion of the balanced market structure that used to obtain. Whether or not this is a better societal outcome is hard to say. We might consider that consumers can vote with their wallets, but if the choice is insignificant and temporary then choice is simple. Brand owners need to be realistic about the positions their strategies must confront. So too they must be realistic where the increasing global purchasing power of the retailer is concerned. As global expansion began over the past two decades, intense pressure has existed on retailers themselves to maintain margins, especially in home markets where the retailers need funding for expansion. Tesco (UK) and Carrefour (France) are examples. Growing discounter share adds to this pressure. Retailers are now resorting to using their wider global presence to deliver better costs and pricing from suppliers – Wal-Mart, Carrefour, Tesco and others can all now do this. While the results are still fragmented, since brands are not uniform across national boundaries, and retailers themselves have local structures and requirements in many cases, the future pattern is emerging. Retailers will look to the manufacturer to deliver the lower prices – from source A in its portfolio rather than the higher costs from source B. Initially these can be negotiated in a spirit of joint experiment or even partnership. When major brands have visibly sought to help with these processes or at least adopted an open mind in considering them, retailers have been keen to suggest that specific brand owners be singled out on a merit basis, as Unilever UK has been through four recent years of Tesco global expansion.

Private label is not only here to stay, but it is here to grow, perhaps to dominate. In many markets it does so already, and Britain, given retailer capability as well as concentration, is foremost in demonstrating this. Some years ago, the president of Coca-Cola was heard to say that he did not like talking about market share, since he didn't see why he had to share his market with anybody. It is safe to say that, however strong the brand, this philosophy can now be ignored. Some level of accommodation will be reached. What it is, in individual markets, will depend on the distinctiveness and long-term strategic capability of the – for the moment at least usually but not invariably – global brand owner. Where there is clear focus, and a strategic performance lead can be perceived by consumers, the brand will still exert major influence and in some cases lead the market. Where there is not, there is a limited future for brand owners, and if their main role is to produce volume for retailer brands they are already living on borrowed time. Retailers will and do know how to source more cheaply from elsewhere.

A good note of open-mindedness comes from Justin King, CEO of Sainsbury's. He says: 'Innovation should come from brands and private label. We have no agenda to push private label beyond what our shoppers want it to be. Knock on our door and ask how we can help you build your brand.' These are not empty words, since five years ago an entrepreneur took her Plum Baby brand, invented in her kitchen, to Sainsbury's buyers, who found its credentials compelling and took it straight into 300 of their biggest stores. The inventor concerned knew very little about business, brands or planning, but she knew a lot about baby food, and Sainsbury's buyers were sharp enough to spot this. Innocent is another well-crafted and distinctive example. There is a moral here for other brands – and maybe also for other retailers.

It is in the end about seeking to preserve elements of balance in the market. The argument depends on three steps:

1 Manufacturer competition is healthy, as it leads to product and process innovation, improved products and wider choice.

2 Own label threatens this healthy competition by removing brand revenue without incurring the costs of innovation, development and marketing.

3 Brand owners will either reduce investment or engage in continuous – and wasteful – differentiation. In the long run the effect is that consumer choice is reduced.

(Dobson, 1998a, 1998b)

This outcome would, in our view, be undesirable. It is the responsibility of the brand manufacturers to invest and innovate and to ensure their brands have discernible and enduring consumer benefits. It is then the responsibility of the retailer to act in the kind of way described above in the Innocent and Plum Baby examples. This is summarized by Stephen King, doyen of JWT: 'A product is something that is made in a factory; a brand is something that is bought by a customer. The product can be copied by a competitor; the brand is unique. A product can be quickly outdated; a successful brand is timeless.' Of course, what is different today is the facility retailers have to start creating brands.

Farmers and produce suppliers

Perhaps the area where the existence of retailer power has been seen to be exercised with the most apparent inequality has been in relation to farmers. In most areas where controversy exists between supplier and the supermarket group there is some room for manoeuvre and the possibility for compromise. This is not a feature of the relationship in this instance, where the two sides appear mostly at daggers drawn. Suppliers are normally focused and primary producers in one local area, and some are very small. The contrast between such small and – in the eyes of the public – defenceless units and the supermarket organizations, individually or en masse, could not be greater. This is reflected in stated public attitudes, which reflect a widespread and strongly held belief that 'supermarkets do not pay farmers enough for their food' and that 'supermarkets should sell UK grown products in season in preference to imported products', in each case by a margin of at least four to one in favour of the farming viewpoint (Friends of the Earth poll, 18 November 2002). The emphasis is put on the qualification 'stated', since it is well known that people are generally willing to choose a higher-cost option if not required to pay the price when responding. Nevertheless even in metropolitan Britain it is clear where public sympathies lie. The trends have been apparent for some time. Verdict Research showed that, over a 10-year period to 1992, while farm incomes fell by 35 per cent, food prices to consumers rose by 52 per cent but farm gate prices received by farmers rose by only 18 per cent (quoted in Raven and Lang, 1995). This in essence is the farmers' case. They feel that the entire benefit from cost increases in their producer areas has gone to the distributors, which would no doubt be able to argue that over a long period their percentage margins have dropped: their absolute returns have improved substantially because of higher volumes and rationalization among suppliers. Meanwhile in some primary areas such as milk, farmers are now apparently having to sell at a continuous net loss.

Of course, it is not that simple. First, retailers rarely buy directly from farmers or produce suppliers; there are layers of intermediaries (in meat, for example, abattoirs, boning and cutting operators, and processors that package the final product that goes on the supermarket shelf). Second, as the Competition Commission pointed out, a variety of factors has influenced returns for farmers in recent years . These include exchange rate variations, reform of the Common Agricultural Policy, food safety and animal health and welfare issues, regulatory arrangements for the sale and marketing of primary products, demand for UK agricultural produce from customers other than UK grocery retailers, and the ability of UK grocery retailers and intermediary purchasers of farm products to exert buyer power so as to extract lower prices from farmers. Nonetheless, it is generally true that, over the years, grocery retailers have received an increasing share of the retail price of agricultural products (the Competition Commission gives detailed figures for milk, red meat, pig meat and fruit in its 2008 report, Appendix 9).

As the relations between supermarket groups and suppliers have been so fraught, and following comments in the Competition Commission report of October 2000, the DTI published in 2001 its long-awaited Code of Practice for Supermarkets in their conduct of business with farmers. The new code's provisions were uniformly and rapidly felt to be too weak by farmers. The National Farmers Union (NFU) president claimed that 'it will do little or nothing to give our members any protection', a viewpoint shared by the Consumers' Association, which described the code's practices as 'objectionable' and its content as 'weak, extremely vague and loosely worded'. The subsequent history of the code did little to assuage critics.

What the OFT found in the early years was that no one – not one single supplier – came forward with a complaint. To critics, this was ample evidence of the climate of fear that they claimed existed: no supplier would complain, because they feared reprisals from the supermarket buyers. After a review in 2005, the OFT decided to commission its own research, but this too was inconclusive. Gradually, however, the situation seemed to improve. Some suppliers did come forward with complaints or to seek advice and, in general, relations were better. Since small producers, especially farmers, did not normally deal directly with supermarkets, a belief spread, anecdotally at least, that well-run suppliers could cope with supermarket buyers.

In its 2008 report, the Competition Commission decided to replace the old code of practice with a new one, the Grocery Supply Code of Practice (GSCOP). Recognizing the problems of the old scheme, it also advised the setting up of an ombudsman with powers to investigate and enforce good practice. The government accepted this advice, but at the time of writing there had been no legislation; as a general election took place in May 2010, this may have to wait.

The arrival of the recession in 2008 made the situation worse. Alongside comments from NFU president Peter Kendall that the big four supermarkets were collectively engaged in 'beating up' farmers and growers, there were complaints about specific and aggressive 'demands for over-riders, sudden price reductions and changes in payment terms'. It is worth observing that, in the economic downturn, there were indeed panic moves, not by any means confined either to small suppliers or to farmers and growers – the demand for lower prices had become the order of the day almost everywhere. There was a widely noted belief that the big retailers had started to ditch their focus on food quality and provenance and were competing in a fierce price war to stop consumers drifting away to lower-price operators (Julia Finch, *Guardian*, 14 November 2008). One exception Peter Kendall had noted earlier, however, was Waitrose, which he praised for fair dealing with suppliers, and he asked the big four to behave more like Waitrose (*Independent*, 26 February 2007) (see below).

What is crystal clear is that we are dealing with two industries ('disciplines' might be a better word) that are intrinsically different from each other. Farmers and growers are at the mercy of world supply and demand cycles in agriculture, where recent years – many would say most years – have seen high unpredictability. Retailers are much better able to manage and hold stable their prices, through years of experience, a well-equipped procurement team, and simply their massive scale, with considerable help from their suppliers. This is a process that they have become more adept at managing in their favour over many years now. Farmers and growers are quite another matter, as we have observed. They are often small primary producers and have little chance to consolidate or to generate sufficient scale to affect their costs critically. What they certainly can and would like to do is to improve their yield and particularly their quality and earn more. With this level of permanent process difference between two types of organization, conflict is almost certain to occur and is probably systemic. It is also well beyond any government's capabilities to arbitrate or to create a set of procedures that will make everyone happy, as some of the more recent attempts confirm. It is, however, not beyond the capabilities of the retailers themselves to exercise measures of self-restraint, and in the last resort they are aware that they must do this, and they show increasing awareness of this responsibility. If for nothing else, they must ensure their own survival. According to the *Guardian* report of 14 November 2008 (noted above), during the first days of the economic recession Tesco admitted that it had asked for some prices to be lowered – because it had paid more when oil and other commodity prices had risen and wanted equivalent reductions now that these prices had returned to 2006 levels. It noted: 'We are having the usual round of supplier negotiations to get the best deal for consumers.' Tesco went on to deny that its buyers were being aggressive, thus indicating awareness of its ongoing responsibility to ensure the survival of a robust supply chain. It stated: 'The last thing we want to do is to put any supplier in a position where they can't supply us any more.' Note that 'any supplier' was the phrase used, not 'some suppliers'.

It is worth looking at some examples of the supplier relationship from the retailer point of view. We begin with Tesco and an interview with Lucy Neville-Rolfe. She referred to the anonymously derived 2009 survey of over 2,300 Tesco suppliers, which showed a consistent level of response to such questions as 'Are you treated with respect?', 'Are we professional in our dealings with you?', 'Do we maintain the highest quality standards?' and several more to the same effect. In every case, more than 90 per cent of Tesco suppliers replied in the affirmative. Turning to the issue of farmers specifically, she pointed to the Sustainable Beef Project, helping suppliers with science-based approaches to beef cattle farming, and to the Tesco Dairy Centre of Excellence, providing with academic help and funding the latest information and expertise on dairy technologies and testing of new ideas. This is behaviour we should expect from a market leader, and there is genuine progress here.

However, it is the smaller Waitrose that provides the best case of an individual retailer going out of its way to promote constructive business dealings with farmers, an approach endorsed, as noted, in this instance by both sides. Waitrose strategy in this regard is not new, since it believes its own knowledge enables it to understand and even speak for the farmer. Mark Price can point to a rooted and long-term commitment to organic production over 20 years. Waitrose alone adopts the Linking Environment and Farming (LEAF) Marque certificate for fruit, vegetable and flower growing. Its milk and organic milk schemes go well beyond basic industry requirements, and actively encourage the promotion of natural habitats in its supplier farms. Sustainable agriculture means something distinctive to Waitrose, and the company senses its commitment has already proved a valuable addition to its overall quality and capacity to brand the business, noted in Chapter 5. The other development that will help the smaller supplier is that, to meet consumer demand, the supermarkets are increasing their range of local produce. Several have identified dependable suppliers that can deliver a quality, differentiated product, which will in its turn help the supermarket to differentiate itself from its competitors.

Conclusions on suppliers

The discussion in parts of this chapter may suggest inconsistency. On the one hand we admire the British supermarkets both individually and as a collective, and argue that they have done a great job over many years, reaching with little doubt world-class standards in many areas of their operation. A cogent case can be made for the British industry today leading the world, and there are knowledgeable people in the United States as well as Europe who would concur with this appraisal. More importantly, consumers who have lived in these markets can speak with some element of confidence of the level of consumer approval in the relative markets. On the other hand we can appreciate that the success of British supermarkets – and indeed of the biggest chains elsewhere, such as Wal-Mart – has brought in its train some undesirable effects. We further accept, as do the more enlightened supermarket leaders, that business practices have from time to time been inadequate. Few industries or companies are perfect. However, the paradox must be recognized. It is possible to admire Rupert Murdoch as a consummate businessman while deploring some of the results of his success. He is a decisive and strategic global thinker and a major risk taker, who deserves the rewards that successful risk taking creates. We are, however, appalled at the effect that he has had on British newspapers, and indeed on the calibre of news reporting in the civilized world (Fox News in the United States is a further example). It is possible to be a business leader without equal, but reduce the content value of the product at the same time. The analogy is not in our view perfect, as we see the food retailers as having mainly, albeit not entirely, benign effects. It shows that it is quite possible to hold quite differing views about different aspects of the same organization.

The supermarket groups are businesses, and they must act in the interests of shareholders. Within the industry as a whole their success has led, and is continuing to promote, a major shift in the balance of power but this is not necessarily a bad thing. There have been cases where the supermarket groups have abused their power, and this has probably happened on more occasions in the past decade than before. (The arrival at the outset of the world's biggest retail brand, while not ignoring new discounter entries, must have some effect in this regard, merely by adding to the number of available 'culprits'.) However, some of the more strident press and TV reporting has been somewhat one-sided – in this instance the media prefer instinctively *not* to be on the side of what they see as the big battalions.

In general we believe that the retailers are to be congratulated on their strategies and their operations. It is a truism now that they have great power, and with that power goes responsibility. They will have to show, consistently, that they can behave as industry leaders.

Conclusions

11

What have we learnt from our most recent review of the British food retailing industry? To some degree, the changes in the past 10 years have been modest. Many of the lessons learnt were already on the record then. But there has been significant movement. In summary, the strong have become stronger and the weak weaker, even in some cases leading to their disappearance. This is not an easy playground in which to operate, as was obvious 10 years ago.

There are now three outstanding British business winners, all of which can point to major progress over the past decade. They are Tesco, Morrisons and Waitrose. They are all intrinsically and fascinatingly different from each other. There is not just one way to succeed in this market.

Let us start with Tesco, a company with excellent performance. Tesco exhibits a consistently high level of customer focus. It is adding to this the multinational process discipline that has enabled it to occupy a dozen or more major world markets at speed and with precision. Yet in doing so it has somehow managed to accommodate the need for local and national innovation and response, which is an area where many other powerful multinationals have failed. This is a high skill, which has been acquired through attention to the global, national and local elements of brand and organization building. In some ways, it could be Tesco's greatest single achievement. Under Terry Leahy's guidance, Tesco have rejoiced in a driving, winning culture, which – so far at least – has avoided stultifying autocracy or lock-step responses from far-flung and diverse worldwide managements. This will be a tough act to follow.

Meanwhile, however, and well as it may have performed in the round in its crucial home market, Tesco is not the decade's overall British market winner. That title falls, unarguably we would suggest, to

Morrisons. Surprising as it may seem, it is a company that 10 years ago was not in the big four that now takes the palm, and has held it against ferocious competition for perhaps two or three years. Building from the cohesive but admittedly narrow, price-sensitive, north of England base created by Ken Morrison, this company weathered a very difficult period in the middle years of the last decade when it acquired, failed sensibly to digest, and finally succeeded in integrating Safeway. The resultant fully national chain has been remodelled, given a well-differentiated brand and business strategy, and is delivering growth figures and margins that are industry-leading. The Morrisons fresh food offer is now recognized as top of the class among the main market performers, and the company's integrated food focus approach has set it apart from the multi-product companies with which it competes. In a short time, Marc Bolland provided new edge and impetus to Ken Morrison's well-positioned company and gave his successor a fine platform for the future.

Our third overall winner is again very different from either of the first two and is perhaps the most surprising of all. Looking at the market share of Waitrose one might be tempted to ignore it, and classify this company as a niche player, certainly more than a pygmy, but emphatically no giant. It may be a non-quoted and basically regional company with a market share of under 5 per cent, but it is a company to take seriously. Waitrose has used the past decade quietly but steadily to create a brand and store platform that uncompromisingly screams quality in every aspect, all the time. Waitrose is now a brave and well-run business with a level of aspiration in its activities that often leaves its bigger rivals gasping for breath. The success of the Waitrose strategy is confirmed by its figures, which have actually accelerated through a recessionary period when economic conditions might have suggested that the high-quality, higher-priced offer might struggle for survival. Waitrose is now putting pressure on the quality offerings of its main market rivals – Waitrose simply does it better – and it is building a range of solid and worthwhile partnerships to promote its brand outside its own stores. Most of all in the Waitrose record of achievements, we would now point to the capacity of this company to create a recognizable and even loved food brand, based on best market quality.

Looking ahead, we see each of these three companies as high-performing future winners that are well able to maintain above-average growth performance. Tesco will do this on the world stage and will have the most exciting portfolio to exploit, but it also has the toughest competition (Wal-Mart, Carrefour, Aldi and Metro) and the most to lose if it starts to lose its way in the world's biggest markets – but there is not the slightest sign of that happening. In the UK, Morrisons' new leader can maintain the momentum that the company now has, and the business has sufficient resources and confidence to take part of the share from others, as it has been doing. Finally Waitrose, small as it is today, has perhaps – in percentage terms at least – the most inspiring capabilities. It knows it is tackling things differently, and so far at least consumers emphatically like what it does. Given economic recovery, this winning formula, comfortably owned by the John Lewis Partnership, appears to be well positioned for the race ahead.

What of the others? Asda cannot be discounted, and we can be sure that, if there are signs of faltering, Wal-Mart will take quick and decisive action to protect and strengthen its franchise. Our long-term view remains that Asda is a well-placed number two food business, which will continue to pressure Tesco through pricing policies, now EDLP, and this will attract a solid following. Clothing is probably the area where Asda can do pre-eminently well – here Tesco can probably be beaten by Asda's well-sourced George branded offer. It is hard to see much headway for the European discounters in Britain's demanding conditions. There is at least a reasonable chance now that the Co-operative movement may be in a position to hold the fort, something it has conspicuously failed to do for at least half a century. Stability would be an achievement in its own right. Then there is yesterday's bright star in the firmament, Marks and Spencer, whose food offer was once the toast of the chattering classes. Its food company has lost its way, and is now constrained by price, space, range and direct competition, all of which has made its recent life something of a misery. The arrival of Marc Bolland from Morrisons may inject the excitement and innovative flair it desperately needs.

Finally we come to Sainsbury's, at one time the seemingly impregnable market leader, now apparently engaged in the unending uphill task of 'making Sainsbury's great again'. So far it has not worked. Encouragingly for the present team, it is just about keeping up with its main competitors, but results are still at a sub-average level in terms of profits. More concerning perhaps is the fact that it is difficult to point to any area where Sainsbury's has a lead based on innovation – and many sectors stand out where it is at best a weak number two or three. Lastly, management must lie awake at night wondering how if ever they can recapture the best-quality food reputation they once owned. First attacked by M&S and then challenged by Tesco Finest, Sainsbury's is now under continual assault from the Waitrose food brand. This is not a good place for Justin King's team to be.

What will happen? This is hard to say. If, five years since the new team took over, Sainsbury's can accelerate growth and find innovative strategies, it still has a committed, even devoted, consumer following. If it cannot – and time may be running out for the present leaders – Sainsbury's looks like a worthwhile acquisition prospect, no doubt coveted, fruitlessly, by Wal-Mart and Carrefour, but probably more available to rich, developing, new-market purchasers from the Gulf, India or China. This might be a sad ending to so long-running and successful a company, but the Sainsbury's brand may be strong enough to survive acquisition and live longer under new owners.

So much for the market players, but what challenges ahead do they face? There are many in this very big and visible industry. Prominent among them we would place the need to avoid complacency and arrogance. Wal-Mart's German foray and Sainsbury's 1980s and 1990s triumphalism show what happens when overconfidence takes over. Wal-Mart has learnt quickly. Tesco is run by an understated realist who calls for performance based on merit. The rest know they have little yet to be comfortable about.

Food itself is a commodity that is showing signs of maturity. As real prices have, in the long term at least, declined, growth becomes harder to find. Not unnaturally therefore clothing is seen – by most – as a better place to gain share. Other non-food categories also hold promise. Finance is an opportunity where prospects for a strong trusted consumer offer can succeed. As the grocers head for these new pastures, two risks present themselves. First, will they know enough and have the experience to win there? Second, as they channel precious resources into new sectors, where does food provision – a demanding and moving target – fit? Can the grocers be all things to all people across such wide swathes of territory? It will not be easy.

There are many other demands too. Worldwide sourcing has opened up astonishingly large prospects of cost reduction and scale advantage. Can this be married to motivated sets of local teams seeking on-the-spot advantage in their local stores? Alongside cost reduction, there is the countervailing power of local consumers wanting to buy their fruit, meat and bread – everything perhaps – from local sources of supply. Delicacy of approach is required to balance these conflicting elements.

Virtually every new brave sally forward on which these commercially minded retailers decide brings its own new challenges. The high street penetration, which has added marginal volume and share to their sales, creates sizeable new issues. Consumers probably do not want scaled-down superstores on their local high street, and they will want a lot more as time passes. Meanwhile the owners cannot generate the scale to protect margins in these smaller units. How will this be resolved? At the moment it is unclear. What *is* clear is that everyone now wants a piece of the action, and customers will be given more choice. Will it be real choice, and will the plethora of offers be differentiated and genuine? If not, patronage will go elsewhere, even to unlikely new venues like farm stores. (See Box 11.1.)

Box 11.1 Now is the time for localness

Kate James-Weed

As the economy bites and takes a sharp downward path, my local high street is beginning to feel the heat. There are already two vacant stores with 'To Let' signs posted in the window, and there is talk in the library that the sports shop is looking very empty. Mick the grocer continues to sell dull and rather wizened fruit and veg, whilst the baker's display of doughnuts and white floured rolls remains doggedly unaltered.

I am describing the average face of my local village high street, consisting of about 20 shops, which remains fatally unchanged to cope with the demands of 21st-century living. My high street is truly an uninspiring sight and yet has deep roots within the community that it serves. Instead of watching its sad and painfully slow demise, wouldn't it be wonderful to see a rejuvenated row of shops selling what we the customers want: delicious, enticing and if at all possible local produce? These shops would be proud of their products, providing convenience and the all-important added value of service to customers whom they have communicated with on an individual and almost daily basis for many years if not decades.

Now is the time for the high street to turn around its fortunes before it is too late and is lost for ever. While it will never be able to compete with the large supermarkets on price, there is an opportunity for the high street to establish a differentiated offer that can compete very favourably with that of the supermarkets.

Only the high street can offer localness, with convenience of easy access and savings on ever more expensive petrol. Arguably, even without the lowest prices you can save money by not being tempted to buy too much on one large shopping visit that could ultimately lead to the wasteful disposal of out-of-date food. But more than this, the high street can also react to the very real needs of consumers for a smaller, friendlier shopping experience with assistants who know and

Box 11.1 continued

personally value your custom. The huge impersonal superstores find it hard to replicate this service, which is crying out to be exploited.

I am not naive enough to believe that there can ever be a return to the single post office serving a small village without enough people to support the costs associated with the breadth of products people seek today. Such a loss can be, understood but I find it difficult to accept the loss of an entire high street that is surrounded by more than enough potential customer support. I, like many others, want convenience and choice within my local area. What we really yearn for is long-term customer commitment, good service, quality-based products and easy access.

Perhaps there is a window of opportunity for the opportunists of all opportunities? Tesco or Sainsbury's could possibly take on the mantle of improving our local parade of shops. Rather than a 'store within a store', it could provide a store within the high street. Maybe it could open up small specialist grocers' or bakeries, maybe a fishmonger's or butcher's shop, all of which would provide customers with their quality products in a local environment. This is hardly a new concept. Sainsbury's, after all, started its journey as a local grocer. Maybe the time is right for it to think about returning to its roots.

Perhaps the day will come when petrol is no longer so readily affordable and we shall be forced to rely once again upon our high street. With growing demands for a greener lifestyle, it makes sense to try to cut down on unnecessary journeys and use our local amenities more, but in order for this to be viable amenities have to live up to the demands of the modern customer. The high street will become fully exploited only if it can provide us with what we want. For these shops to gain our loyalty they must start to step up to the mark and supply us with a smaller, more intimate 21st-century marketplace to go to. I crave such a place: a high street that is familiar and friendly that provides the whole community with the advantages of locations selling great products. I believe that there is a real need for this and a genuine wish for such a service, so let's head back to the future and reinstall the new dynamic and forward-looking high street.

Most significant of all, perhaps, is the evolving food-quality revolution taking place in our homes, all the time, and influenced by a multiplicity of diverse factors. Price, quality and service used to be the three essential components of good food retailing. They still are, no doubt, but the capacity of consumers to ring the changes, become more demanding, state personal requirements, and espouse and desert brands and products overnight has made this a much more exacting game. It is just not possible to see where this will end or which of the ways we want to shop, provide and eat are going to be the most long-standing in the end. Inside this revolutionary process – a maelstrom of changing activities, attitudes and requirements – we see a picture of company managements trying to create, promote and strengthen their single brands. What a complex world they now inhabit, and what a range of delicately honed talents and skills they will need to possess. Twenty years ago, the internet arrived and became a major new factor in food shopping. Today you can see more than one successful exponent of this strikingly different new facility – and high praise must be accorded to two exponents, Ocado and Tesco, that have used the new channel to build well-positioned new businesses. Where might this go next and how big can it be? Really, we do not know. Overall, in assessing the response to these issues, at the end of the day one or two brand owners will simply have more vision, have clearer strategies, and engender a stronger, deeper set of processes, and their consumer approach will help them to win through against their simpler, less well-equipped, and less visionary rivals. So it should be, so it always was and so perhaps it always will be.

What the authors would unhesitatingly put on record is our view that the collection of UK supermarkets is a well-run and highly efficient industry. The food retailers are wide-ranging and powerful certainly, but against absolute or relative standards (other British industries and global retailers) they are high performing. Judged against the question 'Have the supermarkets done a good, average or poor job for British consumers?', the industry emerges with a predominantly well-rated report card. We are strengthened in this overall appraisal by successive judgements of the UK's own highly active Competition Commission, which has given successive judgements in a similar vein on several recent occasions.

However, success can bring complacency. Looking at the industry as a whole today, and through a global lens, we can see only too clearly what the future, on a global basis, will bring. Food retailing is moving now at some pace from a set of national companies delivering local and national solutions to a global industry. Several big players, Tesco being one, are now present in the world's handful of biggest markets. The processes they will all need will create some megalithic-size enterprises – Wal-Mart already is one, and surely others will follow. Scale and size on these proportions have only rarely been encountered before, and they will create management challenges that are therefore unusual. Efficiency of process will be at a premium and will create of itself huge competitive advantage. Can the suppliers of such efficiency still manage to keep the consumer at the heart of their strategy? Will the discontinuity engendered by scale and distance be a force that will mean consumer satisfaction begins to take a back seat in their deliberations? Of course, the companies will all say this won't happen, but it is a danger. As we have seen in Britain and more visibly in the United States, where Wal-Mart has just received a resoundingly negative court judgment from a collective class action of all its women employees, size is not always perceived as an advantage, and gargantuan size, once perceived, is a big handicap. How the future giants of this industry play this ever-growing reality will be a leadership challenge of significant proportions.

This brings us to our last key point. Leadership is the single component that has appeared to generate long-term strategic success: Sam Walton in the series of follow-up actions to his unprepossessing Newport, Arkansas beginnings; Lord John Sainsbury in his powerful, driving creation of the apparently impregnable Sainsbury's public company in Britain for two decades until 1990; Archie Norman and Allan Leighton in the Asda revival; Sir Ken Morrison in his half-century of Yorkshire tenacity that created his own famous store; Sir Terry Leahy with his remarkable transformation of Tesco from UK supermarket leader to multi-product global competitor. All of these leaders were placed, in most cases for many years, at the front of their companies, and all of them were able to aspire and inspire, to chase and cajole, to drive and push big management and staff teams to do stellar jobs in delivering successful consumer response. More of the same, and in tougher, global environments, will be needed in the years ahead. Where will these leaders be found? And will they – above all else – have the learning and listening capabilities to hear the still small voice of the customer as they drive their retail behemoths forward? It will not be easy, and sometimes the response will need to be both considered and quick.

REFERENCES

Burt, S and Sparks, L (1997) 'Performance in Food Retailing: A cross-national consideration and comparison of retail margins', *British Journal of Management 8*, pp 133–50

Competition Commission (2000) *Supermarkets: A report on the supply of groceries from multiple stores in the UK*, Competition Commission, London

Competition Commission (2008) *The Supply of Groceries in the UK Market Investigation*, Competition Commission, London

Deutsche Morgan Grenfell (1998) *Analysis of Food Retailer Results in Britain, France, Belgium and the USA*

Dobson, P (1998a) The economic welfare implications of own label goods, School of Management and Finance Discussion Papers IV, University of Nottingham

Dobson, P (1998b) The competition effect of look-alike products, School of Management and Finance Discussion Papers VIII, University of Nottingham

Dobson, P, Waterson, M and Chu, A (1998) *The Welfare Consequences of the Exercise of Buyer Power*, Office of Fair Trading, London

Marks and Spencer (2009) *M&S How We Do Business Report 2009: Doing the right thing*, Marks and Spencer, London

Peston and Ennew, C (eds) 1998 *Neighbourhood Shopping in the Millennium*, University of Nottingham Business School, Nottingham

Raven, H and Lang, T (1995) *Off Our Trolleys? Food retailing and the hypermarket economy*, Institute of Public Policy Research, London

Rose, S (2009) Chairman's introduction, in *M&S How We Do Business Report 2009: Doing the right thing*, Marks and Spencer, London

Rowthorn, R (1998) Private communication to the authors

Wrigley, N (1994) 'After the store wars? Towards a new era of retail competition?' *Journal of Retail and Consumer Series I*, pp 5–20

INDEX